BLACK HAMMER

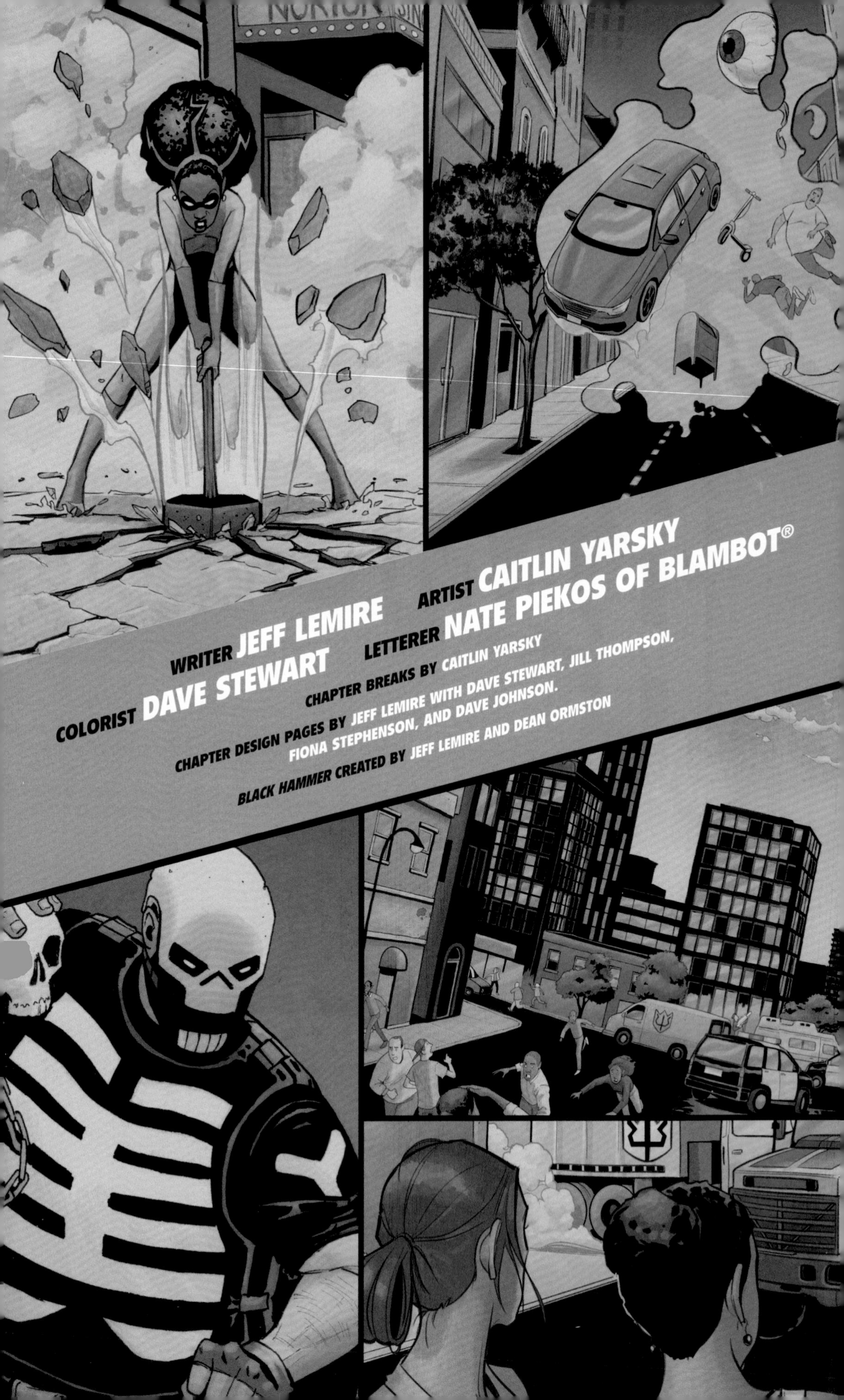

WRITER **JEFF LEMIRE** ARTIST **CAITLIN YARSKY**

COLORIST **DAVE STEWART** LETTERER **NATE PIEKOS OF BLAMBOT®**

CHAPTER BREAKS BY CAITLIN YARSKY

CHAPTER DESIGN PAGES BY JEFF LEMIRE WITH DAVE STEWART, JILL THOMPSON, FIONA STEPHENSON, AND DAVE JOHNSON.

BLACK HAMMER CREATED BY JEFF LEMIRE AND DEAN ORMSTON

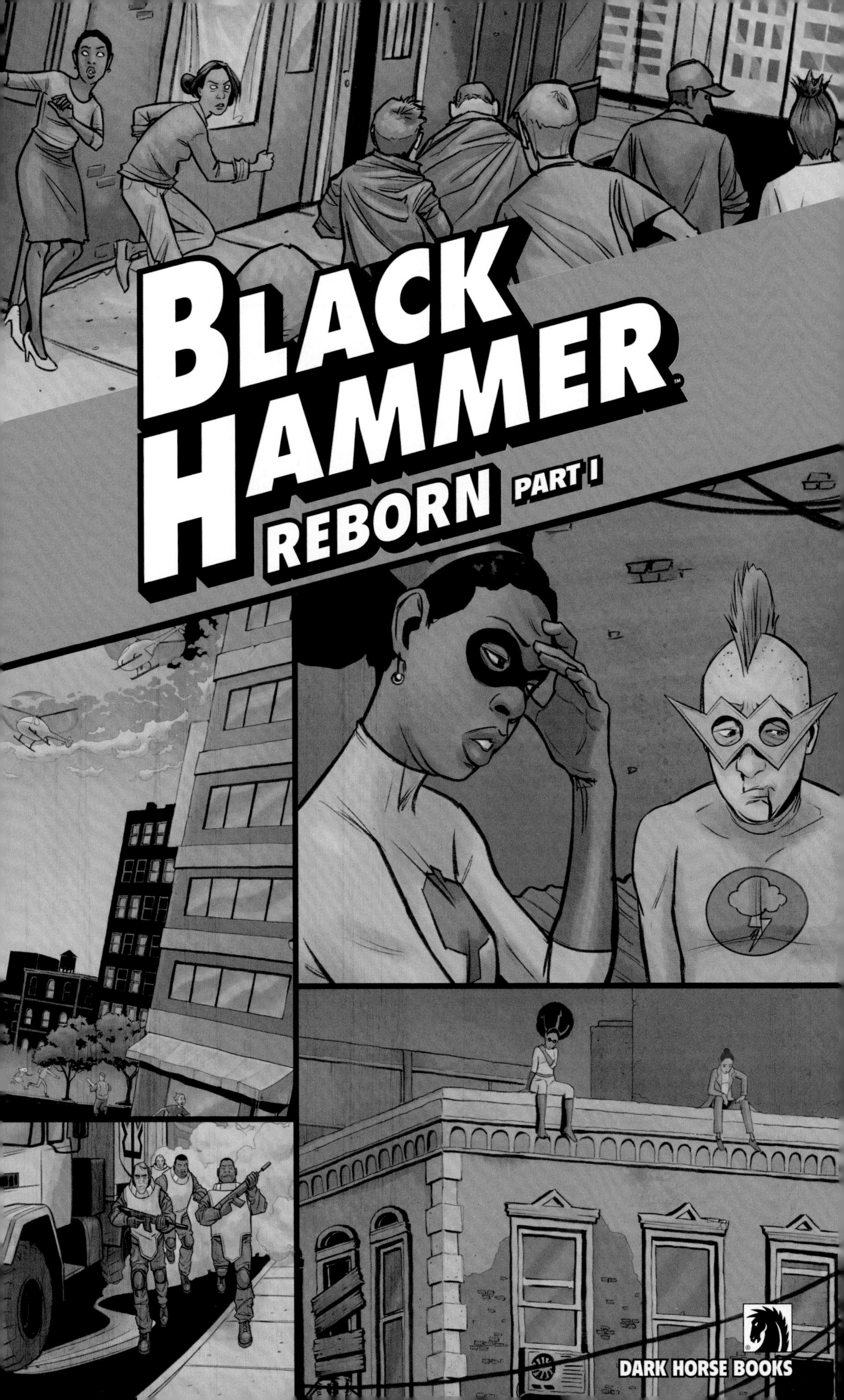
BLACK HAMMER™
REBORN PART I
DARK HORSE BOOKS

PRESIDENT & PUBLISHER
MIKE RICHARDSON

EDITOR
DANIEL CHABON

ASSISTANT EDITORS
CHUCK HOWITT
AND KONNER KNUDSEN

DESIGNER
ETHAN KIMBERLING

DIGITAL ART TECHNICIAN
JOSIE CHRISTENSEN

BLACK HAMMER VOLUME 5: REBORN PART I

Collects issues #1–#4 of the Dark Horse Comics series *Black Hammer Reborn*.

Library of Congress Cataloging-in-Publication Data

Names: Lemire, Jeff, writer. | Yarsky, Caitlin, artist. | Stewart, Dave,
  colourist. | Piekos, Nate, letterer.
Title: Reborn Part one / writer, Jeff Lemire ; artist, Caitlin Yarsky ;
  colorist, Dave Stewart ; letterer, Nate Piekos.
Other titles: Black Hammer reborn
Description: First edition. | Milwaukie, OR : Dark Horse Books, 2022. |
  Series: Black Hammer ; volume 5 | "Black Hammer Created by Jeff Lemire
  and Dean Ormston" | Summary: "In 1986, Black Hammer and the rest of
  Spiral City's greatest superheroes seemingly died defeating the cosmic
  despot known as Anti-God and saving the world. But one woman refused to
  believe they were truly gone: Lucy Weber, the daughter of Black Hammer.
  Learning that her dad had sacrificed himself to save the other heroes,
  Lucy soon took up the mantle of Black Hammer and carried on the legacy
  of her father as the world's greatest superhero"-- Provided by
  publisher.
Identifiers: LCCN 2021035801 (print) | LCCN 2021035802 (ebook) | ISBN
  9781506714264 (trade paperback) | ISBN 9781506714271 (ebook)
Subjects: LCGFT: Paranormal comics. | Superhero comics. | Fantasy comics.
Classification: LCC PN6728.B51926 L45 2022 (print) | LCC PN6728.B51926
  (ebook) | DDC 741.5/973--dc23
LC record available at https://lccn.loc.gov/2021035801
LC ebook record available at https://lccn.loc.gov/2021035802

Published by
Dark Horse Books
A division of Dark Horse Comics LLC
10956 SE Main Street
Milwaukie, OR 97222

DarkHorse.com

To find a comics shop in your area, visit comicshoplocator.com

First Edition: January 2022
Ebook ISBN 978-1-50671-427-1
Trade Paperback ISBN 978-1-50671-426-4

10 9 8 7 6 5 4 3 2 1
Printed in China

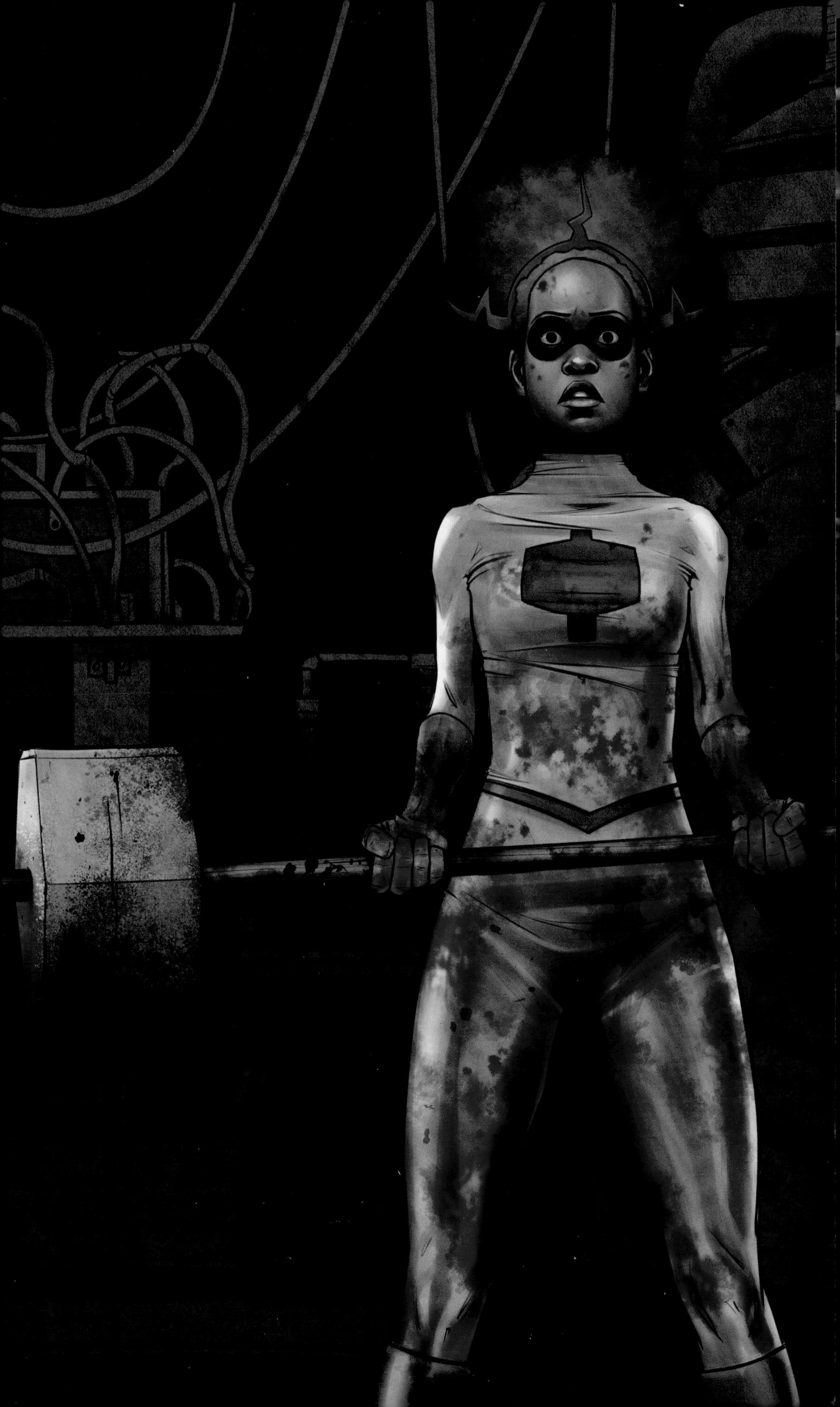

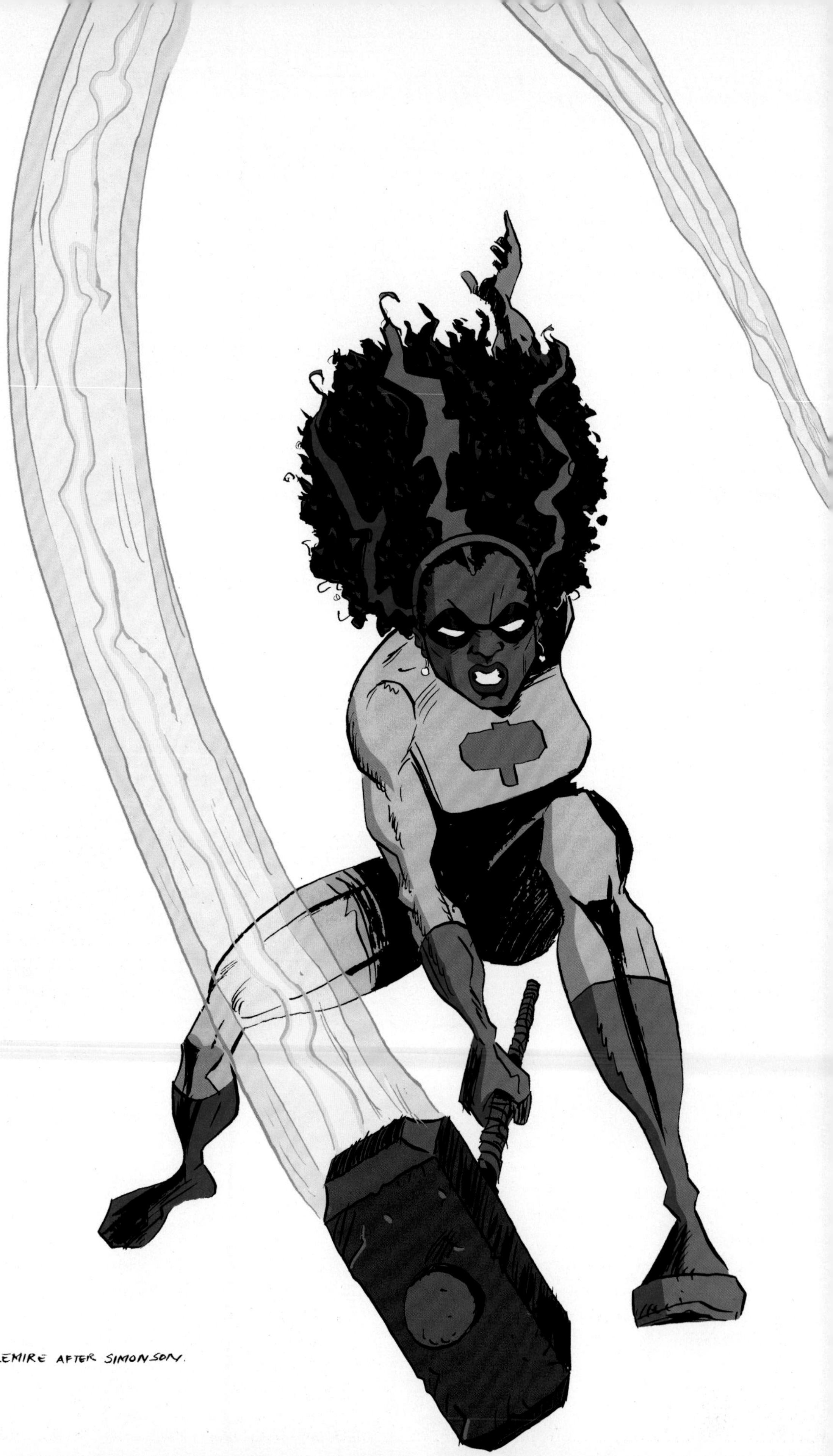

LEMIRE AFTER SIMONSON.

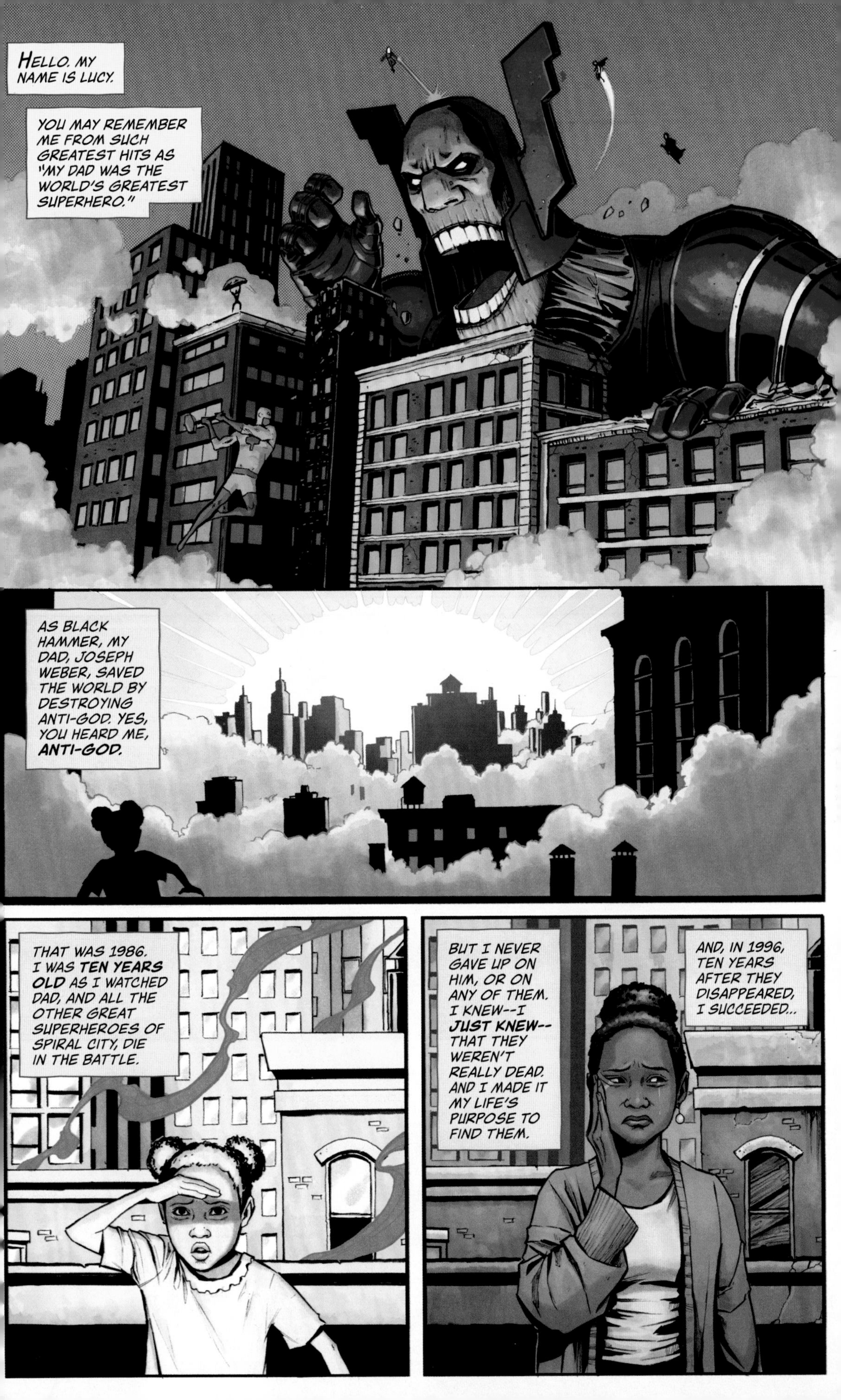

HELLO. MY NAME IS LUCY.
YOU MAY REMEMBER ME FROM SUCH GREATEST HITS AS "MY DAD WAS THE WORLD'S GREATEST SUPERHERO."
AS BLACK HAMMER, MY DAD, JOSEPH WEBER, SAVED THE WORLD BY DESTROYING ANTI-GOD. YES, YOU HEARD ME, **ANTI-GOD.**
THAT WAS 1986. I WAS **TEN YEARS OLD** AS I WATCHED DAD, AND ALL THE OTHER GREAT SUPERHEROES OF SPIRAL CITY, DIE IN THE BATTLE.
BUT I NEVER GAVE UP ON HIM, OR ON ANY OF THEM. I KNEW--I **JUST KNEW--** THAT THEY WEREN'T REALLY DEAD. AND I MADE IT MY LIFE'S PURPOSE TO FIND THEM.
AND, IN 1996, TEN YEARS AFTER THEY DISAPPEARED, I SUCCEEDED...

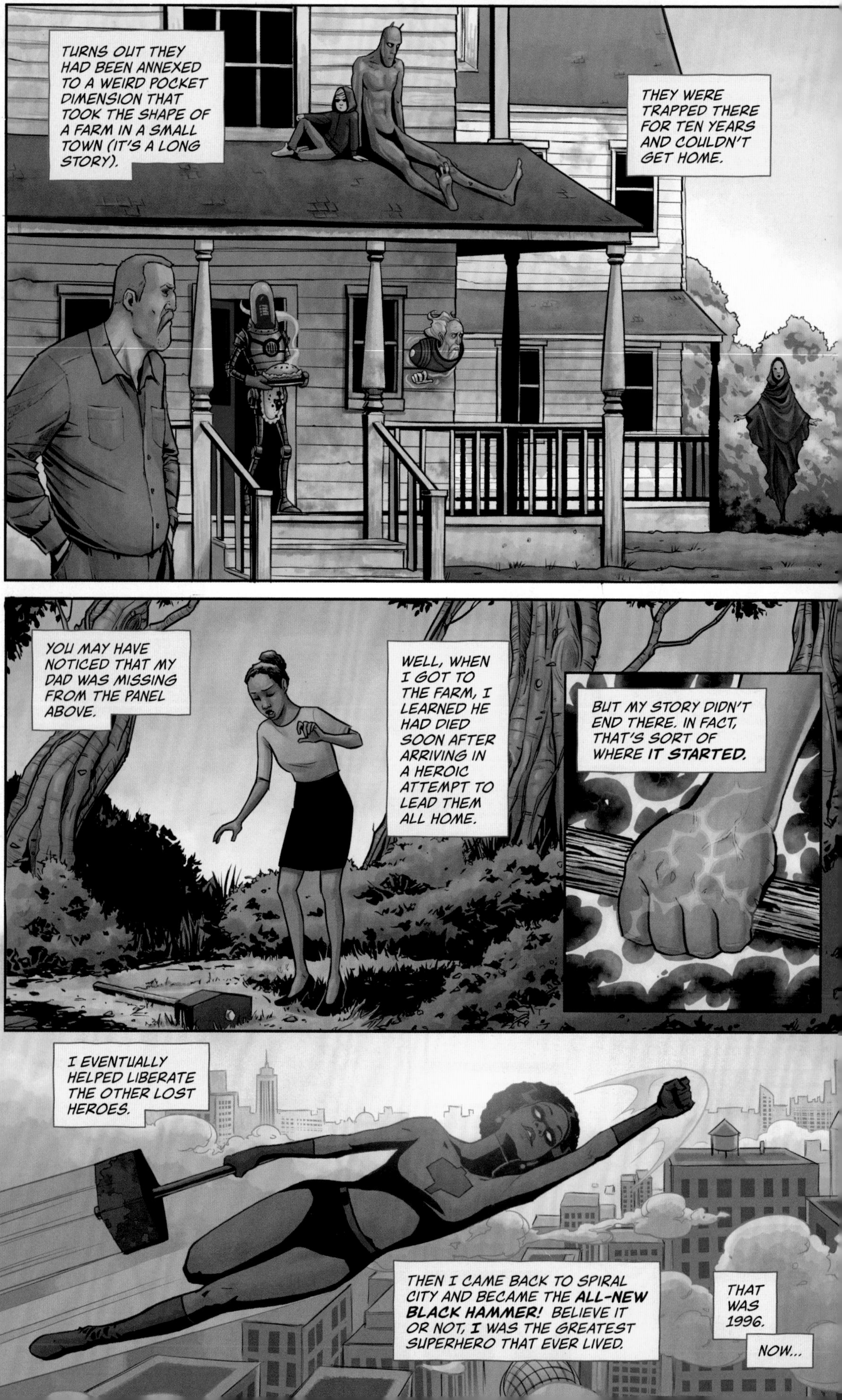
TURNS OUT THEY HAD BEEN ANNEXED TO A WEIRD POCKET DIMENSION THAT TOOK THE SHAPE OF A FARM IN A SMALL TOWN (IT'S A LONG STORY).
THEY WERE TRAPPED THERE FOR TEN YEARS AND COULDN'T GET HOME.
YOU MAY HAVE NOTICED THAT MY DAD WAS MISSING FROM THE PANEL ABOVE.
WELL, WHEN I GOT TO THE FARM, I LEARNED HE HAD DIED SOON AFTER ARRIVING IN A HEROIC ATTEMPT TO LEAD THEM ALL HOME.
BUT MY STORY DIDN'T END THERE. IN FACT, THAT'S SORT OF WHERE **IT STARTED.**
I EVENTUALLY HELPED LIBERATE THE OTHER LOST HEROES.
THEN I CAME BACK TO SPIRAL CITY AND BECAME THE **ALL-NEW BLACK HAMMER!** BELIEVE IT OR NOT, **I** WAS THE GREATEST SUPERHERO THAT EVER LIVED.
THAT WAS 1996.
NOW...

TWENTY YEARS LATER...

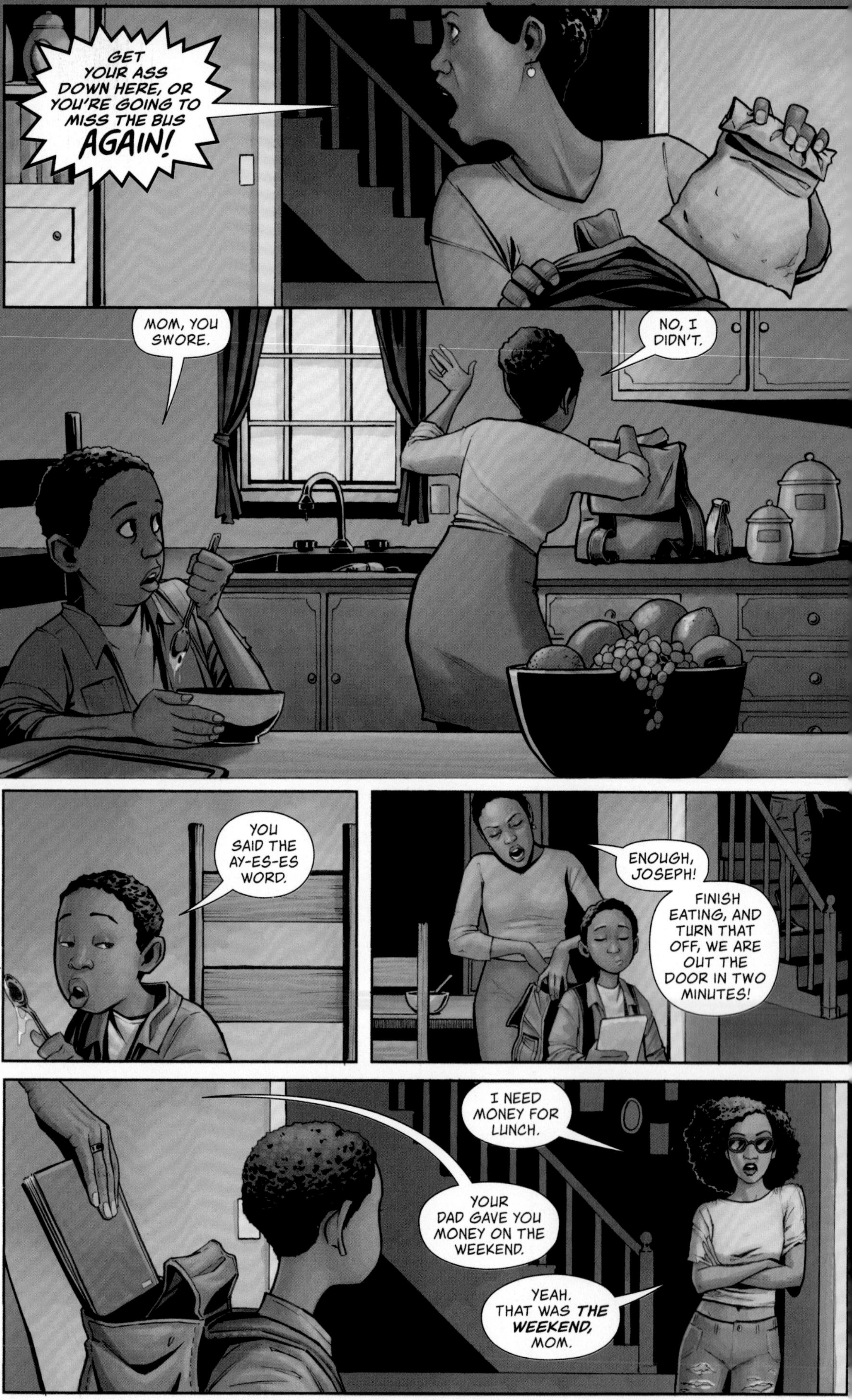
GET YOUR ASS DOWN HERE, OR YOU'RE GOING TO MISS THE BUS AGAIN!
MOM, YOU SWORE.
NO, I DIDN'T.
YOU SAID THE AY-ES-ES WORD.
ENOUGH, JOSEPH!
FINISH EATING, AND TURN THAT OFF, WE ARE OUT THE DOOR IN TWO MINUTES!
I NEED MONEY FOR LUNCH.
YOUR DAD GAVE YOU MONEY ON THE WEEKEND.
YEAH. THAT WAS THE WEEKEND, MOM.

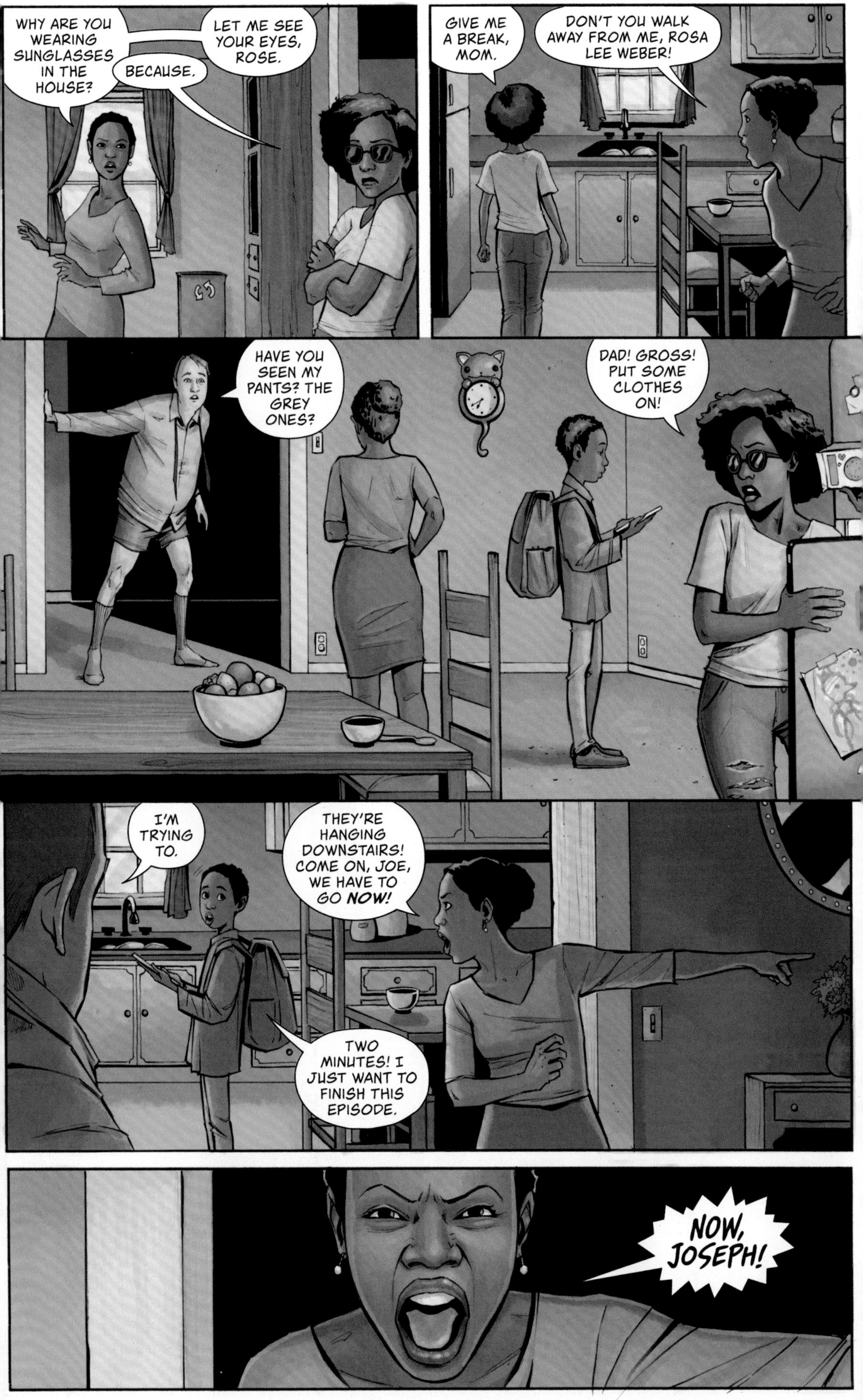
WHY ARE YOU WEARING SUNGLASSES IN THE HOUSE?
BECAUSE.
LET ME SEE YOUR EYES, ROSE.
GIVE ME A BREAK, MOM.
DON'T YOU WALK AWAY FROM ME, ROSA LEE WEBER!
HAVE YOU SEEN MY PANTS? THE GREY ONES?
DAD! GROSS! PUT SOME CLOTHES ON!
I'M TRYING TO.
THEY'RE HANGING DOWNSTAIRS! COME ON, JOE, WE HAVE TO GO **NOW!**
TWO MINUTES! I JUST WANT TO FINISH THIS EPISODE.
NOW, JOSEPH!

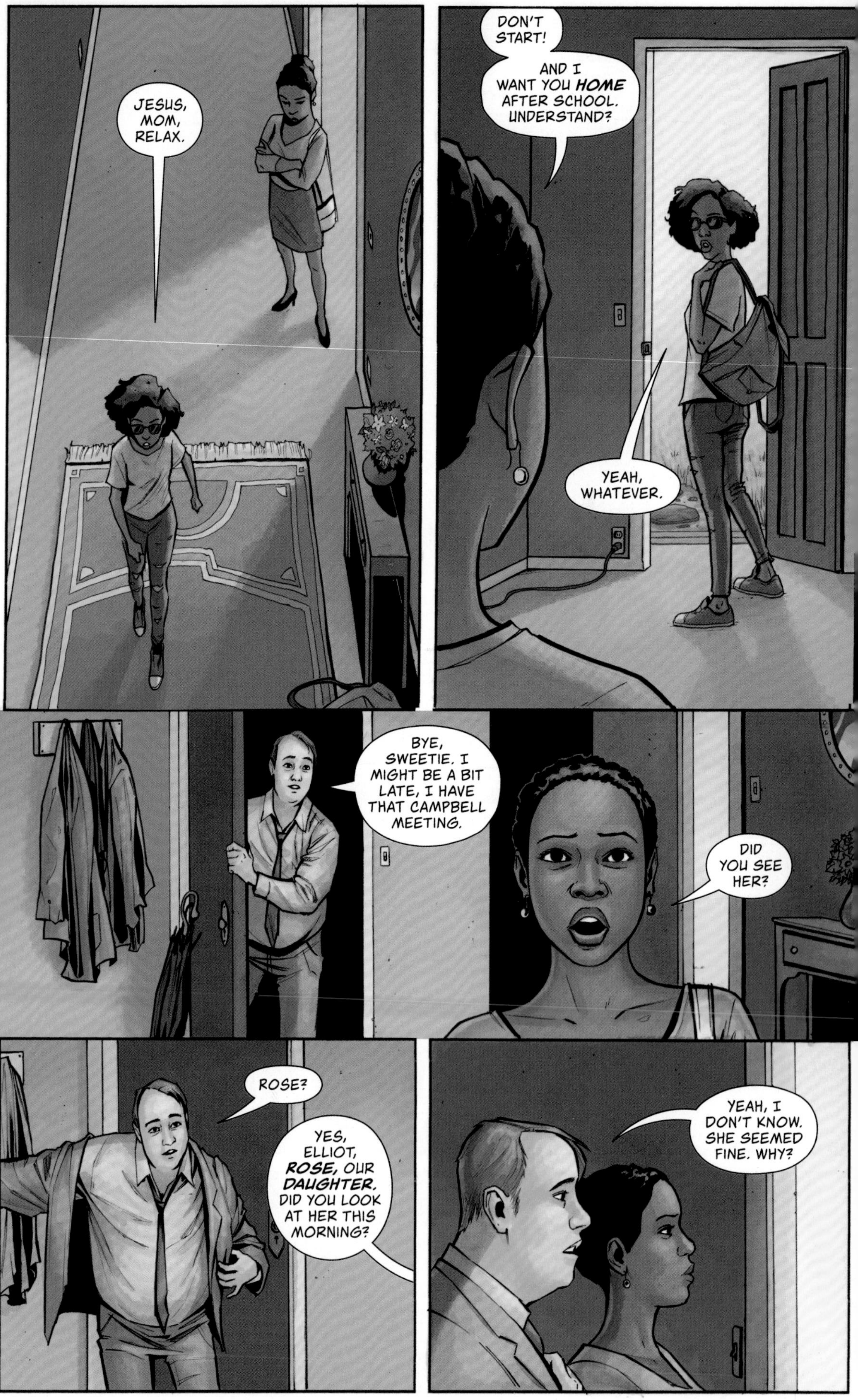
JESUS, MOM, RELAX.
DON'T START!
AND I WANT YOU **HOME** AFTER SCHOOL. UNDERSTAND?
YEAH, WHATEVER.
BYE, SWEETIE. I MIGHT BE A BIT LATE, I HAVE THAT CAMPBELL MEETING.
DID YOU SEE HER?
ROSE?
YES, ELLIOT, ***ROSE,*** OUR ***DAUGHTER.*** DID YOU LOOK AT HER THIS MORNING?
YEAH, I DON'T KNOW. SHE SEEMED FINE. WHY?

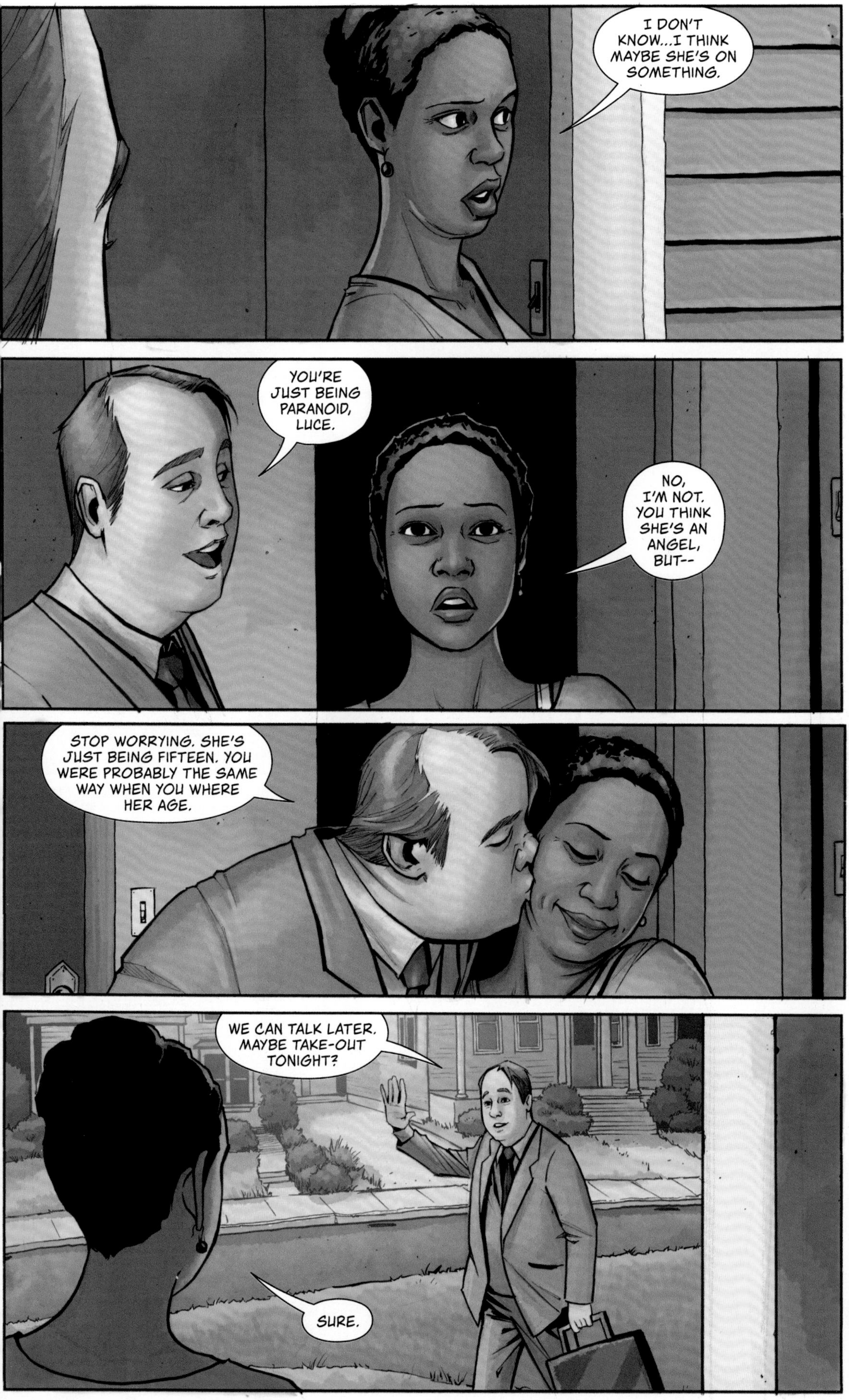
I DON'T KNOW...I THINK MAYBE SHE'S ON SOMETHING.
YOU'RE JUST BEING PARANOID, LUCE.
NO, I'M NOT. YOU THINK SHE'S AN ANGEL, BUT--
STOP WORRYING. SHE'S JUST BEING FIFTEEN. YOU WERE PROBABLY THE SAME WAY WHEN YOU WHERE HER AGE.
WE CAN TALK LATER. MAYBE TAKE-OUT TONIGHT?
SURE.

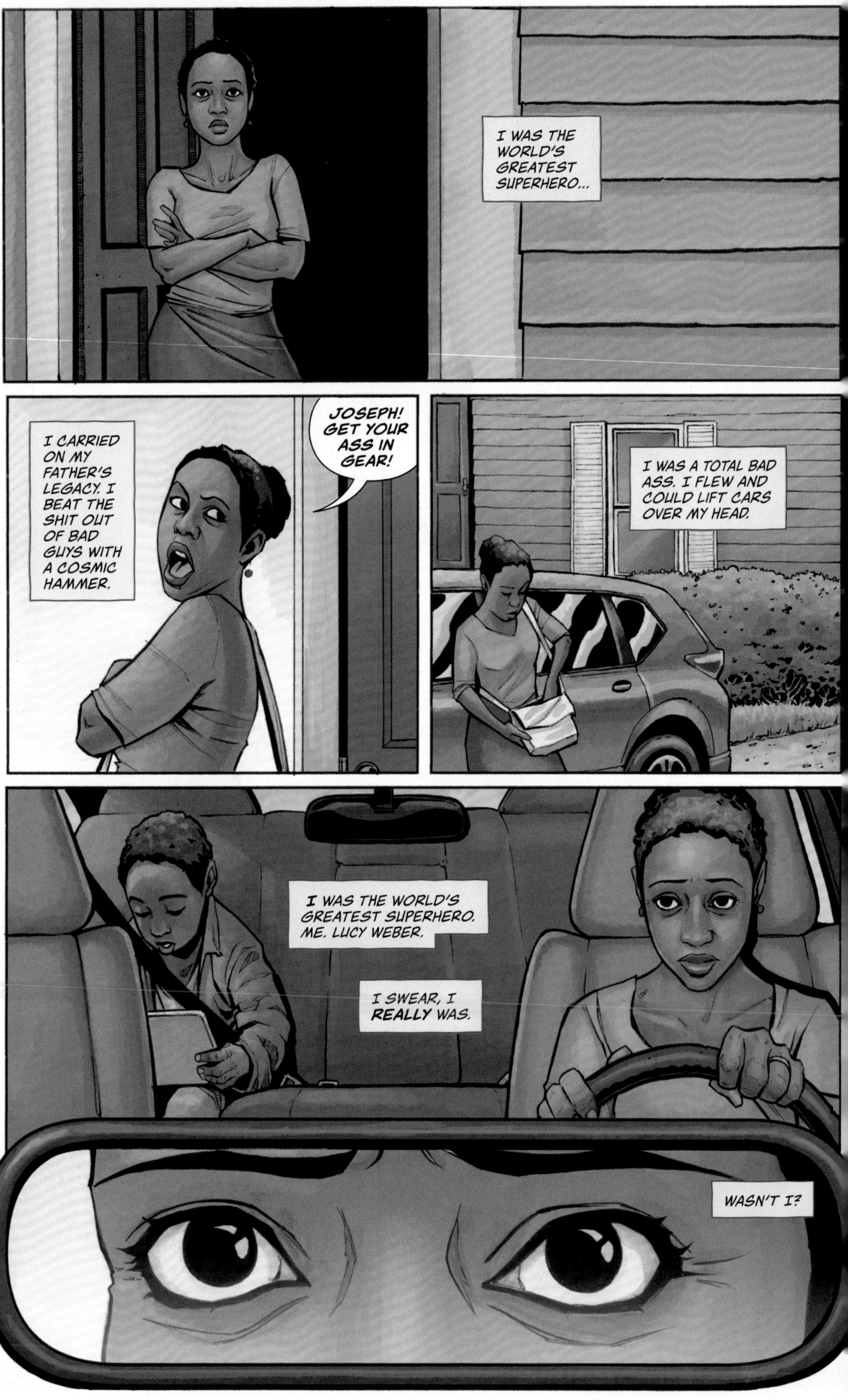
I WAS THE WORLD'S GREATEST SUPERHERO...
I CARRIED ON MY FATHER'S LEGACY. I BEAT THE SHIT OUT OF BAD GUYS WITH A COSMIC HAMMER.
JOSEPH! GET YOUR ASS IN GEAR!
I WAS A TOTAL BAD ASS. I FLEW AND COULD LIFT CARS OVER MY HEAD.
I WAS THE WORLD'S GREATEST SUPERHERO. ME. LUCY WEBER.
I SWEAR, I REALLY WAS.
WASN'T I?

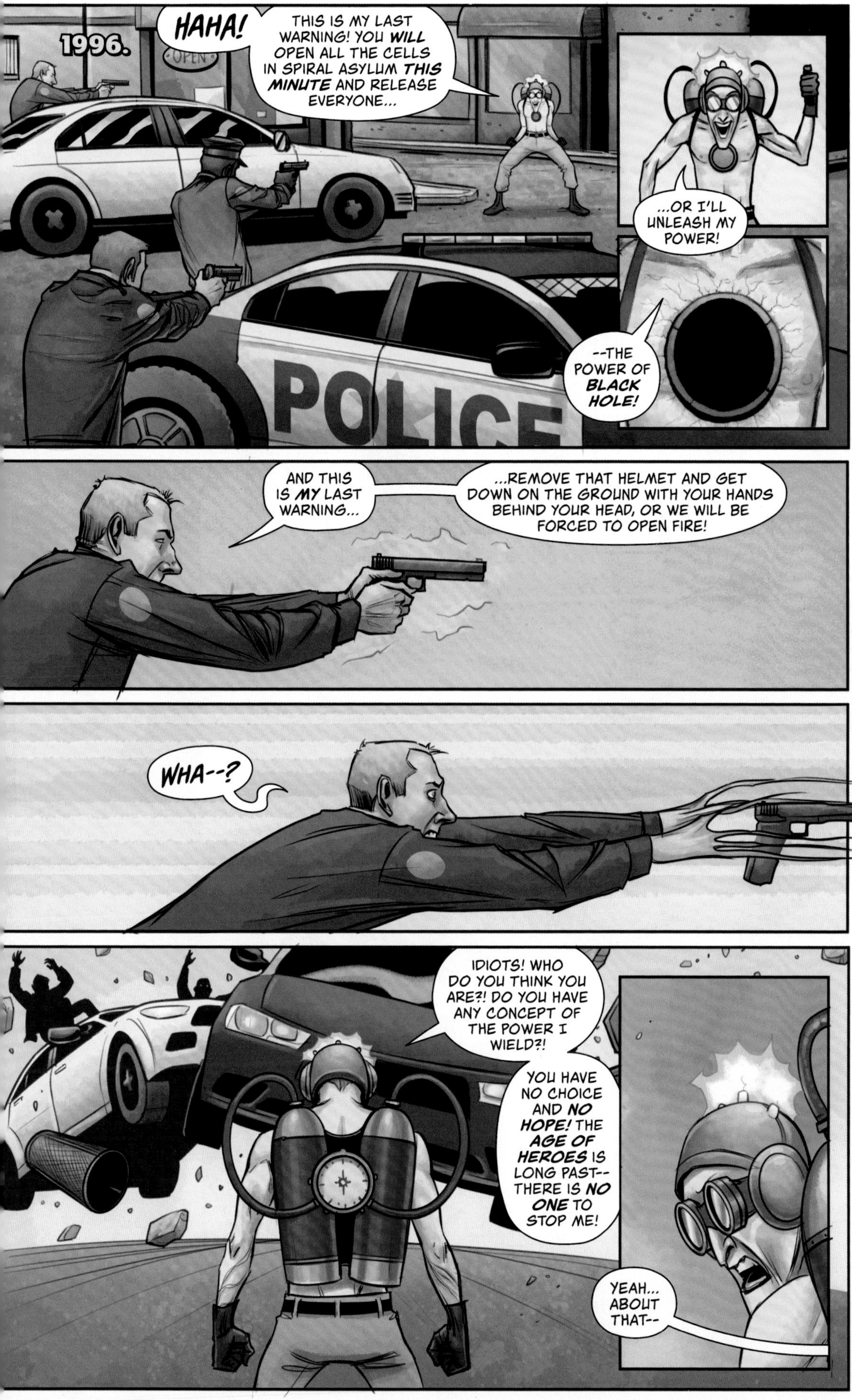
1996.
HAHA!
THIS IS MY LAST WARNING! YOU WILL OPEN ALL THE CELLS IN SPIRAL ASYLUM THIS MINUTE AND RELEASE EVERYONE...
OPEN
...OR I'LL UNLEASH MY POWER!
--THE POWER OF BLACK HOLE!
POLICE
AND THIS IS MY LAST WARNING...
...REMOVE THAT HELMET AND GET DOWN ON THE GROUND WITH YOUR HANDS BEHIND YOUR HEAD, OR WE WILL BE FORCED TO OPEN FIRE!
WHA--?
IDIOTS! WHO DO YOU THINK YOU ARE?! DO YOU HAVE ANY CONCEPT OF THE POWER I WIELD?!
YOU HAVE NO CHOICE AND NO HOPE! THE AGE OF HEROES IS LONG PAST-- THERE IS NO ONE TO STOP ME!
YEAH... ABOUT THAT--

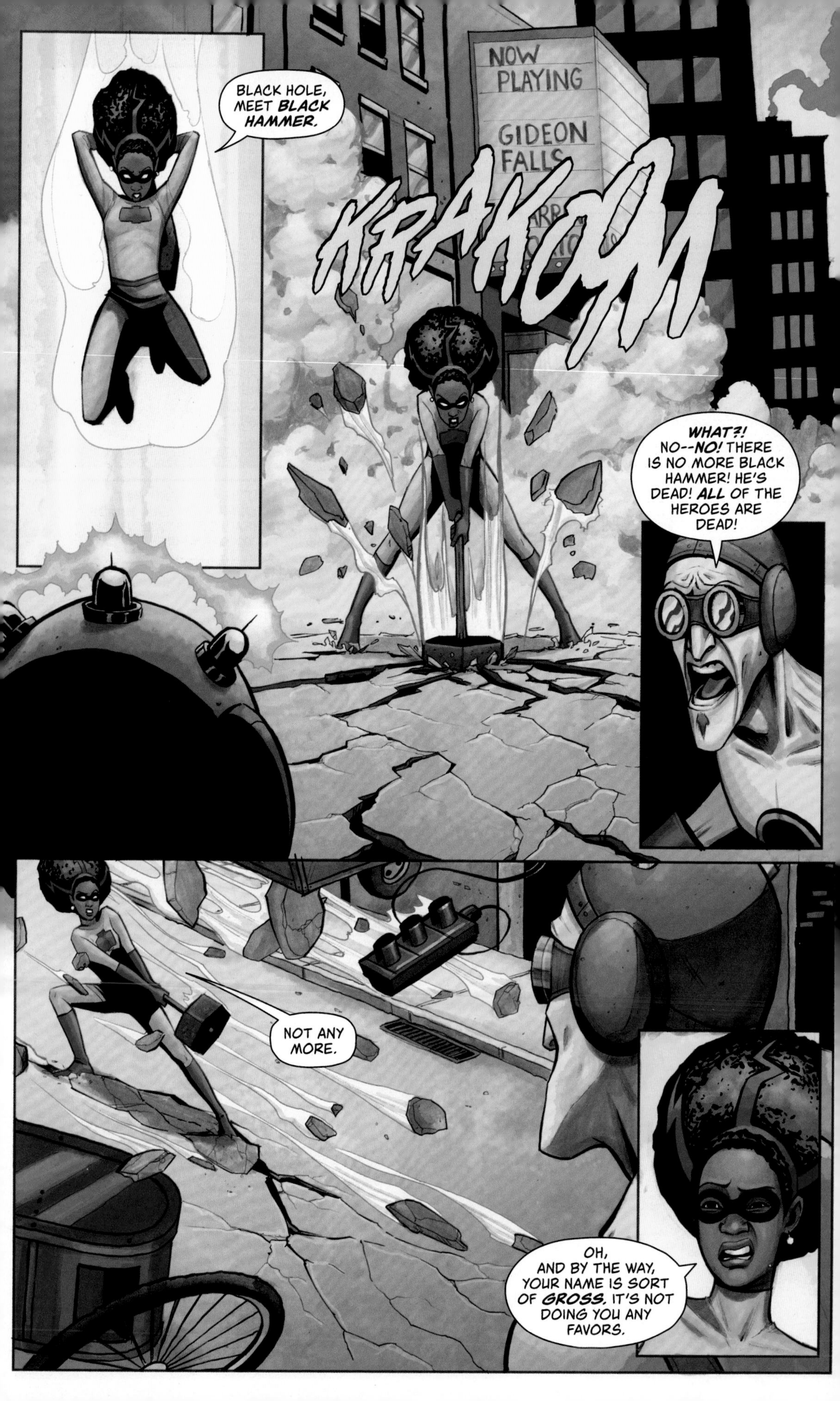

BLACK HOLE, MEET **BLACK HAMMER.**
NOW PLAYING
GIDEON FALLS
KRAKOOM
WHAT?! NO--**NO!** THERE IS NO MORE BLACK HAMMER! HE'S DEAD! **ALL** OF THE HEROES ARE DEAD!
NOT ANY MORE.
OH, AND BY THE WAY, YOUR NAME IS SORT OF **GROSS.** IT'S NOT DOING YOU ANY FAVORS.

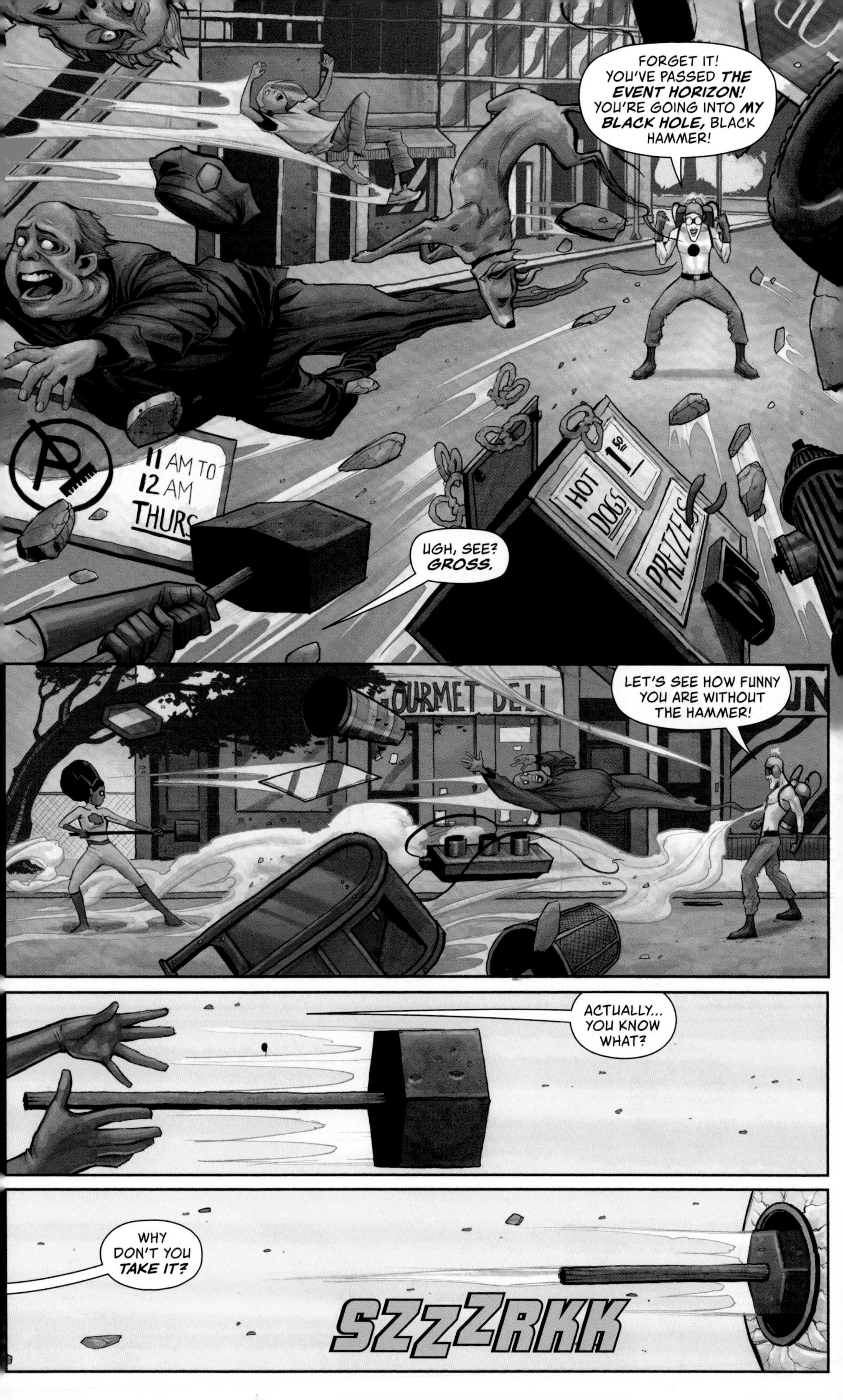

FORGET IT! YOU'VE PASSED THE EVENT HORIZON! YOU'RE GOING INTO MY BLACK HOLE, BLACK HAMMER!
11 AM TO 12 AM THURS
HOT DOGS
PRETZELS
UGH, SEE? GROSS.
GOURMET DELI
LET'S SEE HOW FUNNY YOU ARE WITHOUT THE HAMMER!
ACTUALLY... YOU KNOW WHAT?
WHY DON'T YOU TAKE IT?
SZZZRKK

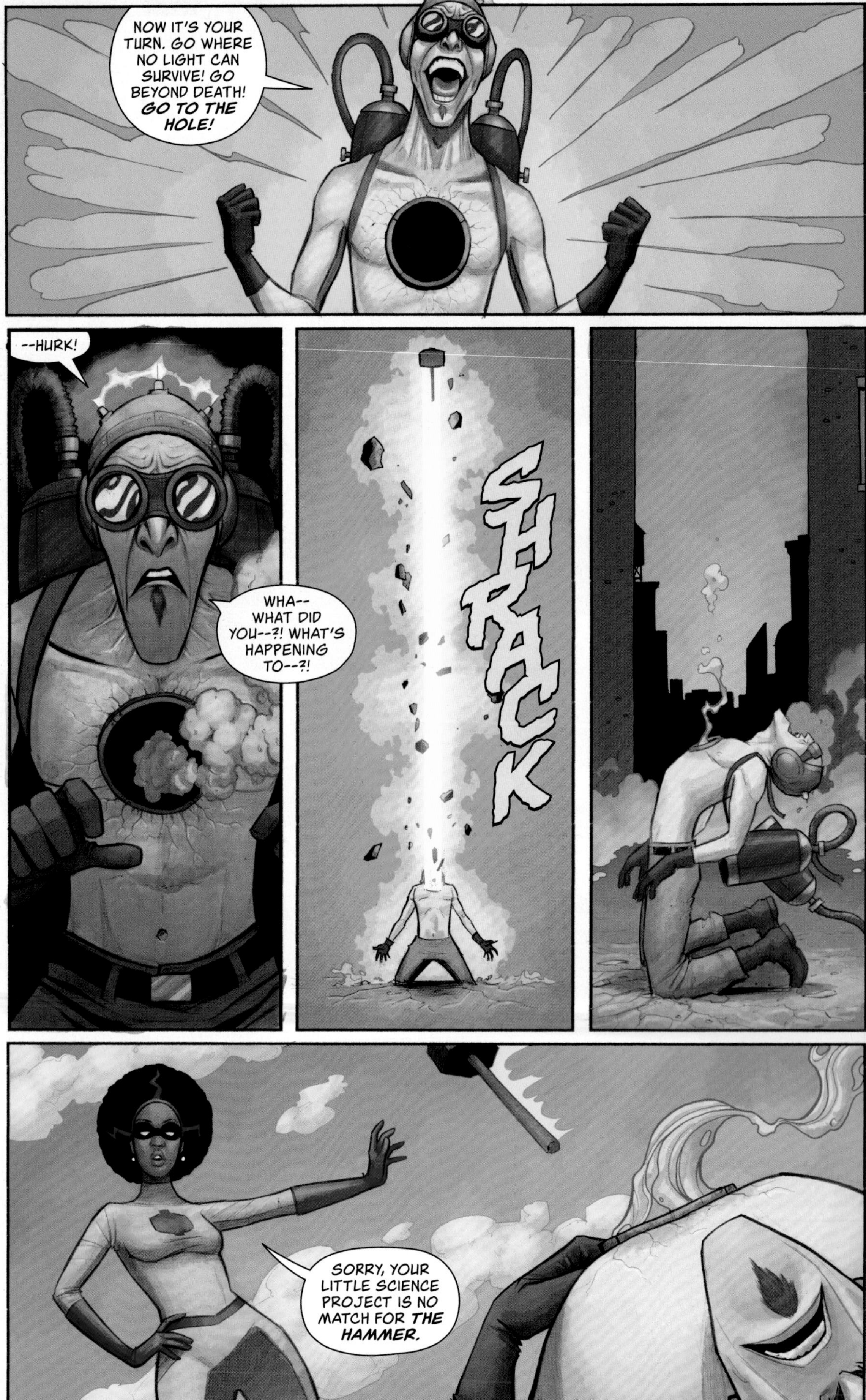
NOW IT'S YOUR TURN. GO WHERE NO LIGHT CAN SURVIVE! GO BEYOND DEATH! GO TO THE HOLE!
--HURK!
WHA-- WHAT DID YOU--?! WHAT'S HAPPENING TO--?!
SHRACK
SORRY, YOUR LITTLE SCIENCE PROJECT IS NO MATCH FOR THE HAMMER.

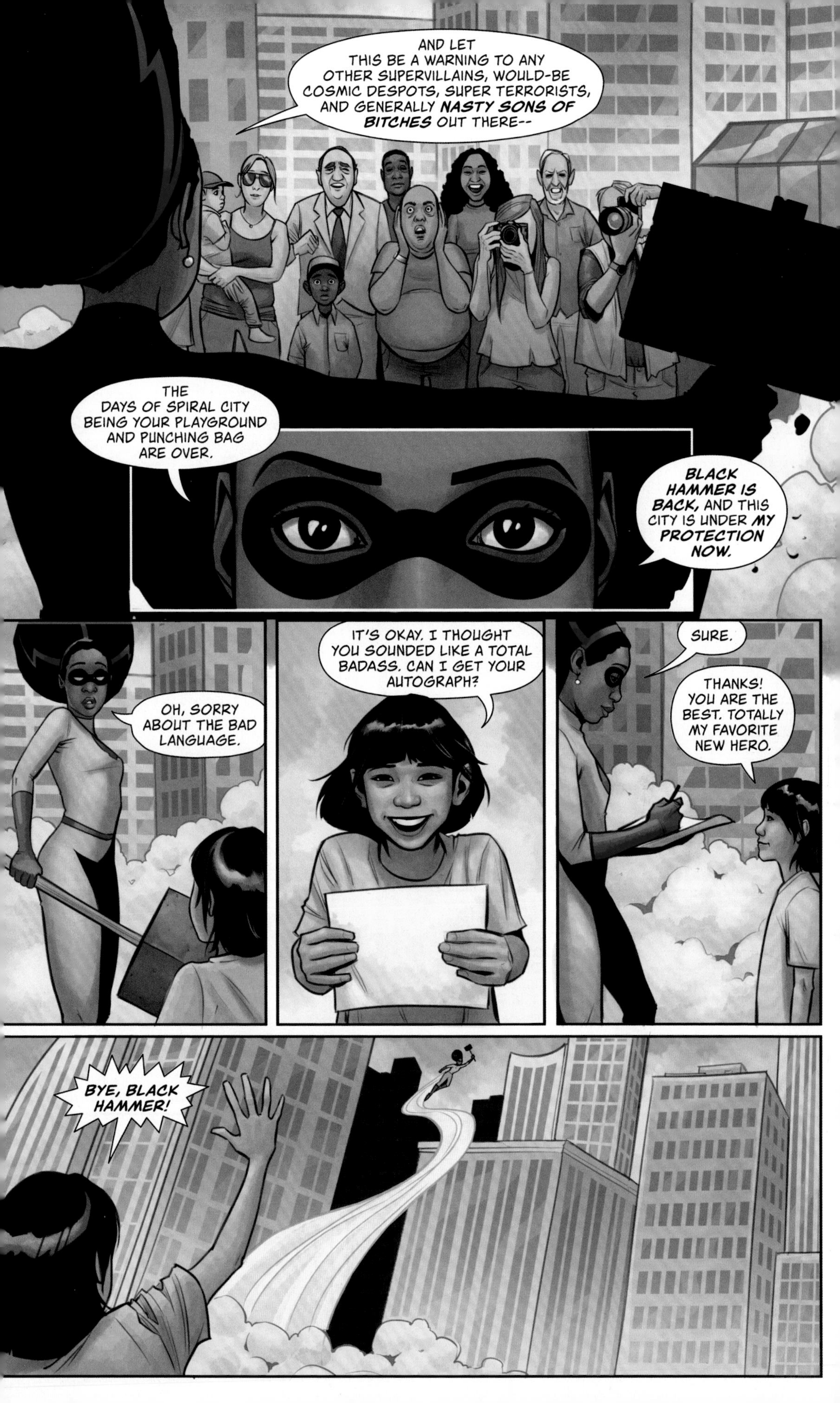
AND LET THIS BE A WARNING TO ANY OTHER SUPERVILLAINS, WOULD-BE COSMIC DESPOTS, SUPER TERRORISTS, AND GENERALLY NASTY SONS OF BITCHES OUT THERE--
THE DAYS OF SPIRAL CITY BEING YOUR PLAYGROUND AND PUNCHING BAG ARE OVER.
BLACK HAMMER IS BACK, AND THIS CITY IS UNDER MY PROTECTION NOW.
OH, SORRY ABOUT THE BAD LANGUAGE.
IT'S OKAY. I THOUGHT YOU SOUNDED LIKE A TOTAL BADASS. CAN I GET YOUR AUTOGRAPH?
SURE.
THANKS! YOU ARE THE BEST. TOTALLY MY FAVORITE NEW HERO.
BYE, BLACK HAMMER!

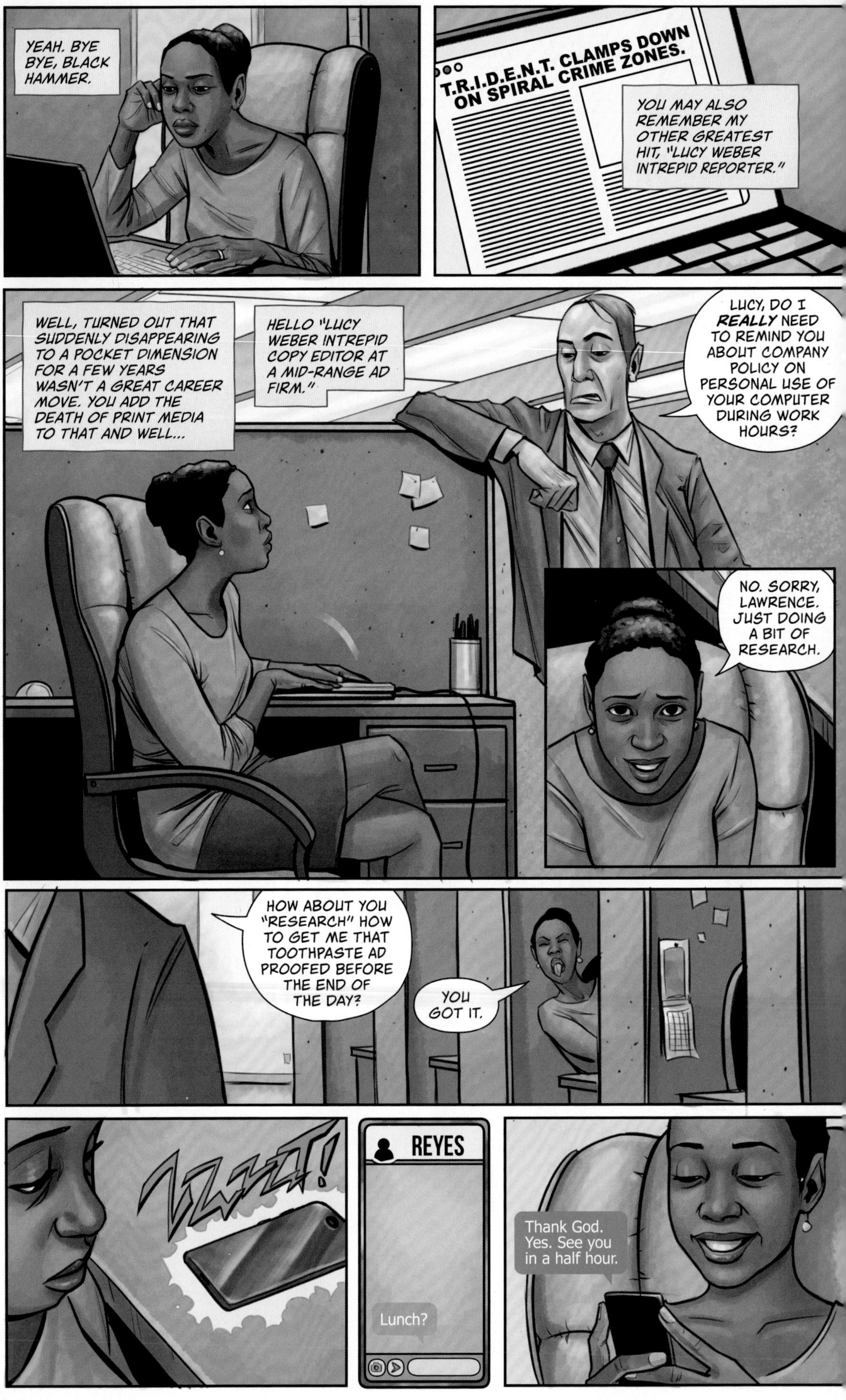
YEAH. BYE BYE, BLACK HAMMER.
T.R.I.D.E.N.T. CLAMPS DOWN ON SPIRAL CRIME ZONES.
YOU MAY ALSO REMEMBER MY OTHER GREATEST HIT, "LUCY WEBER INTREPID REPORTER."
WELL, TURNED OUT THAT SUDDENLY DISAPPEARING TO A POCKET DIMENSION FOR A FEW YEARS WASN'T A GREAT CAREER MOVE. YOU ADD THE DEATH OF PRINT MEDIA TO THAT AND WELL...
HELLO "LUCY WEBER INTREPID COPY EDITOR AT A MID-RANGE AD FIRM."
LUCY, DO I **REALLY** NEED TO REMIND YOU ABOUT COMPANY POLICY ON PERSONAL USE OF YOUR COMPUTER DURING WORK HOURS?
NO. SORRY, LAWRENCE. JUST DOING A BIT OF RESEARCH.
HOW ABOUT YOU "RESEARCH" HOW TO GET ME THAT TOOTHPASTE AD PROOFED BEFORE THE END OF THE DAY?
YOU GOT IT.
VZZZT!
REYES
Lunch?
Thank God. Yes. See you in a half hour.

HOW DO YOU MEASURE ALL THE THINGS YOU'VE LOST?

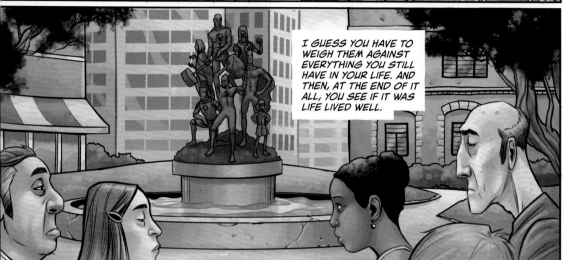

I GUESS YOU HAVE TO WEIGH THEM AGAINST EVERYTHING YOU STILL HAVE IN YOUR LIFE. AND THEN, AT THE END OF IT ALL, YOU SEE IF IT WAS LIFE LIVED WELL.

BUT SOME DAYS... SOME DAYS THE LOSSES JUST FEEL HEAVIER AND HEAVIER.

REYES?

HEY, LUCY. PULL UP A STOOL.

I THOUGHT YOU SAID LUNCH?

THERE'S NUTS.

GREAT.

LOOK AT THIS. TAKES A WHOLE TEAM OF *THOSE IDIOTS* TO ARREST ONE JUNKIE. DON'T YOU JUST FEEL SAFER AT NIGHT?

WELL, SAY WHAT YOU WANT, BUT THERE HASN'T BEEN A NEW SUPER VILLAIN IN NEARLY *THREE YEARS.*

T.R.I.D.E.N.T.* IS DOING SOMETHING RIGHT.

* T.R.I.D.E.N.T.--TACTICAL RESPONSE INTERNATIONAL DEFENSE EXTRANORMAL NEUTRALIZATION TEAM.

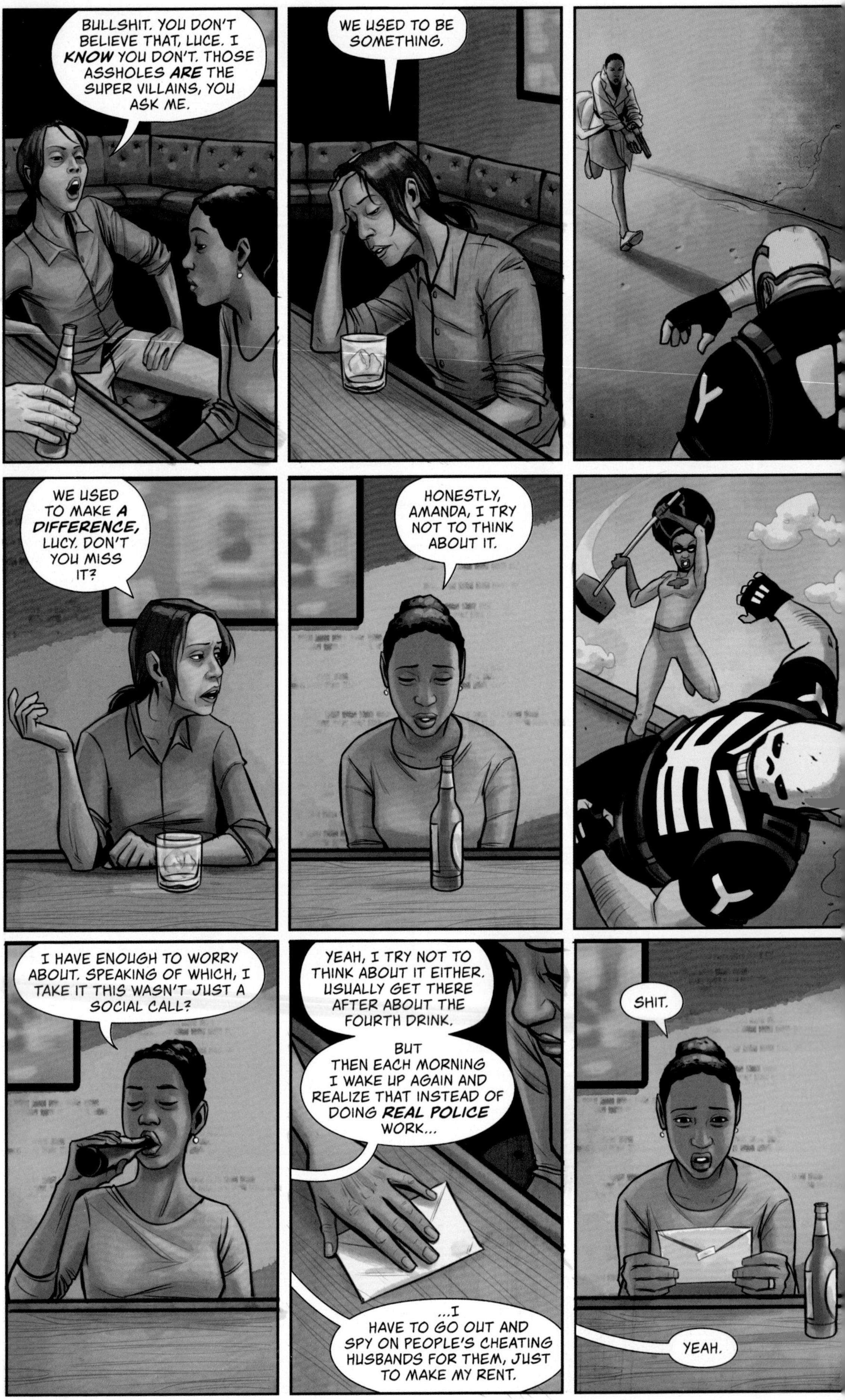
BULLSHIT. YOU DON'T BELIEVE THAT, LUCE. I **KNOW** YOU DON'T. THOSE ASSHOLES **ARE** THE SUPER VILLAINS, YOU ASK ME.
WE USED TO BE SOMETHING.
WE USED TO MAKE **A DIFFERENCE,** LUCY. DON'T YOU MISS IT?
HONESTLY, AMANDA, I TRY NOT TO THINK ABOUT IT.
I HAVE ENOUGH TO WORRY ABOUT. SPEAKING OF WHICH, I TAKE IT THIS WASN'T JUST A SOCIAL CALL?
YEAH, I TRY NOT TO THINK ABOUT IT EITHER. USUALLY GET THERE AFTER ABOUT THE FOURTH DRINK.
BUT THEN EACH MORNING I WAKE UP AGAIN AND REALIZE THAT INSTEAD OF DOING **REAL POLICE** WORK...
...I HAVE TO GO OUT AND SPY ON PEOPLE'S CHEATING HUSBANDS FOR THEM, JUST TO MAKE MY RENT.
SHIT.
YEAH.

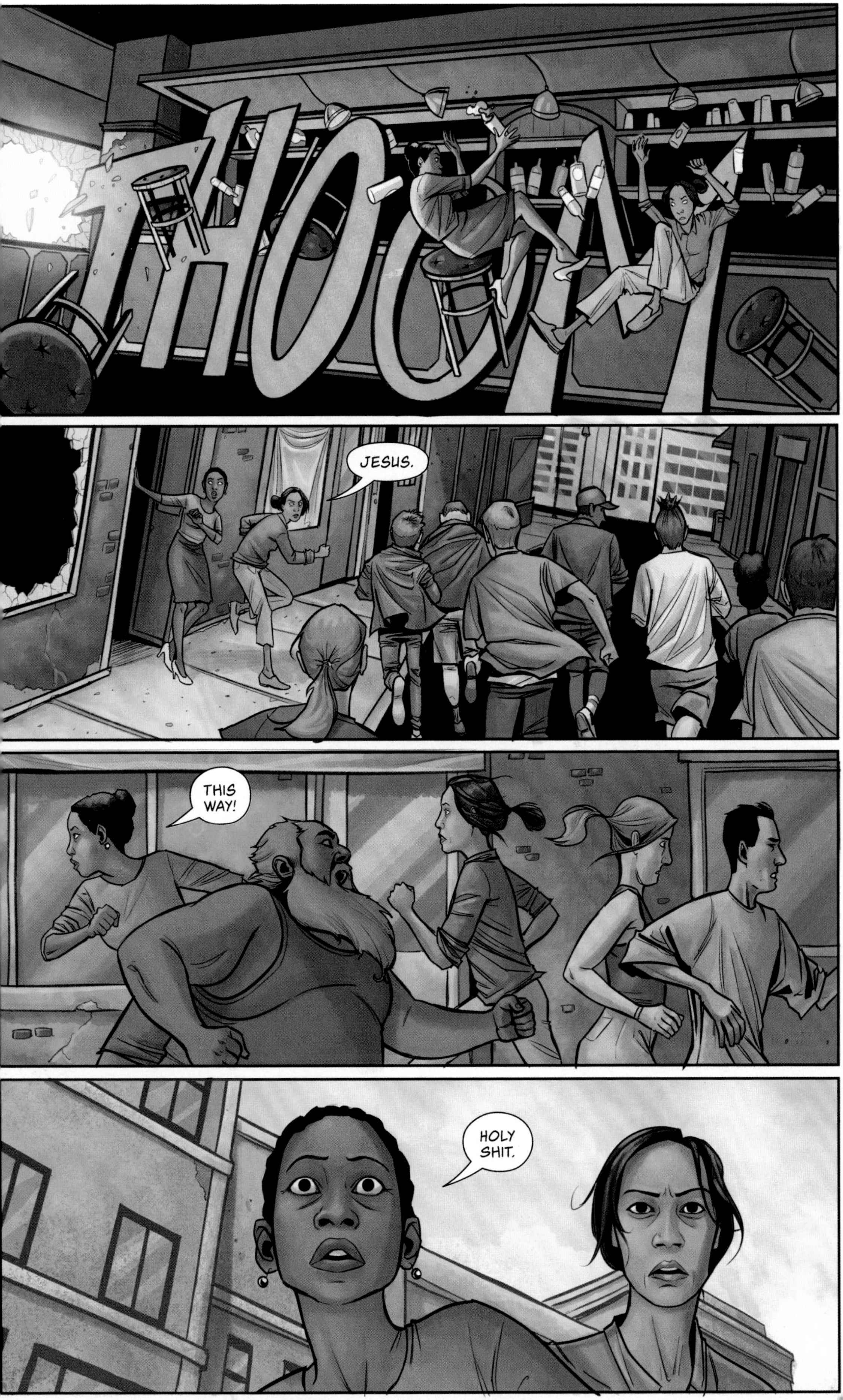
THOOM
JESUS.
THIS WAY!
HOLY SHIT.

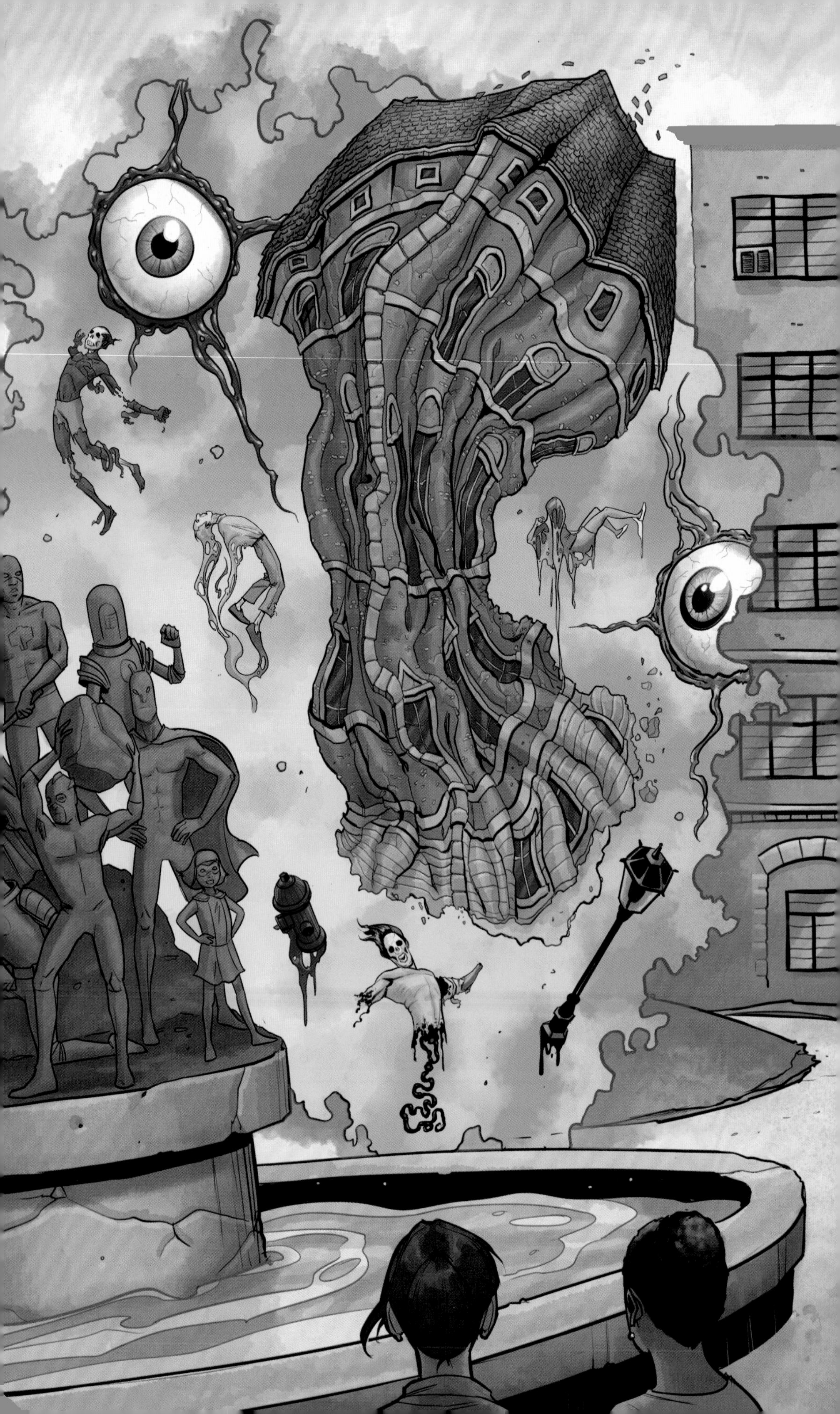

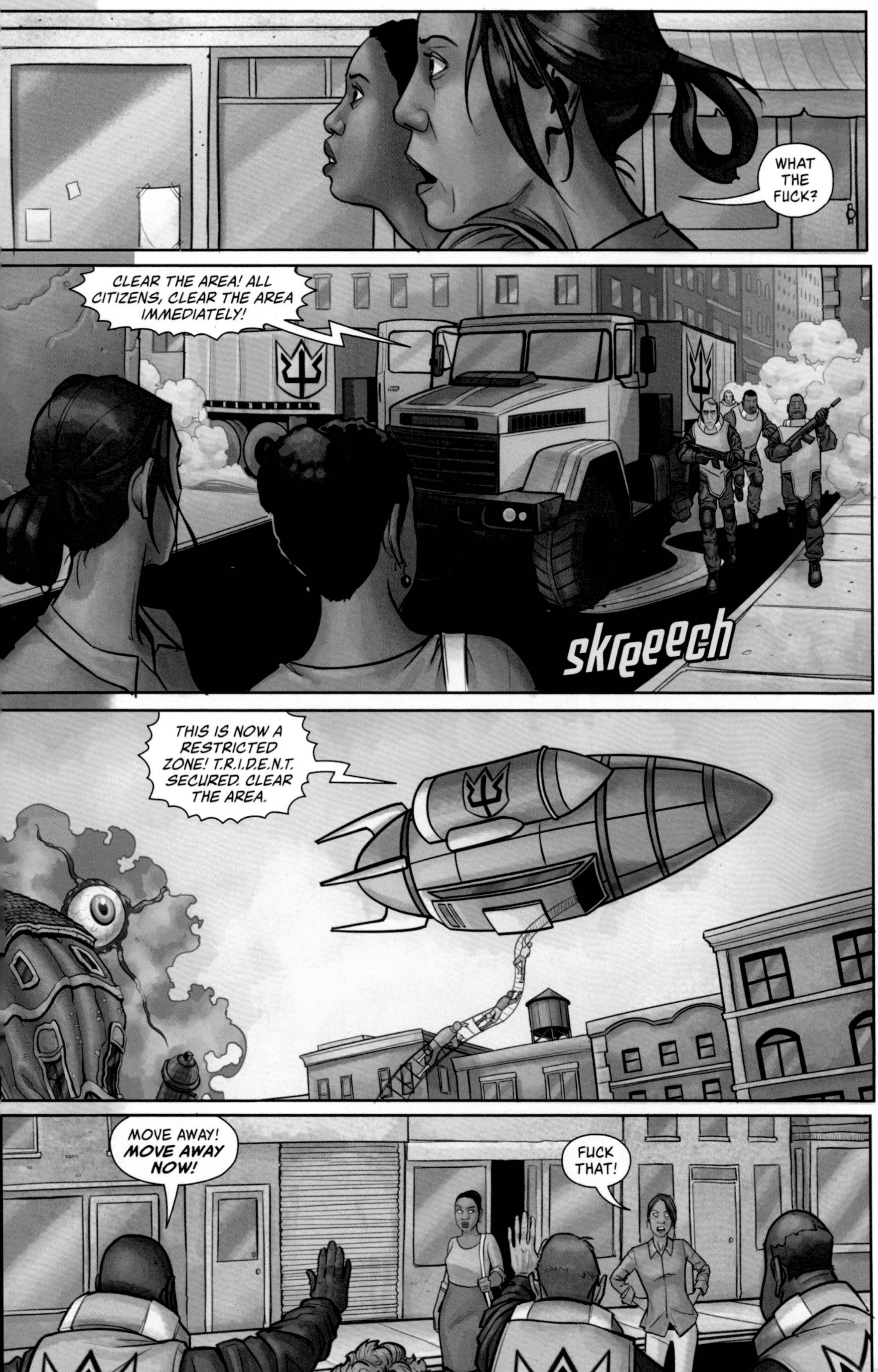

WHAT THE FUCK?
CLEAR THE AREA! ALL CITIZENS, CLEAR THE AREA IMMEDIATELY!
skreeech
THIS IS NOW A RESTRICTED ZONE! T.R.I.D.E.N.T. SECURED. CLEAR THE AREA.
MOVE AWAY! MOVE AWAY NOW!
FUCK THAT!

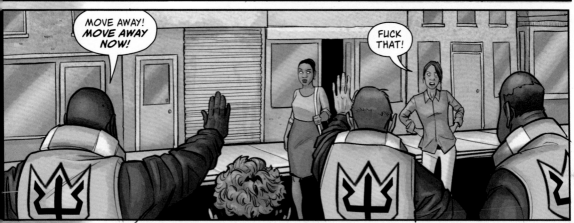

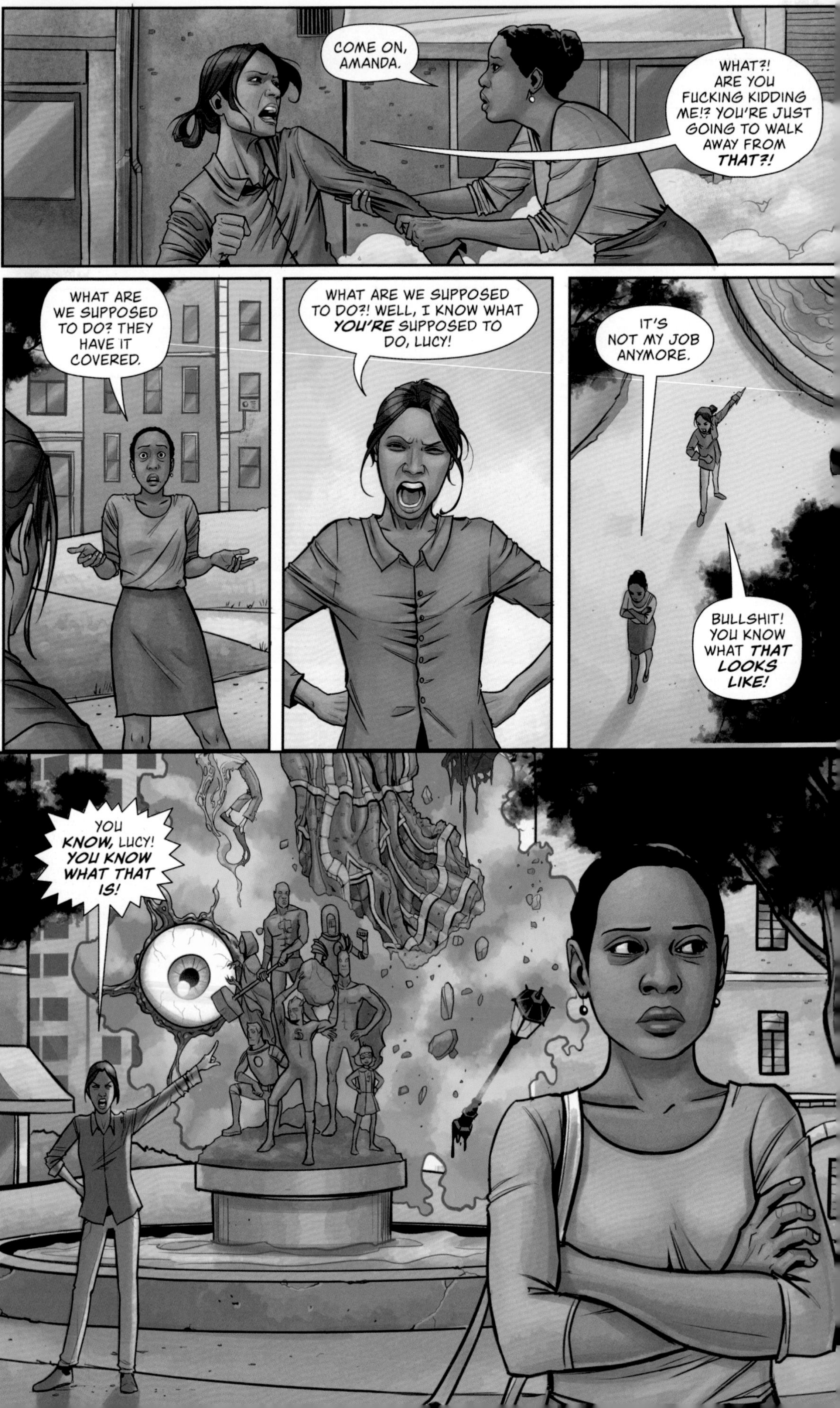
COME ON, AMANDA.
WHAT?! ARE YOU FUCKING KIDDING ME!? YOU'RE JUST GOING TO WALK AWAY FROM THAT?!
WHAT ARE WE SUPPOSED TO DO? THEY HAVE IT COVERED.
WHAT ARE WE SUPPOSED TO DO?! WELL, I KNOW WHAT YOU'RE SUPPOSED TO DO, LUCY!
IT'S NOT MY JOB ANYMORE.
BULLSHIT! YOU KNOW WHAT THAT LOOKS LIKE!
YOU KNOW, LUCY! YOU KNOW WHAT THAT IS!

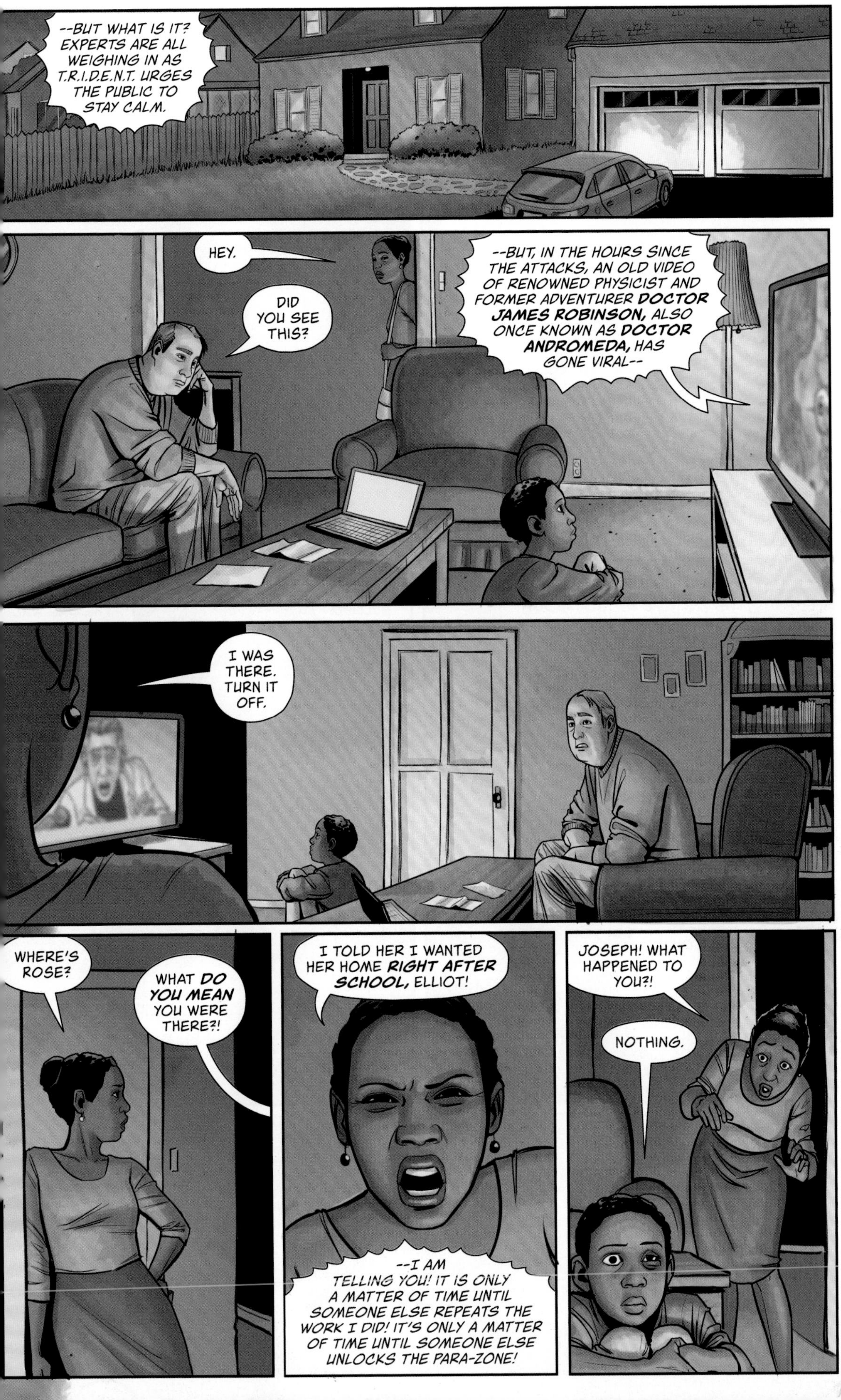
--BUT WHAT IS IT? EXPERTS ARE ALL WEIGHING IN AS T.R.I.D.E.N.T. URGES THE PUBLIC TO STAY CALM.
HEY.
DID YOU SEE THIS?
--BUT, IN THE HOURS SINCE THE ATTACKS, AN OLD VIDEO OF RENOWNED PHYSICIST AND FORMER ADVENTURER DOCTOR JAMES ROBINSON, ALSO ONCE KNOWN AS DOCTOR ANDROMEDA, HAS GONE VIRAL--
I WAS THERE. TURN IT OFF.
WHERE'S ROSE?
WHAT DO YOU MEAN YOU WERE THERE?!
I TOLD HER I WANTED HER HOME RIGHT AFTER SCHOOL, ELLIOT!
--I AM TELLING YOU! IT IS ONLY A MATTER OF TIME UNTIL SOMEONE ELSE REPEATS THE WORK I DID! IT'S ONLY A MATTER OF TIME UNTIL SOMEONE ELSE UNLOCKS THE PARA-ZONE!
JOSEPH! WHAT HAPPENED TO YOU?!
NOTHING.

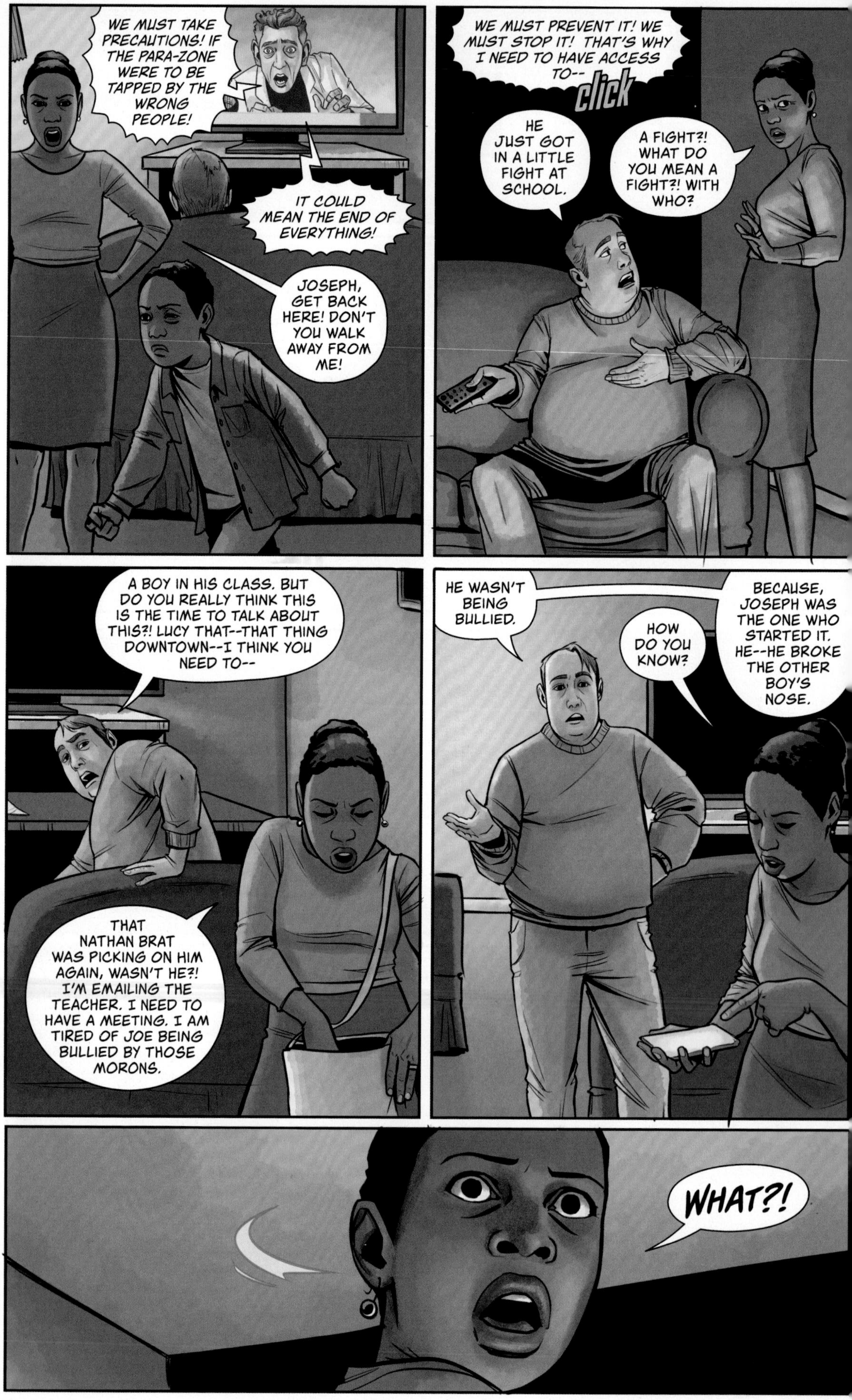
WE MUST TAKE PRECAUTIONS! IF THE PARA-ZONE WERE TO BE TAPPED BY THE WRONG PEOPLE!
IT COULD MEAN THE END OF EVERYTHING!
JOSEPH, GET BACK HERE! DON'T YOU WALK AWAY FROM ME!
WE MUST PREVENT IT! WE MUST STOP IT! THAT'S WHY I NEED TO HAVE ACCESS TO--
click
HE JUST GOT IN A LITTLE FIGHT AT SCHOOL.
A FIGHT?! WHAT DO YOU MEAN A FIGHT?! WITH WHO?
A BOY IN HIS CLASS. BUT DO YOU REALLY THINK THIS IS THE TIME TO TALK ABOUT THIS?! LUCY THAT--THAT THING DOWNTOWN--I THINK YOU NEED TO--
THAT NATHAN BRAT WAS PICKING ON HIM AGAIN, WASN'T HE?! I'M EMAILING THE TEACHER. I NEED TO HAVE A MEETING. I AM TIRED OF JOE BEING BULLIED BY THOSE MORONS.
HE WASN'T BEING BULLIED.
HOW DO YOU KNOW?
BECAUSE, JOSEPH WAS THE ONE WHO STARTED IT. HE--HE BROKE THE OTHER BOY'S NOSE.
WHAT?!

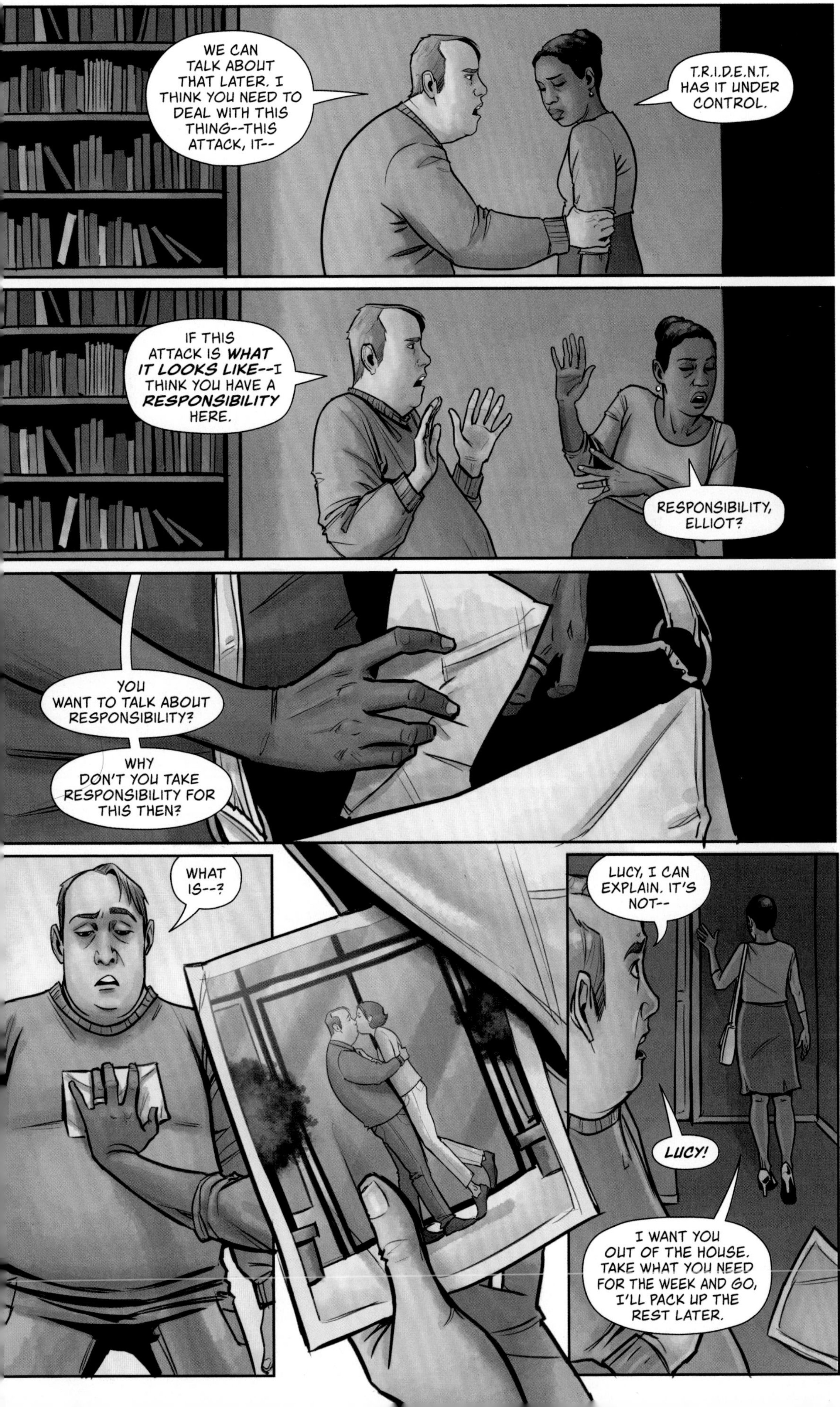
WE CAN TALK ABOUT THAT LATER. I THINK YOU NEED TO DEAL WITH THIS THING--THIS ATTACK, IT--
T.R.I.D.E.N.T. HAS IT UNDER CONTROL.
IF THIS ATTACK IS WHAT IT LOOKS LIKE--I THINK YOU HAVE A RESPONSIBILITY HERE.
RESPONSIBILITY, ELLIOT?
YOU WANT TO TALK ABOUT RESPONSIBILITY?
WHY DON'T YOU TAKE RESPONSIBILITY FOR THIS THEN?
WHAT IS--?
LUCY, I CAN EXPLAIN. IT'S NOT--
LUCY!
I WANT YOU OUT OF THE HOUSE. TAKE WHAT YOU NEED FOR THE WEEK AND GO, I'LL PACK UP THE REST LATER.

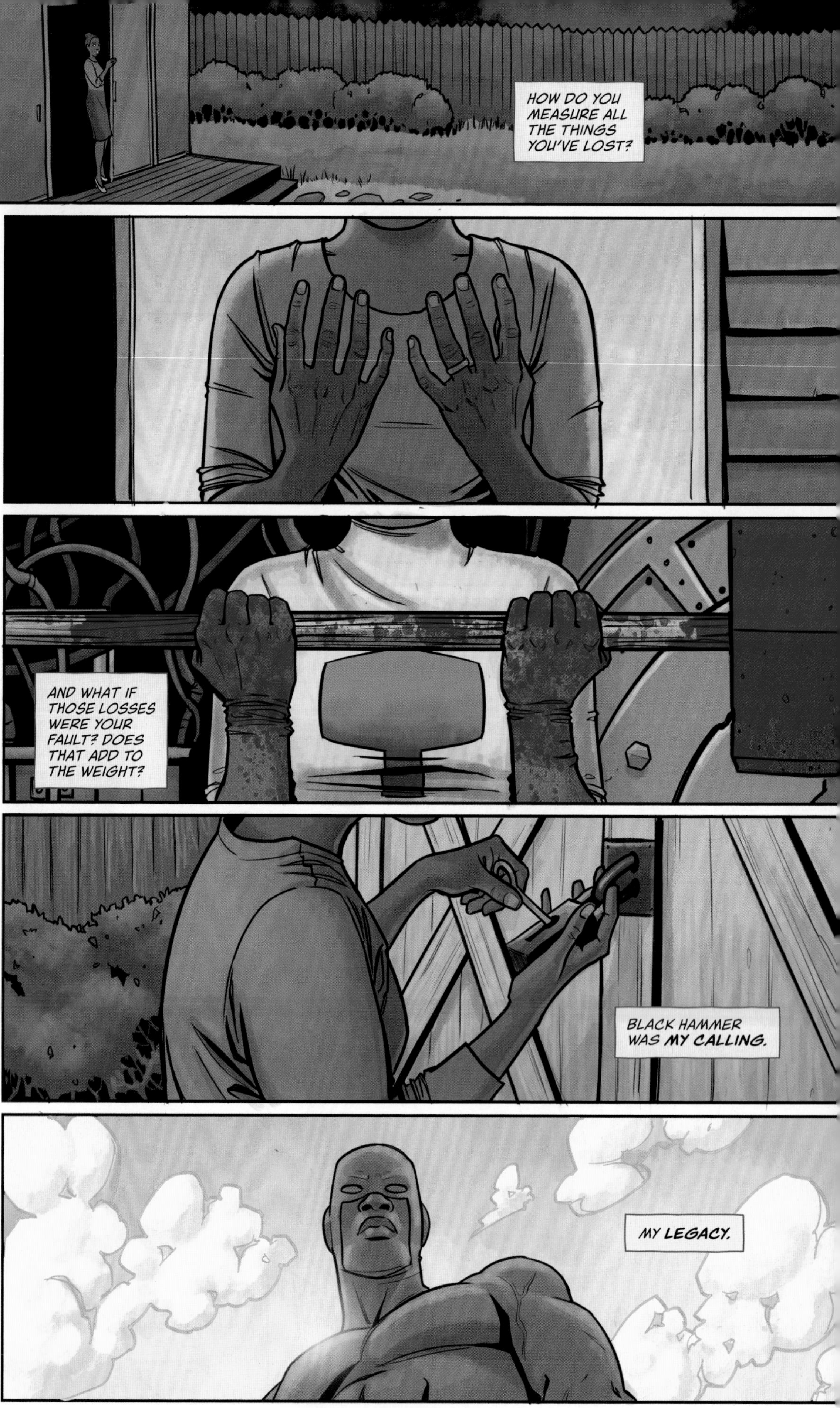
HOW DO YOU MEASURE ALL THE THINGS YOU'VE LOST?
AND WHAT IF THOSE LOSSES WERE YOUR FAULT? DOES THAT ADD TO THE WEIGHT?
BLACK HAMMER WAS MY CALLING.
MY LEGACY.

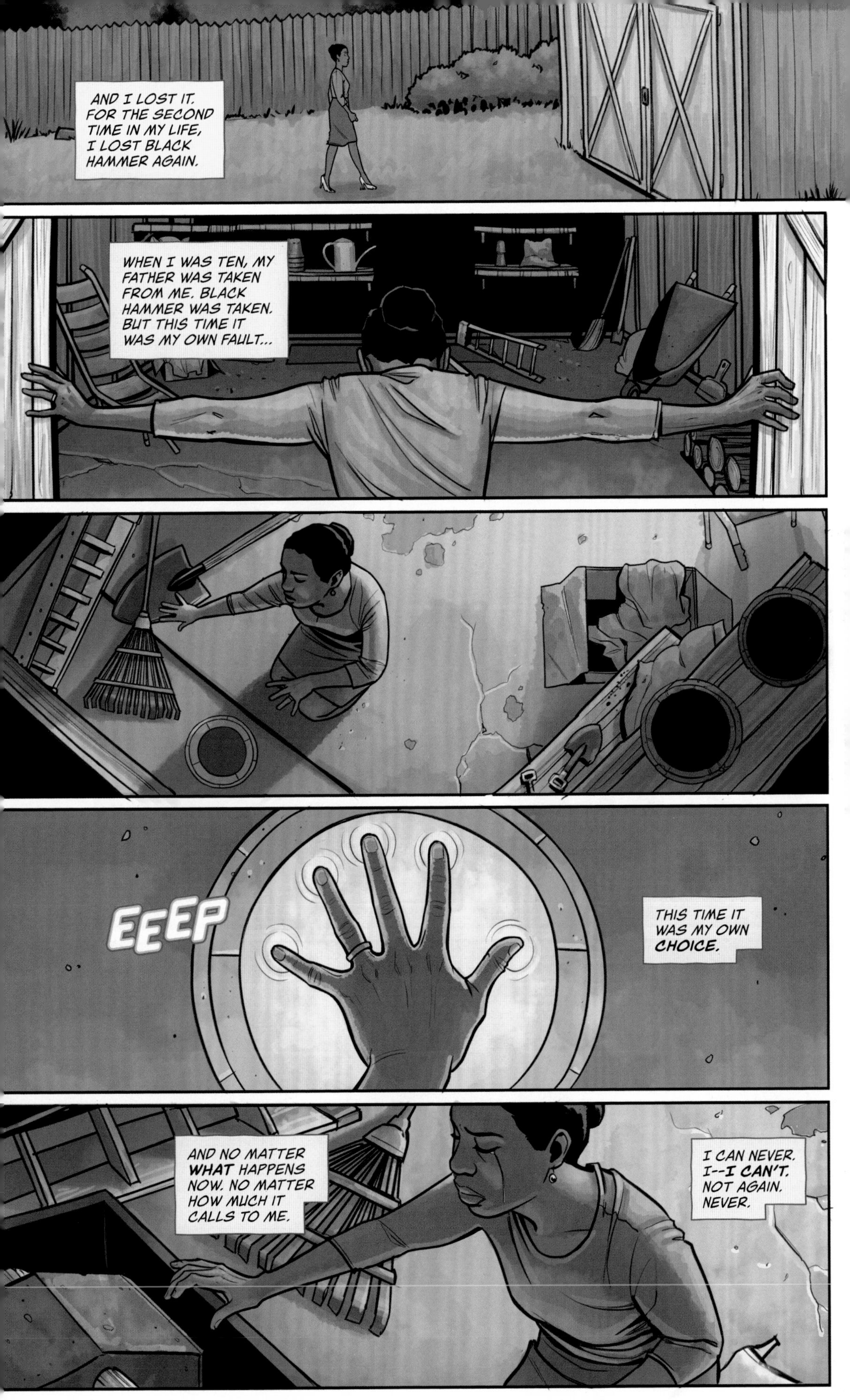
AND I LOST IT. FOR THE SECOND TIME IN MY LIFE, I LOST BLACK HAMMER AGAIN.
WHEN I WAS TEN, MY FATHER WAS TAKEN FROM ME. BLACK HAMMER WAS TAKEN. BUT THIS TIME IT WAS MY OWN FAULT...
EEEP
THIS TIME IT WAS MY OWN CHOICE.
AND NO MATTER WHAT HAPPENS NOW. NO MATTER HOW MUCH IT CALLS TO ME.
I CAN NEVER. I--I CAN'T. NOT AGAIN. NEVER.

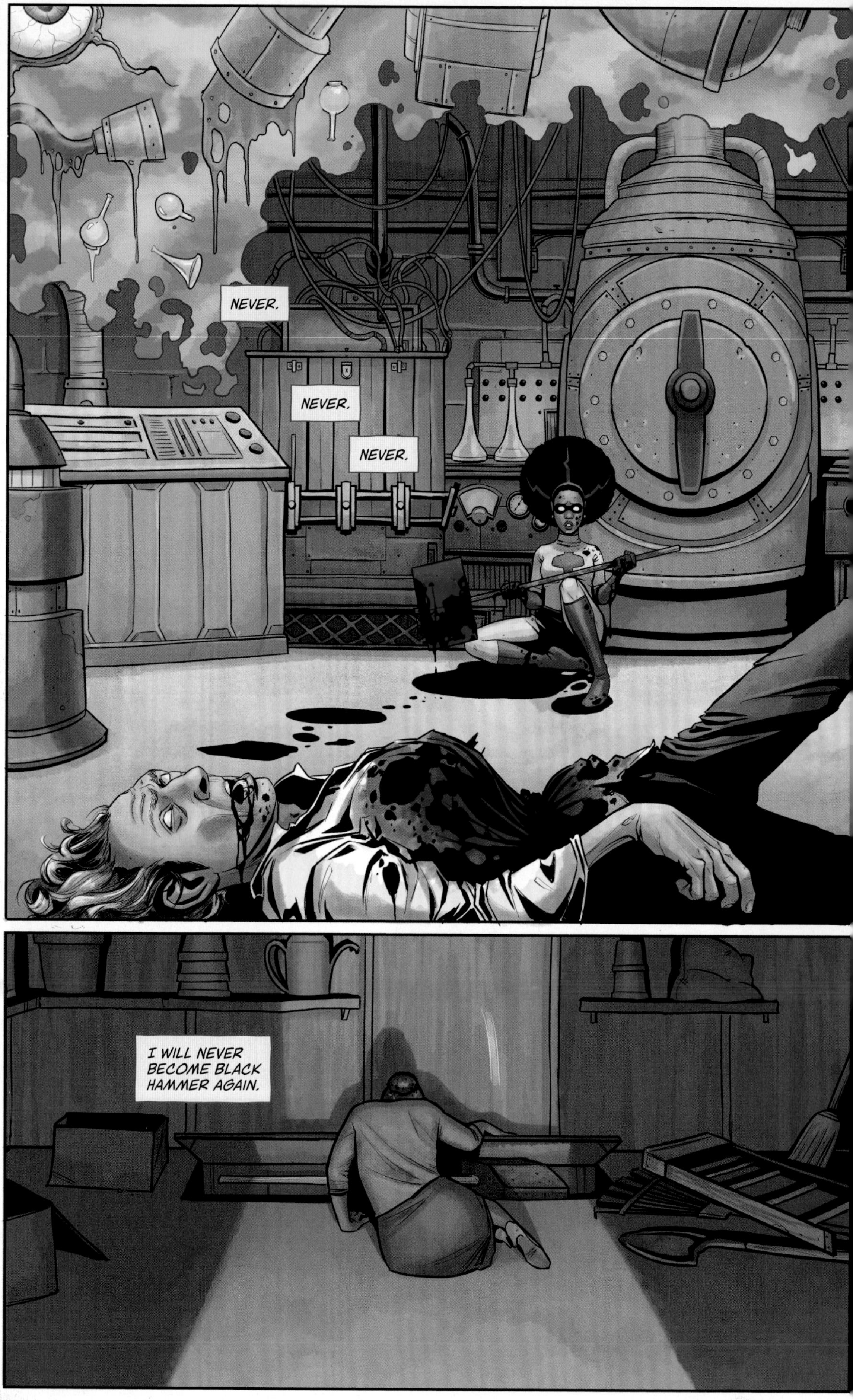
NEVER.
NEVER.
NEVER.
I WILL NEVER BECOME BLACK HAMMER AGAIN.

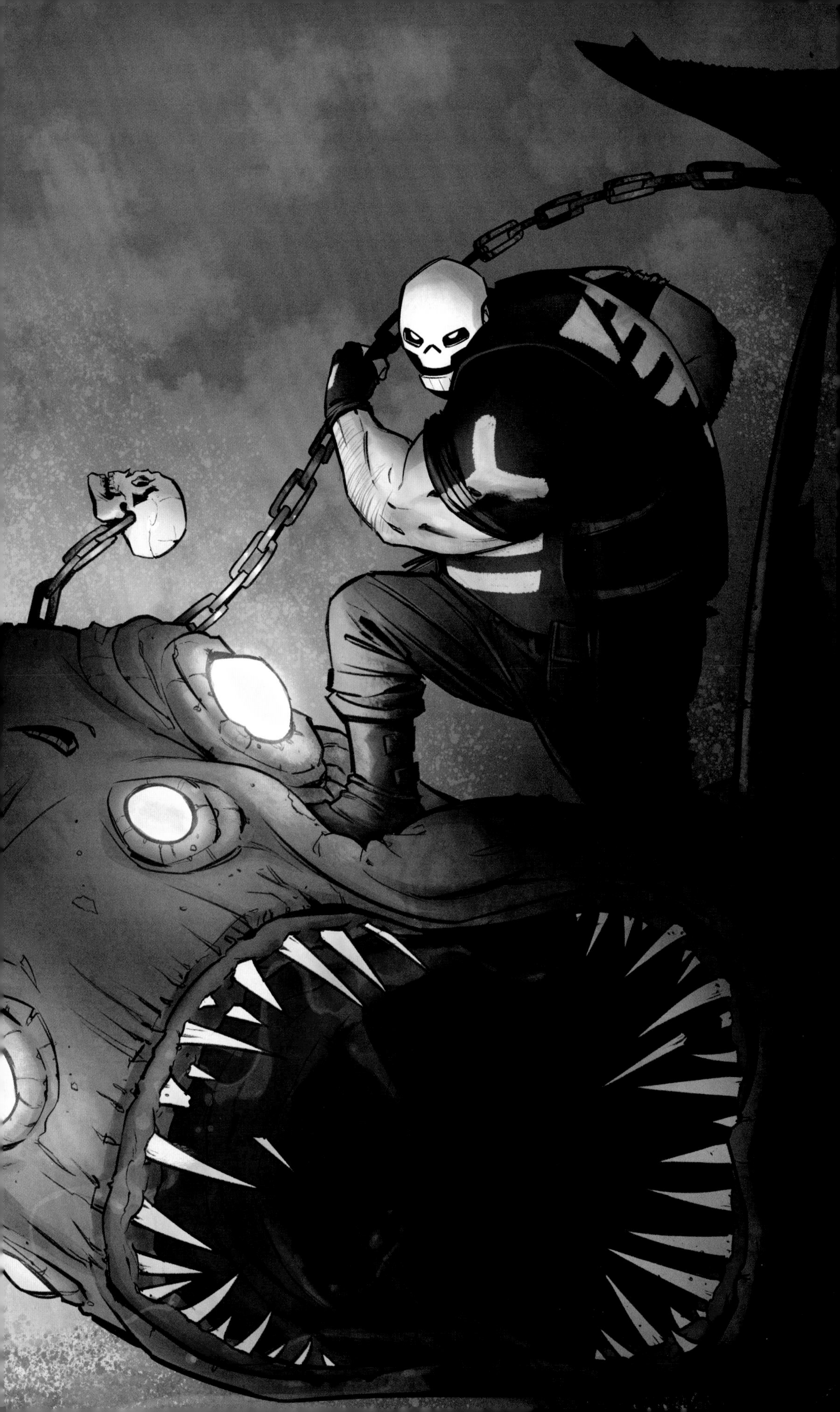

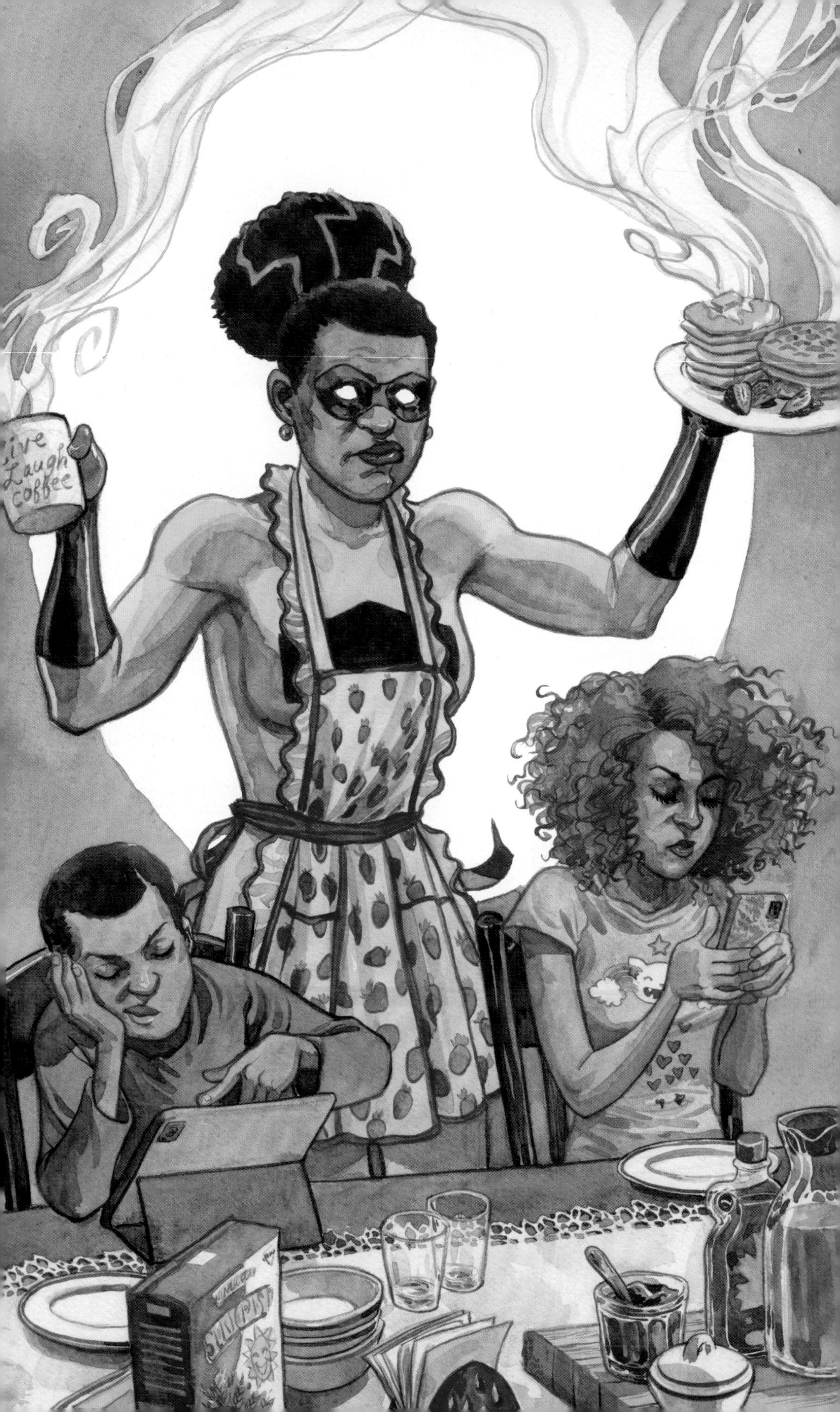
Laugh
coffee

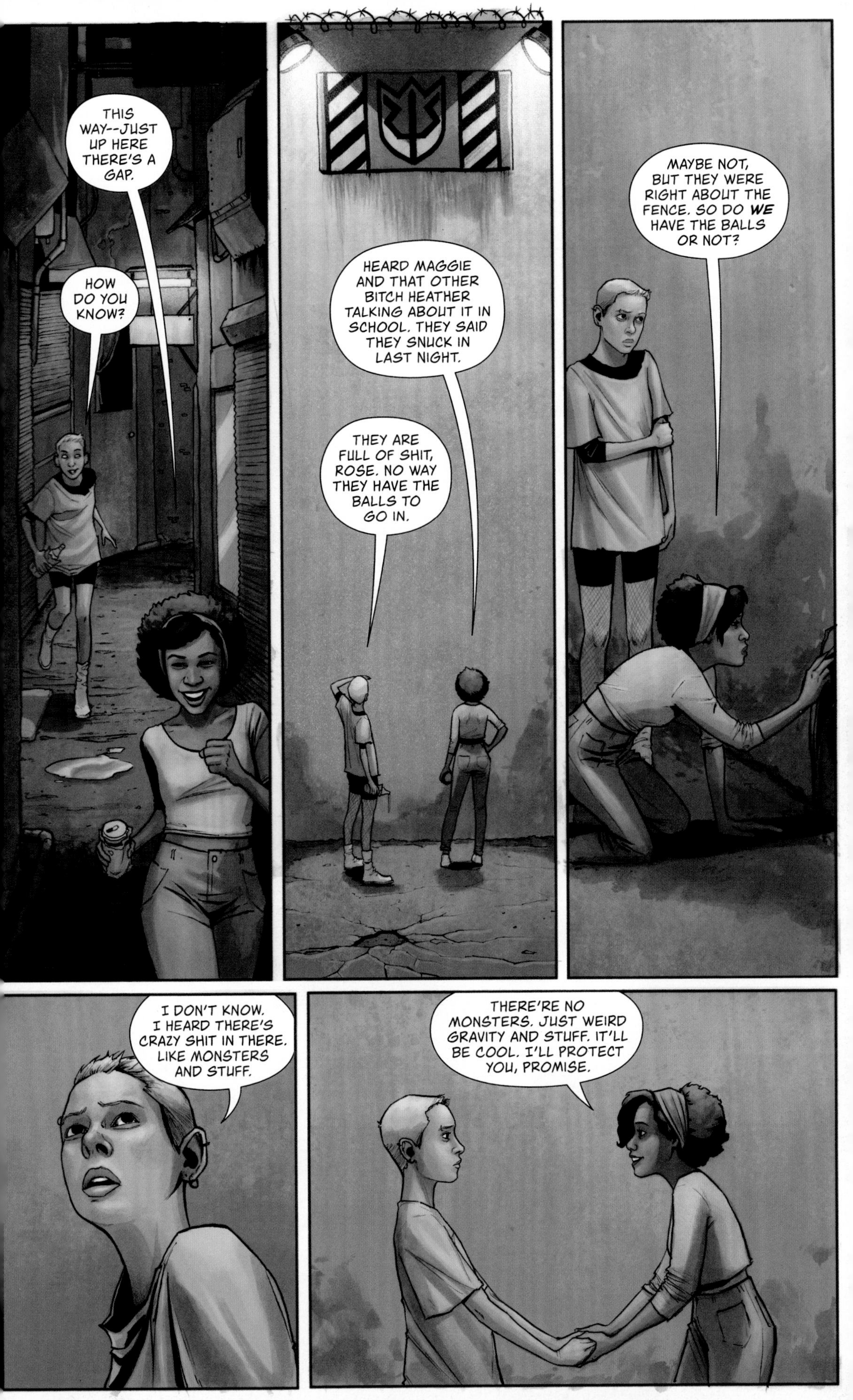

THIS WAY--JUST UP HERE THERE'S A GAP.
HOW DO YOU KNOW?
HEARD MAGGIE AND THAT OTHER BITCH HEATHER TALKING ABOUT IT IN SCHOOL. THEY SAID THEY SNUCK IN LAST NIGHT.
THEY ARE FULL OF SHIT, ROSE. NO WAY THEY HAVE THE BALLS TO GO IN.
MAYBE NOT, BUT THEY WERE RIGHT ABOUT THE FENCE. SO DO **WE** HAVE THE BALLS OR NOT?
I DON'T KNOW. I HEARD THERE'S CRAZY SHIT IN THERE. LIKE MONSTERS AND STUFF.
THERE'RE NO MONSTERS. JUST WEIRD GRAVITY AND STUFF. IT'LL BE COOL. I'LL PROTECT YOU, PROMISE.

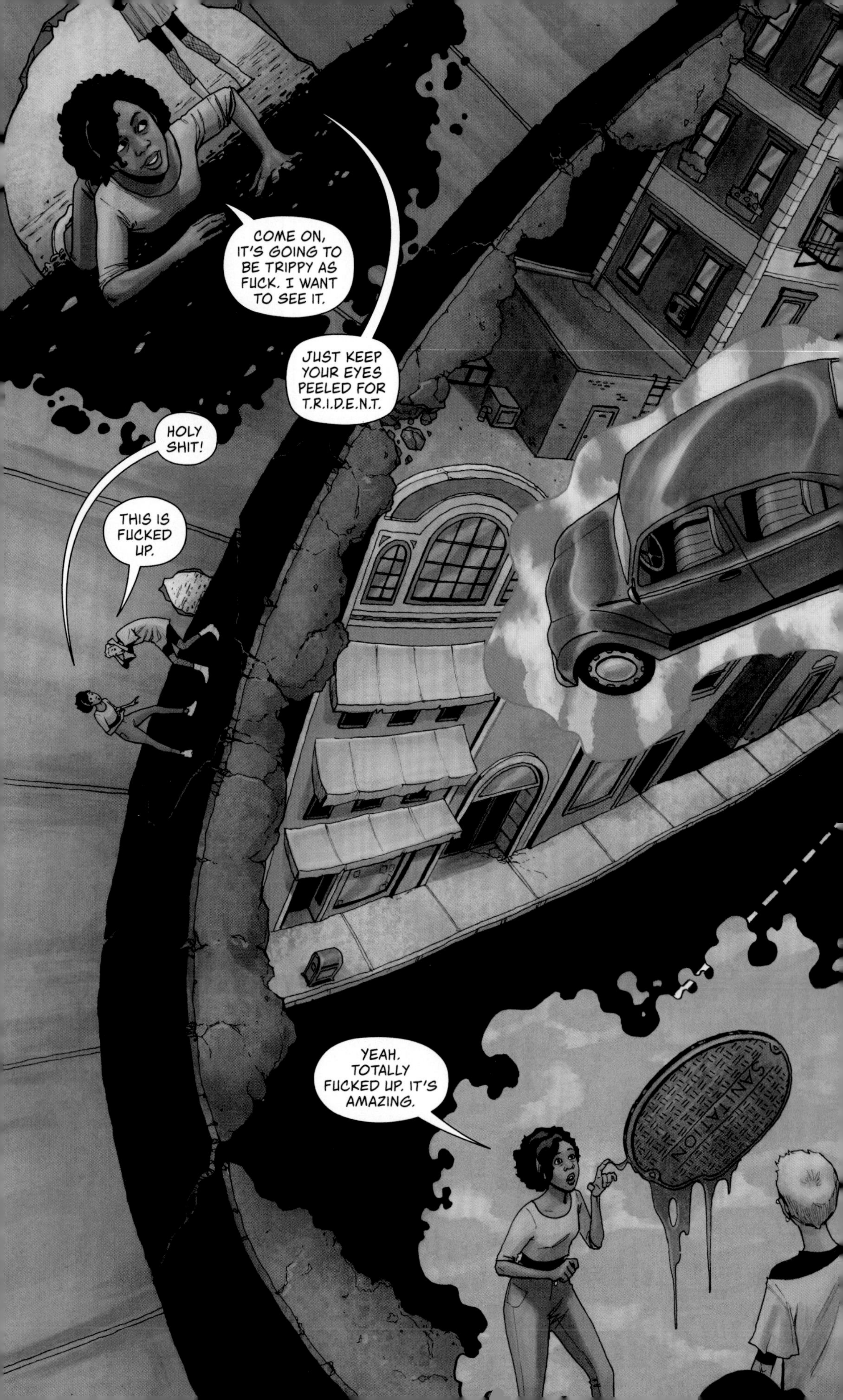
COME ON, IT'S GOING TO BE TRIPPY AS FUCK. I WANT TO SEE IT.
JUST KEEP YOUR EYES PEELED FOR T.R.I.D.E.N.T.
HOLY SHIT!
THIS IS FUCKED UP.
YEAH. TOTALLY FUCKED UP. IT'S AMAZING.
SANITATION

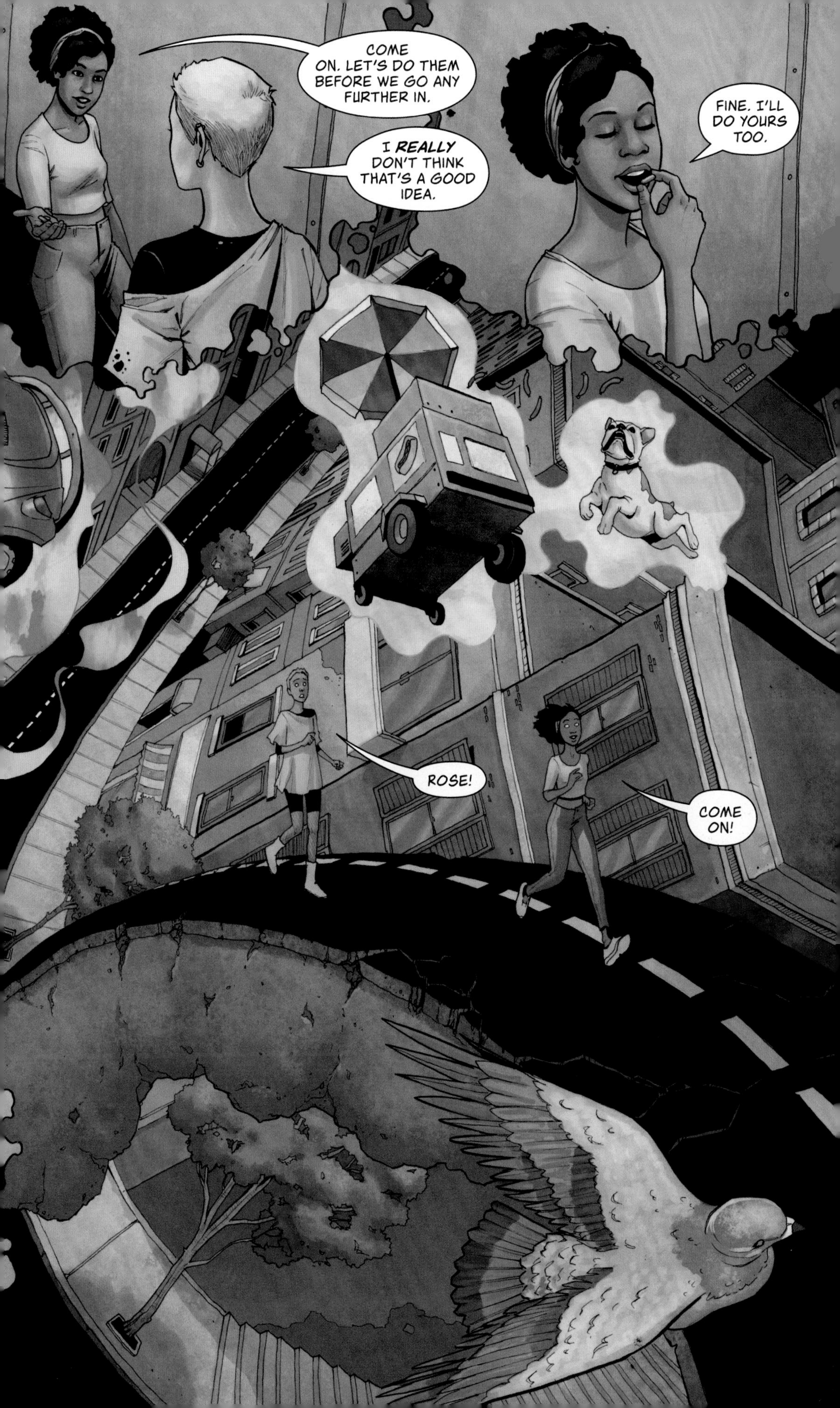
COME ON. LET'S DO THEM BEFORE WE GO ANY FURTHER IN.
I **REALLY** DON'T THINK THAT'S A GOOD IDEA.
FINE. I'LL DO YOURS TOO.
ROSE!
COME ON!

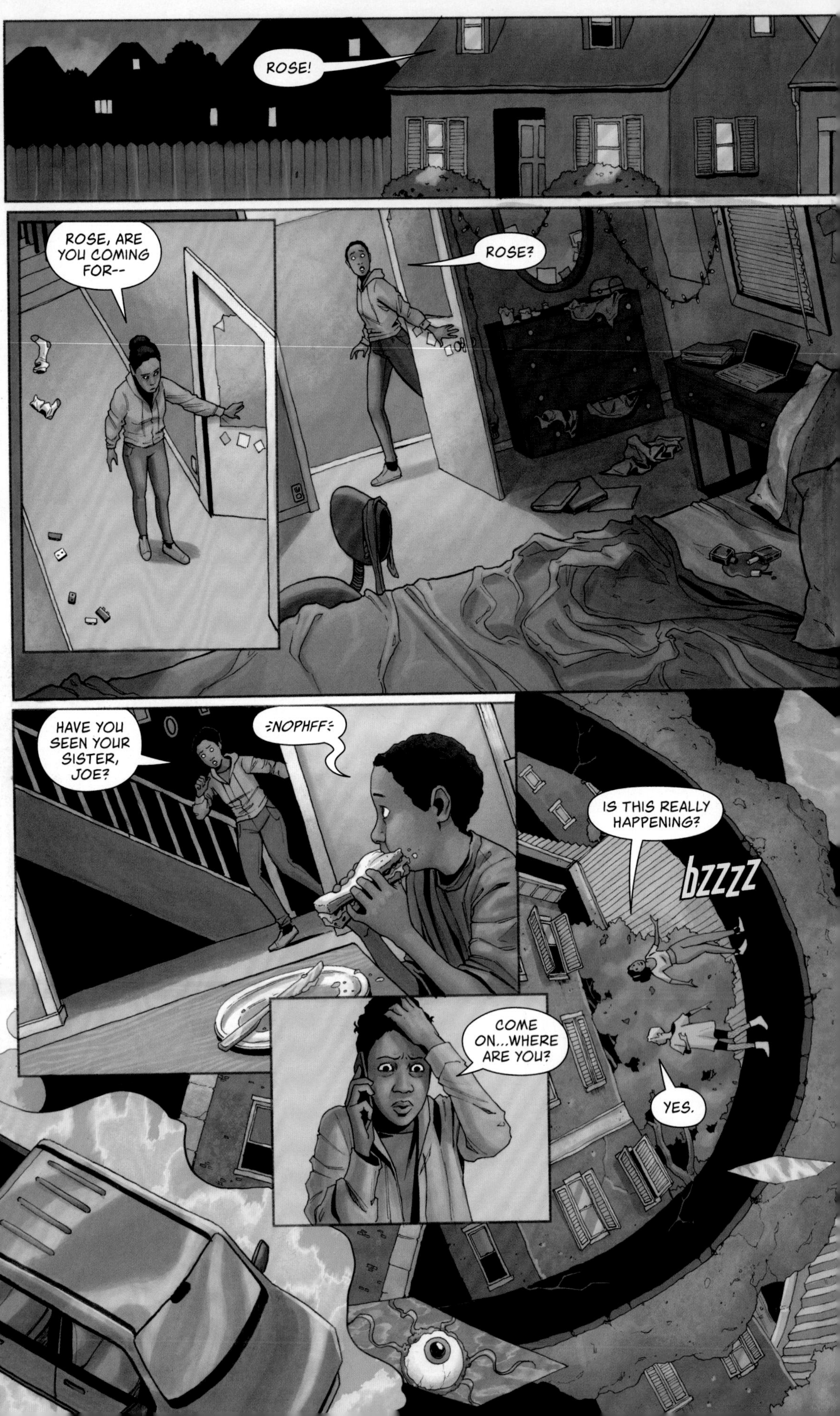
ROSE!
ROSE, ARE YOU COMING FOR--
ROSE?
HAVE YOU SEEN YOUR SISTER, JOE?
=NOPHFF=
IS THIS REALLY HAPPENING?
bzzzz
COME ON...WHERE ARE YOU?
YES.

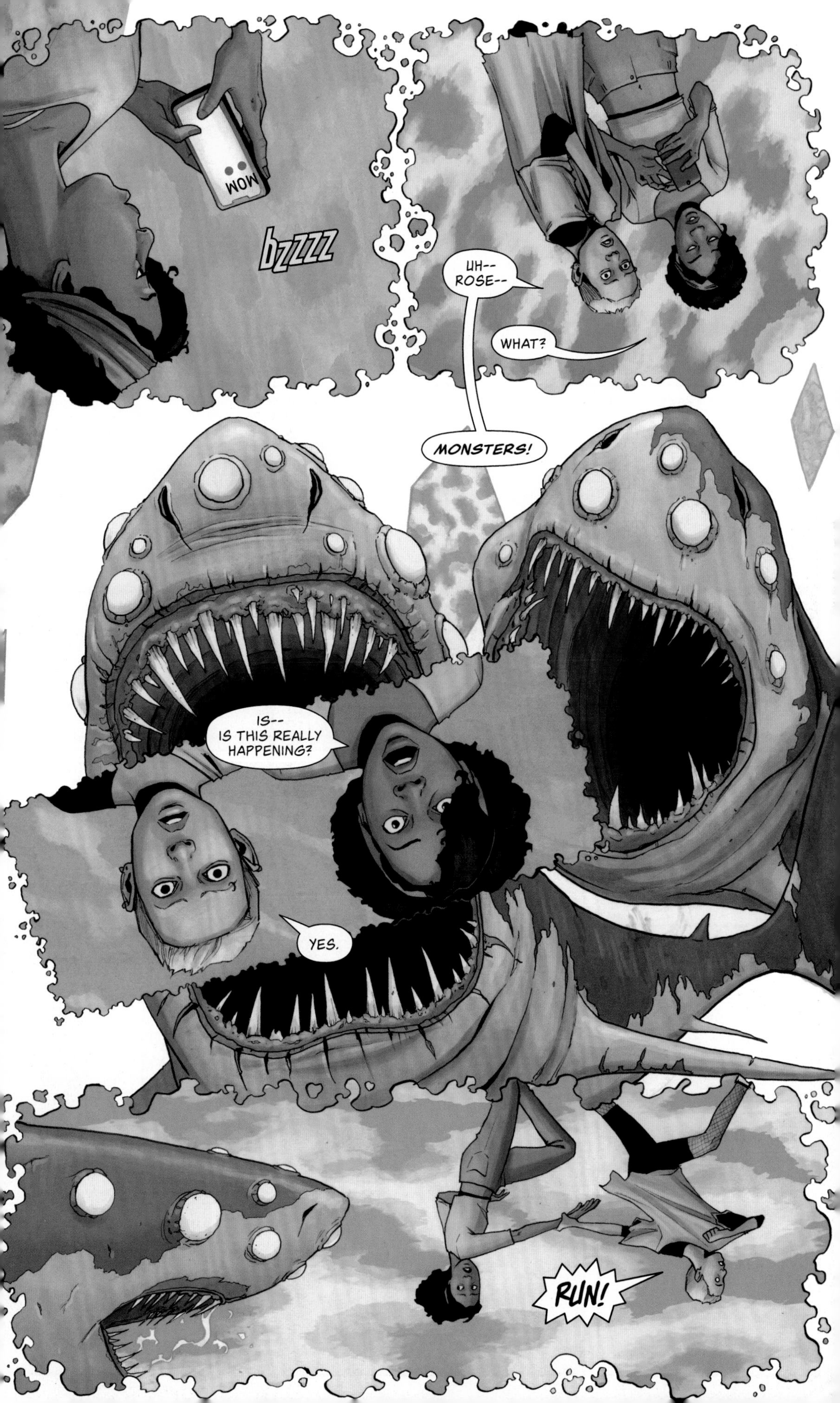
MOM
bzzzz
UH--
ROSE--
WHAT?
MONSTERS!
IS--
IS THIS REALLY
HAPPENING?
YES.
RUN!

TWENTY YEARS AGO.

RUN!

I AM!

HE'S UP THERE. WE GOT THAT ASSHOLE. WE FINALLY GOT HIM, LUCE.

PUT THE GUN AWAY, AMANDA...YOU WON'T NEED IT.

YOU SURE ABOUT THIS?

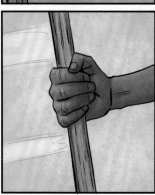

I'M SURE.

JUST KEEP YOUR MEN BACK.

I GOT HIM.

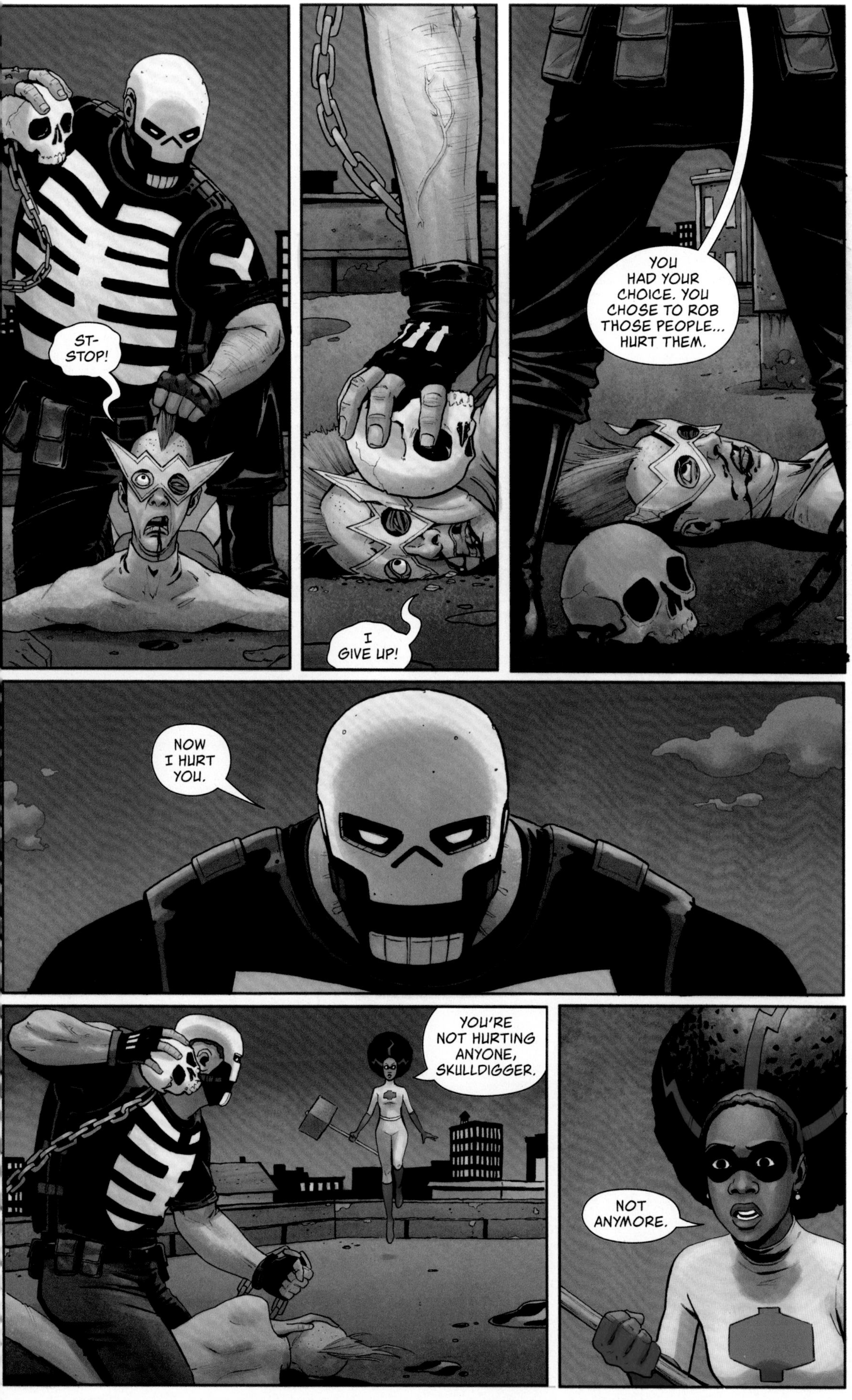
ST-
STOP!
I
GIVE UP!
YOU
HAD YOUR
CHOICE. YOU
CHOSE TO ROB
THOSE PEOPLE...
HURT THEM.
NOW
I HURT
YOU.
YOU'RE
NOT HURTING
ANYONE,
SKULLDIGGER.
NOT
ANYMORE.

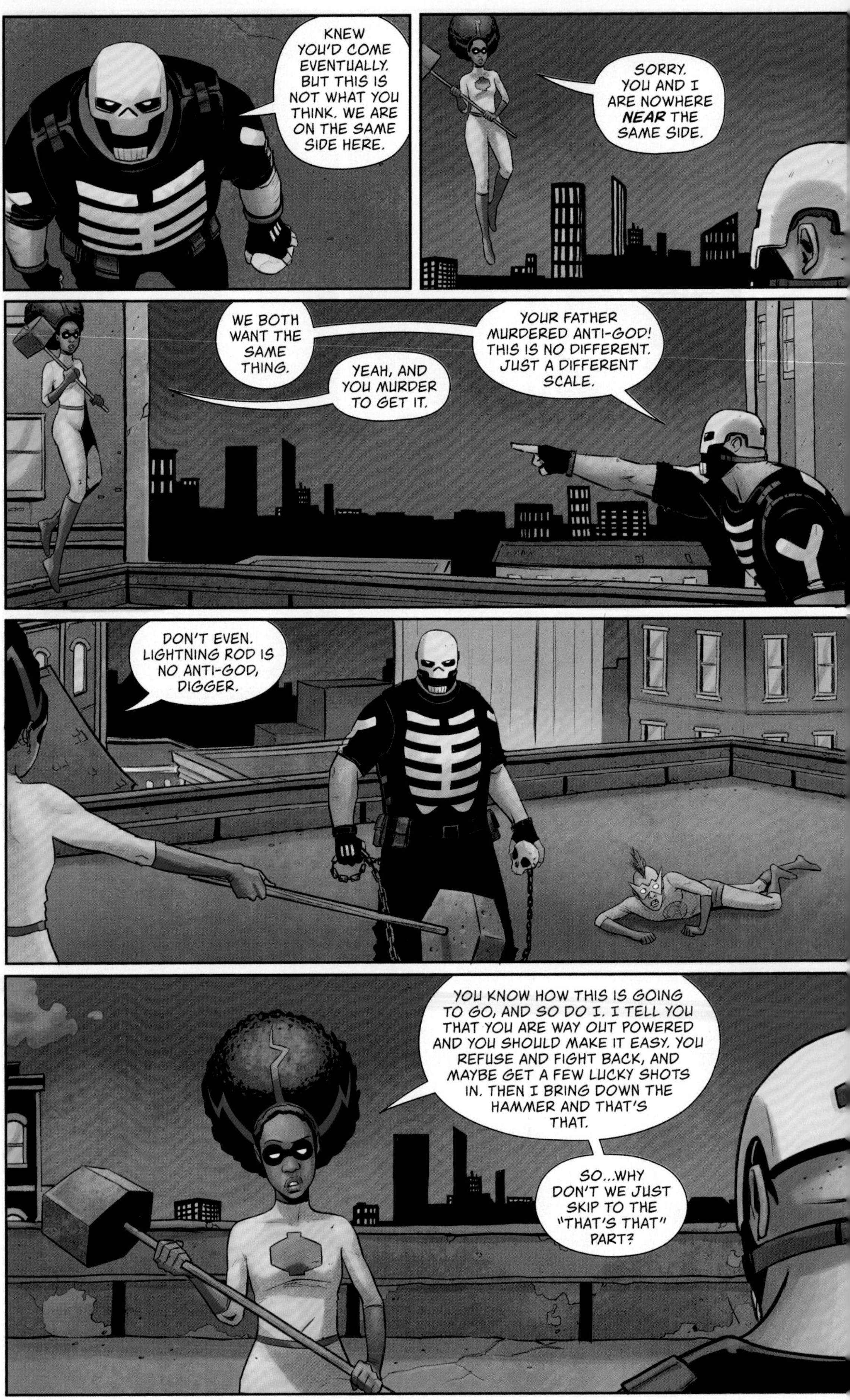

KNEW YOU'D COME EVENTUALLY. BUT THIS IS NOT WHAT YOU THINK. WE ARE ON THE SAME SIDE HERE.
SORRY. YOU AND I ARE NOWHERE **NEAR** THE SAME SIDE.
WE BOTH WANT THE SAME THING.
YEAH, AND YOU MURDER TO GET IT.
YOUR FATHER MURDERED ANTI-GOD! THIS IS NO DIFFERENT. JUST A DIFFERENT SCALE.
DON'T EVEN. LIGHTNING ROD IS NO ANTI-GOD, DIGGER.
YOU KNOW HOW THIS IS GOING TO GO, AND SO DO I. I TELL YOU THAT YOU ARE WAY OUT POWERED AND YOU SHOULD MAKE IT EASY. YOU REFUSE AND FIGHT BACK, AND MAYBE GET A FEW LUCKY SHOTS IN. THEN I BRING DOWN THE HAMMER AND THAT'S THAT.
SO...WHY DON'T WE JUST SKIP TO THE "THAT'S THAT" PART?

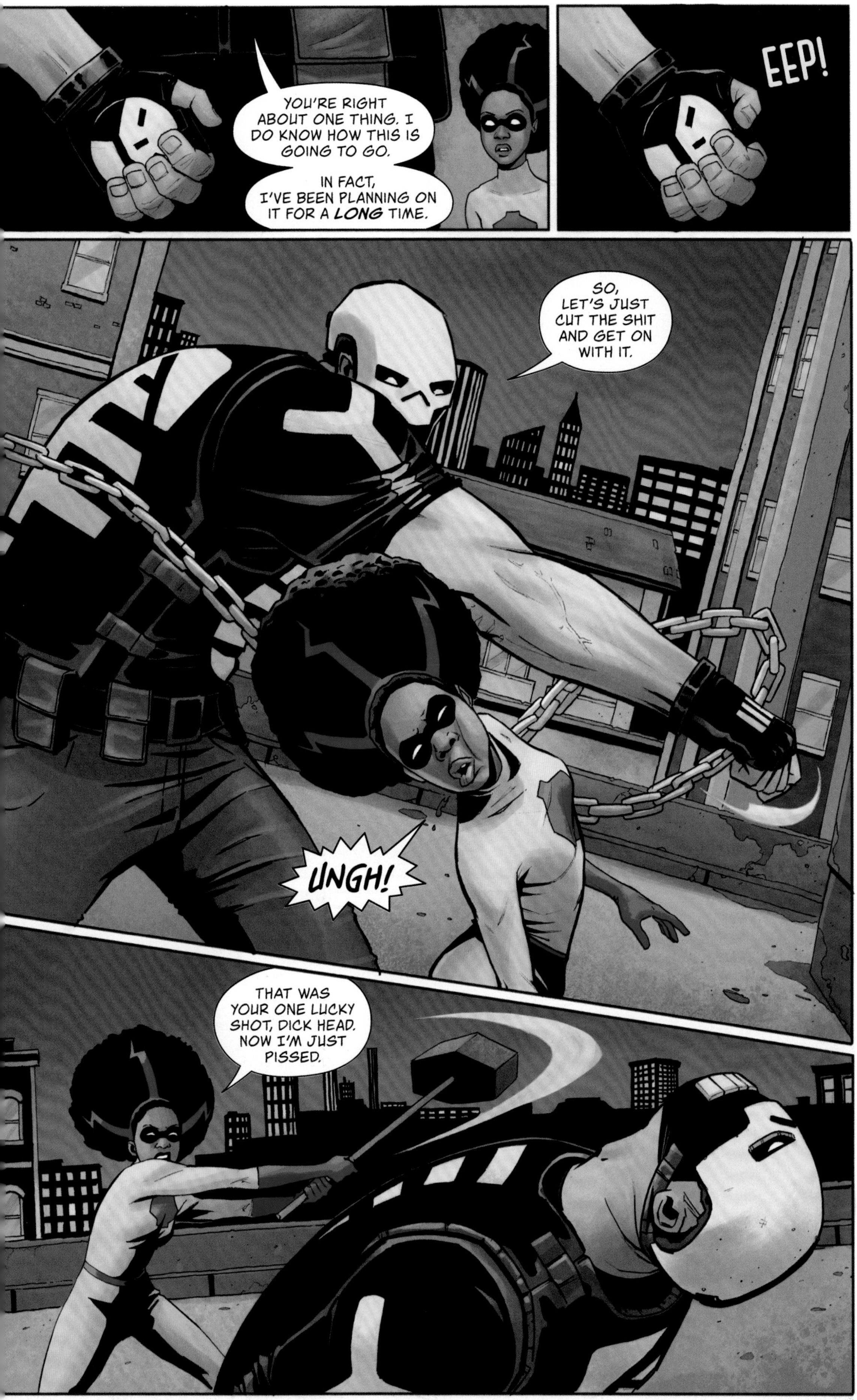

YOU'RE RIGHT ABOUT ONE THING. I DO KNOW HOW THIS IS GOING TO GO.
IN FACT, I'VE BEEN PLANNING ON IT FOR A **LONG** TIME.
EEP!
SO, LET'S JUST CUT THE SHIT AND GET ON WITH IT.
UNGH!
THAT WAS YOUR ONE LUCKY SHOT, DICK HEAD. NOW I'M JUST PISSED.

ARE WE DONE?

NOT EVEN CLOSE.

THE FUCK?

PTOOF

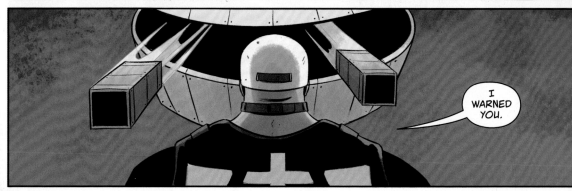

I WARNED YOU.

THWOOP

CHAK

CHAK

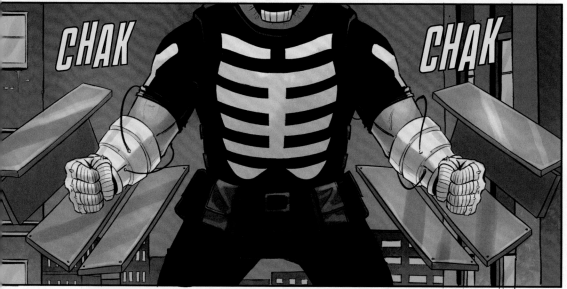

THOSE GLOVES-- THEY'RE JUST LIKE--

UNGH!

YEAH. I KNOW.

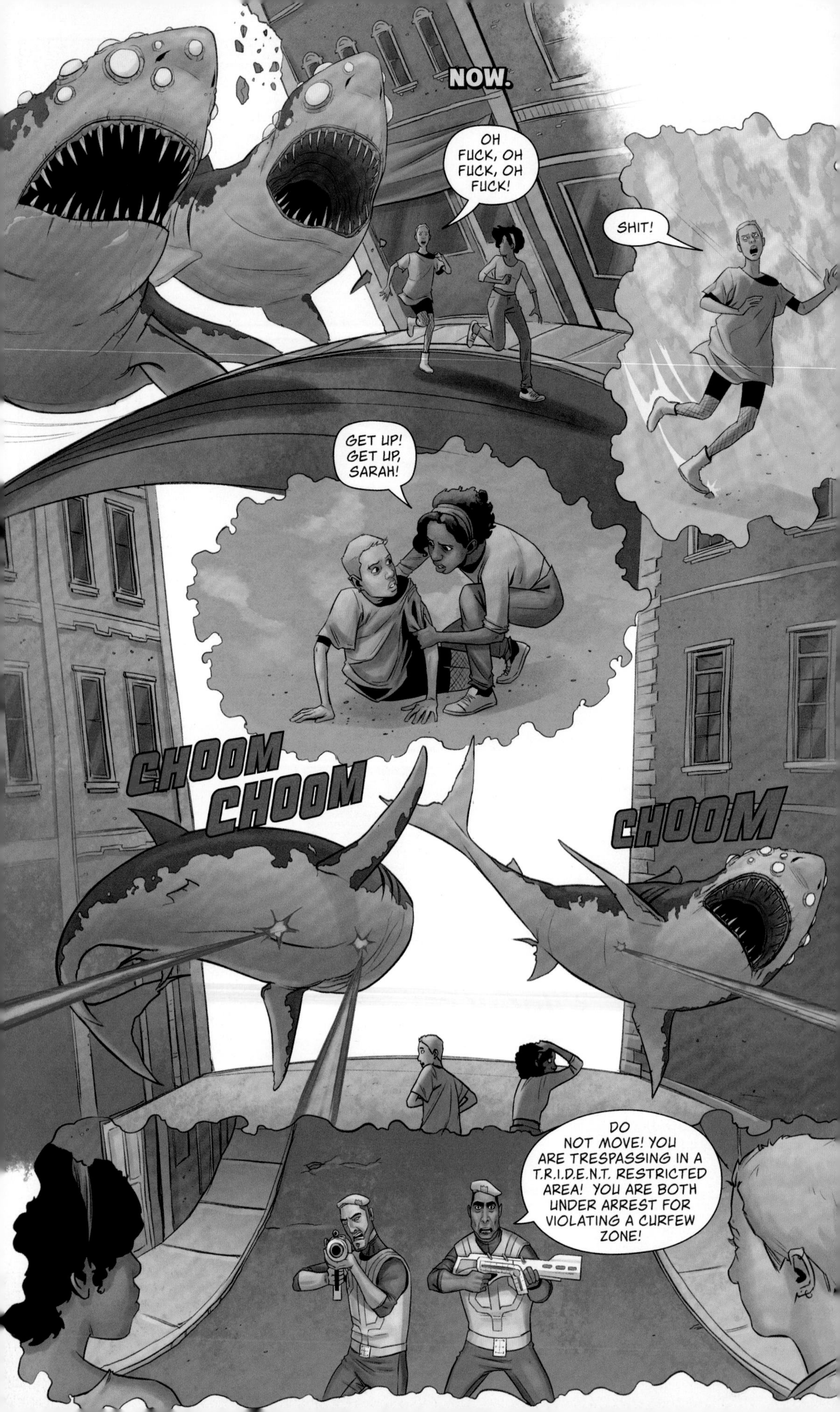
NOW.
OH FUCK, OH FUCK, OH FUCK!
SHIT!
GET UP! GET UP, SARAH!
CHOOM
CHOOM
CHOOM
DO NOT MOVE! YOU ARE TRESPASSING IN A T.R.I.D.E.N.T. RESTRICTED AREA! YOU ARE BOTH UNDER ARREST FOR VIOLATING A CURFEW ZONE!

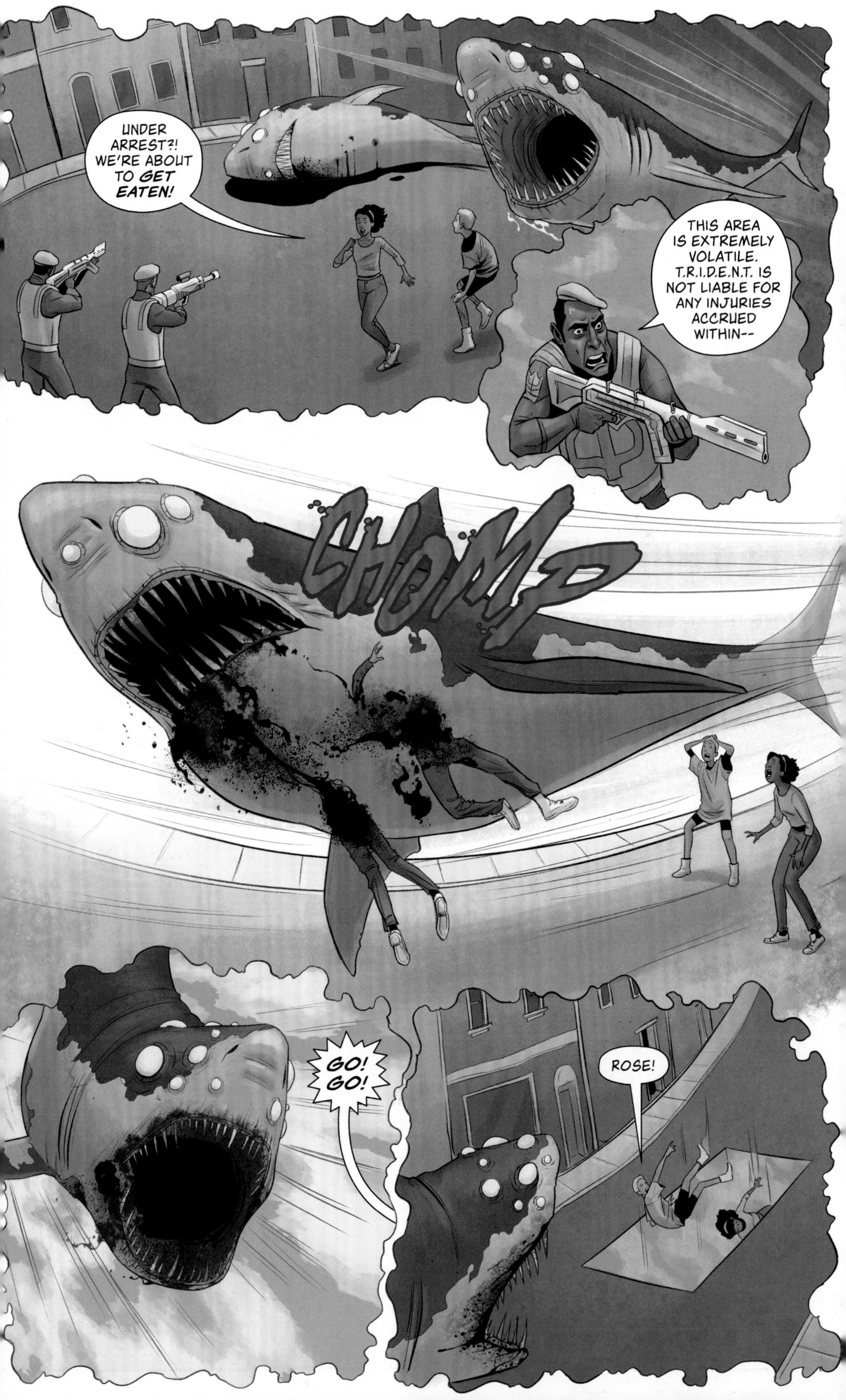
UNDER ARREST?! WE'RE ABOUT TO GET EATEN!
THIS AREA IS EXTREMELY VOLATILE. T.R.I.D.E.N.T. IS NOT LIABLE FOR ANY INJURIES ACCRUED WITHIN--
CHOMP
GO! GO!
ROSE!

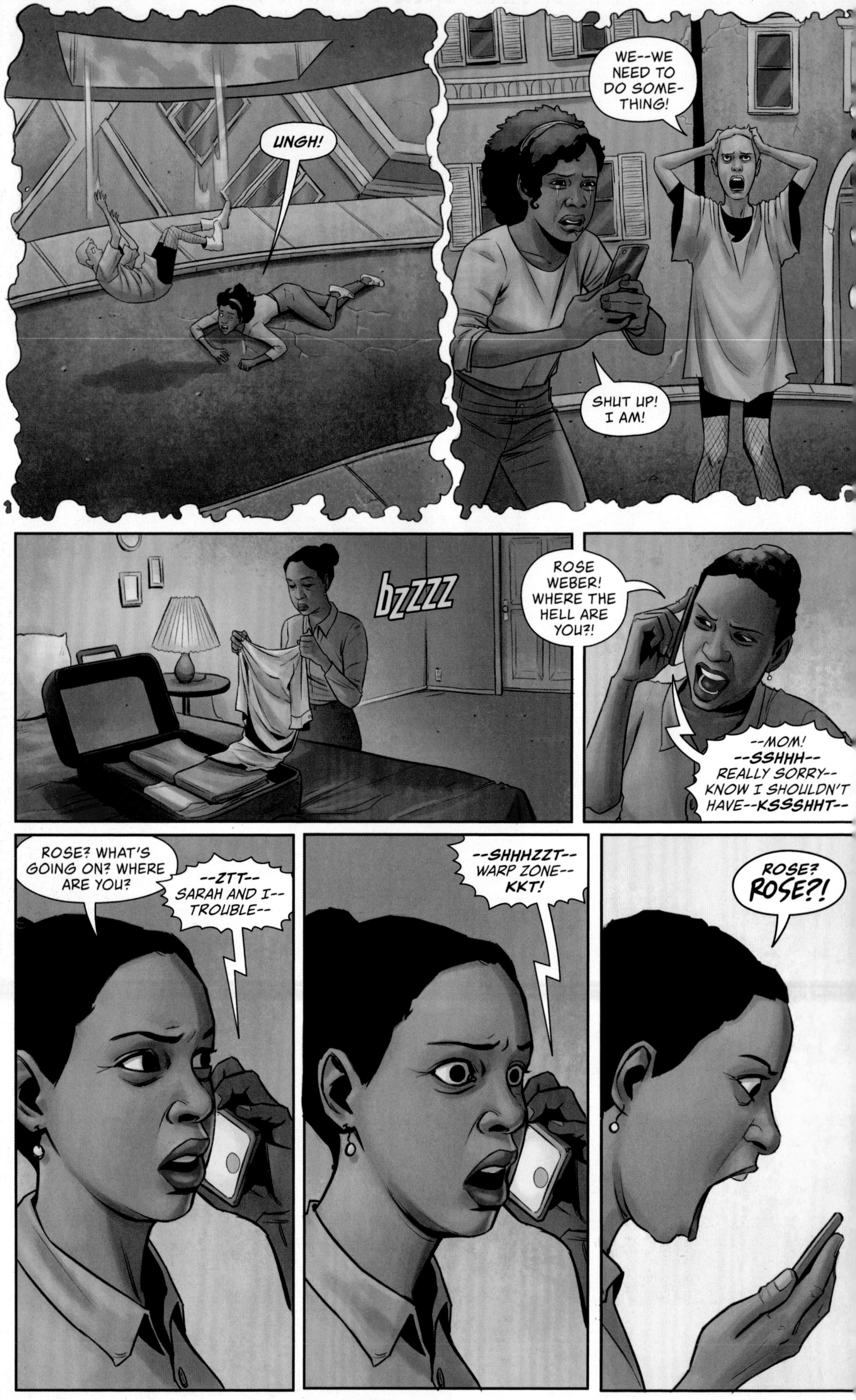
UNGH!
WE--WE NEED TO DO SOME-THING!
SHUT UP! I AM!
bzzzz
ROSE WEBER! WHERE THE HELL ARE YOU?!
--MOM! --SSHHH-- REALLY SORRY-- KNOW I SHOULDN'T HAVE--KSSSHHT--
ROSE? WHAT'S GOING ON? WHERE ARE YOU?
--ZTT-- SARAH AND I-- TROUBLE--
--SHHHZZT-- WARP ZONE-- KKT!
ROSE? ROSE?!

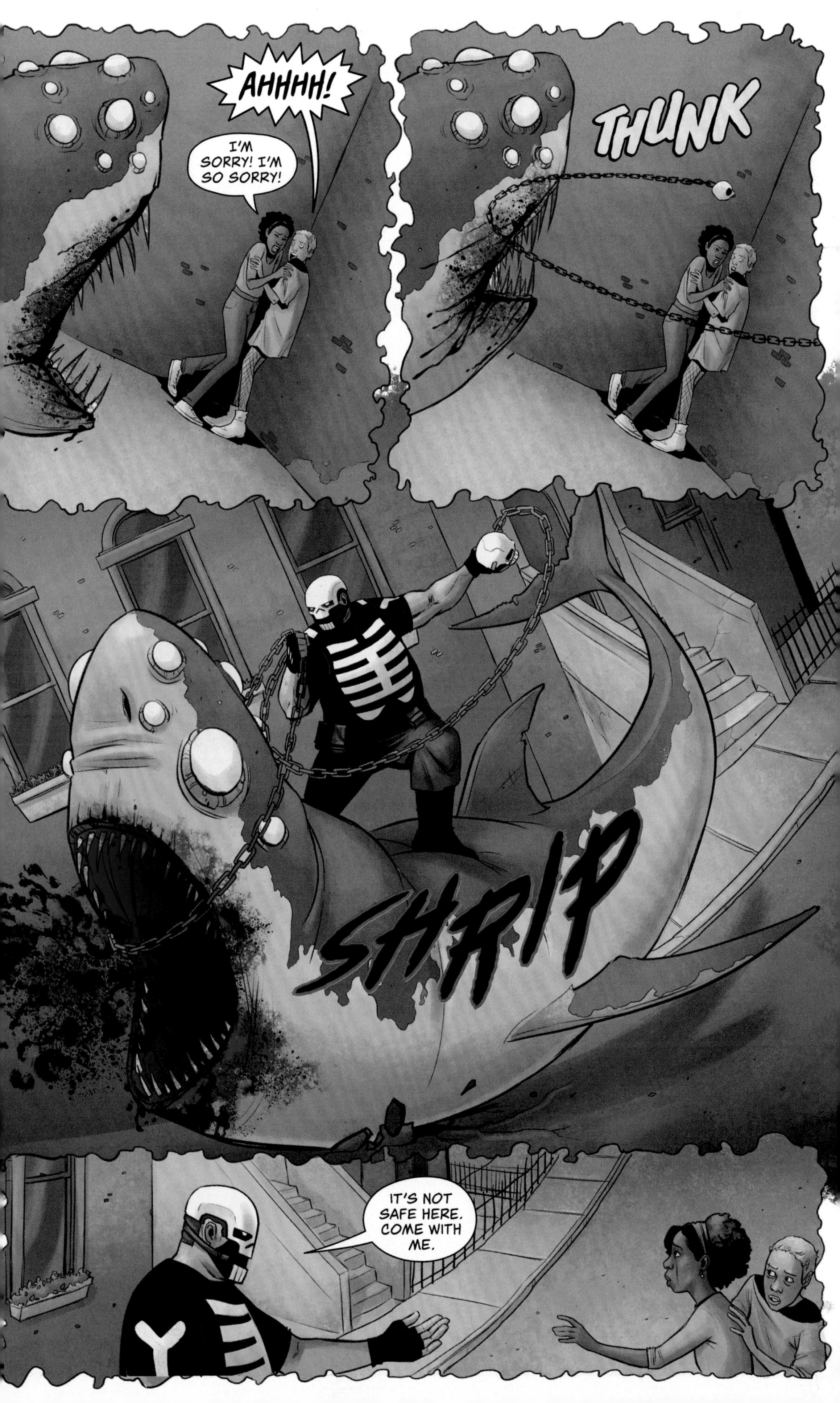
AHHHH!
I'M SORRY! I'M SO SORRY!
THUNK
SHRIP
IT'S NOT SAFE HERE. COME WITH ME.

TWENTY YEARS AGO.

SHIT!

NOW...WILL YOU STOP AND LISTEN TO WHAT I HAVE TO SAY? WILL YOU AT LEAST GIVE ME A CHANCE?

UNGH!

BLAM

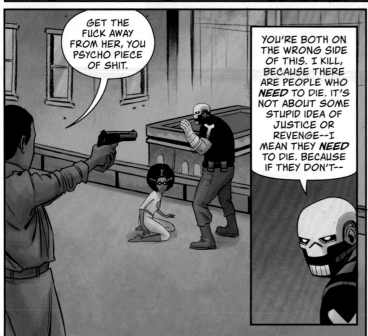

GET THE FUCK AWAY FROM HER, YOU PSYCHO PIECE OF SHIT.

YOU'RE BOTH ON THE WRONG SIDE OF THIS. I KILL, BECAUSE THERE ARE PEOPLE WHO *NEED* TO DIE. IT'S NOT ABOUT SOME STUPID IDEA OF JUSTICE OR REVENGE--I MEAN THEY *NEED* TO DIE. BECAUSE IF THEY DON'T--

OH WOULD YOU JUST SHUT THE FUCK UP.

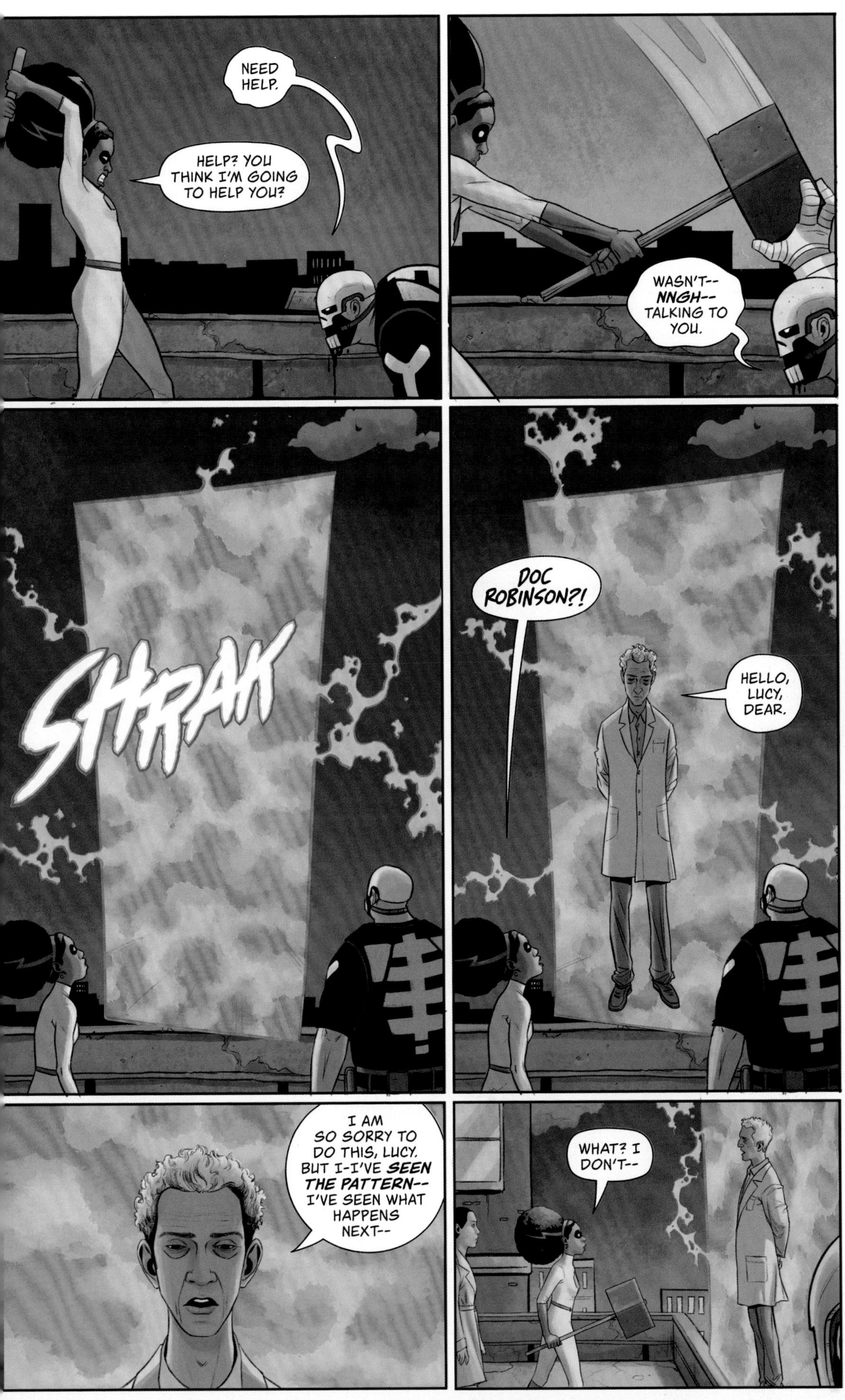
NEED HELP.
HELP? YOU THINK I'M GOING TO HELP YOU?
WASN'T-- NNGH-- TALKING TO YOU.
SHRAK
DOC ROBINSON?!
HELLO, LUCY, DEAR.
I AM SO SORRY TO DO THIS, LUCY. BUT I-I'VE SEEN THE PATTERN-- I'VE SEEN WHAT HAPPENS NEXT--
WHAT? I DON'T--

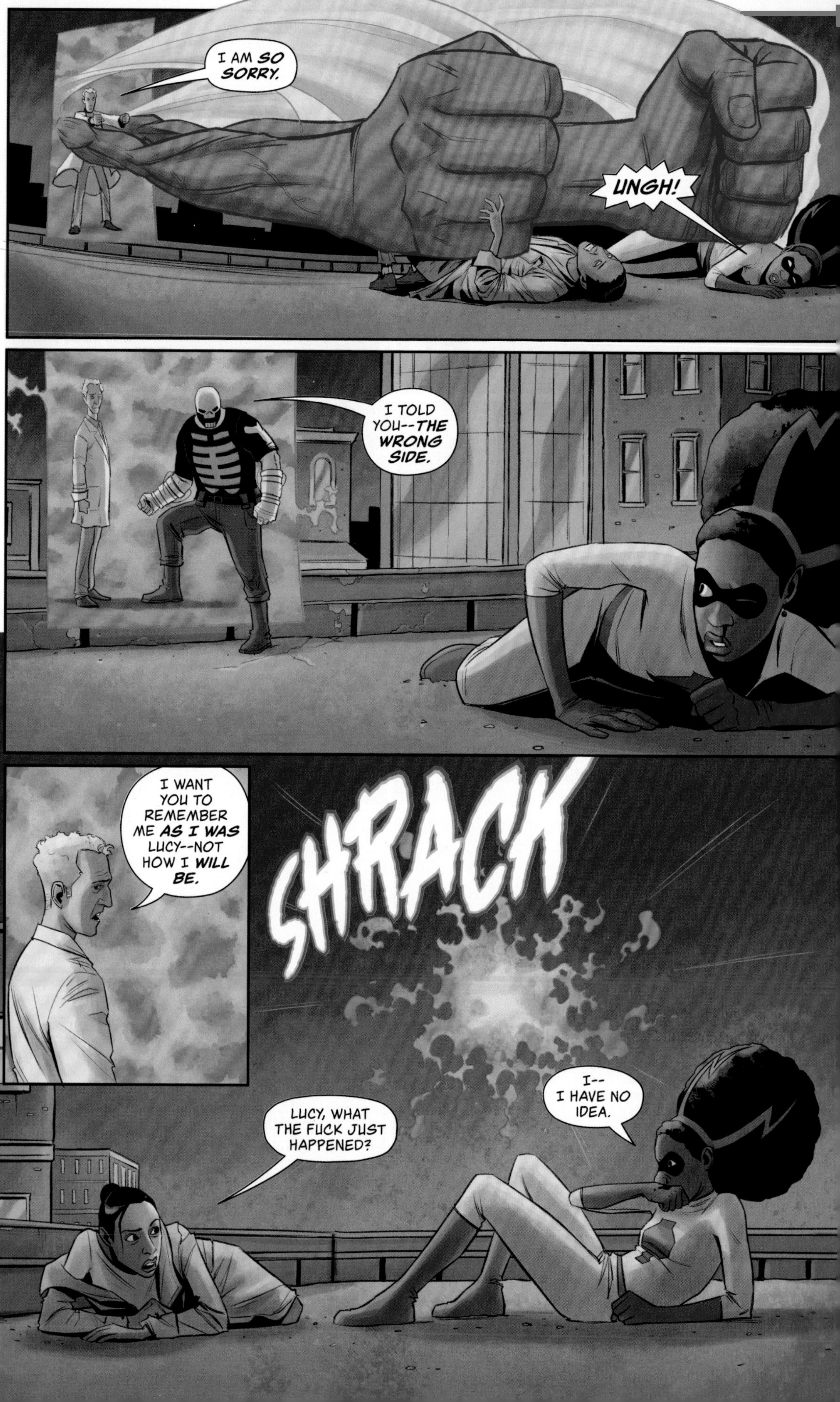
I AM SO SORRY.
UNGH!
I TOLD YOU--THE WRONG SIDE.
I WANT YOU TO REMEMBER ME AS I WAS LUCY--NOT HOW I WILL BE.
SHRACK
LUCY, WHAT THE FUCK JUST HAPPENED?
I-- I HAVE NO IDEA.

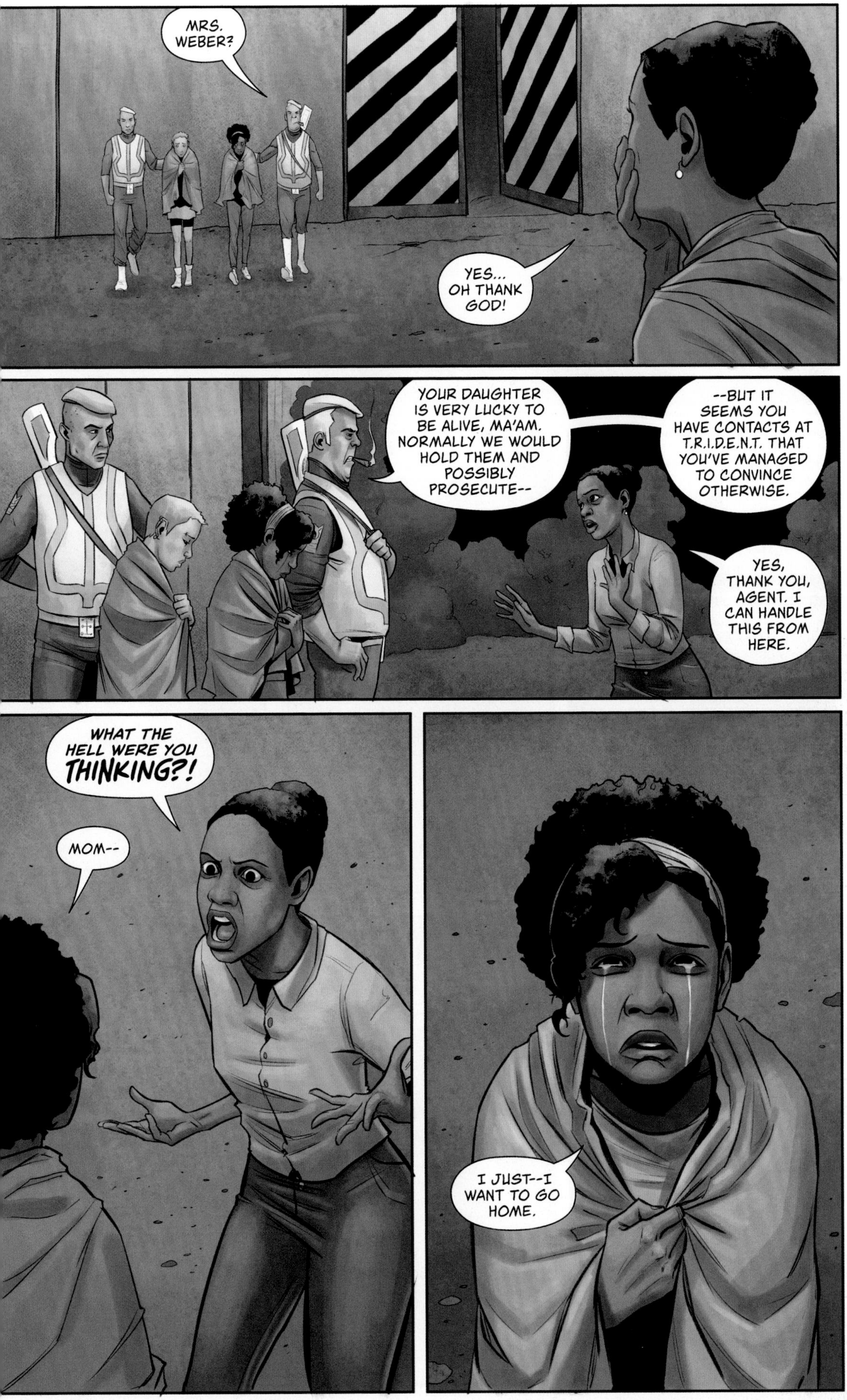
MRS. WEBER?
YES... OH THANK GOD!
YOUR DAUGHTER IS VERY LUCKY TO BE ALIVE, MA'AM. NORMALLY WE WOULD HOLD THEM AND POSSIBLY PROSECUTE--
--BUT IT SEEMS YOU HAVE CONTACTS AT T.R.I.D.E.N.T. THAT YOU'VE MANAGED TO CONVINCE OTHERWISE.
YES, THANK YOU, AGENT. I CAN HANDLE THIS FROM HERE.
WHAT THE HELL WERE YOU THINKING?!
MOM--
I JUST--I WANT TO GO HOME.

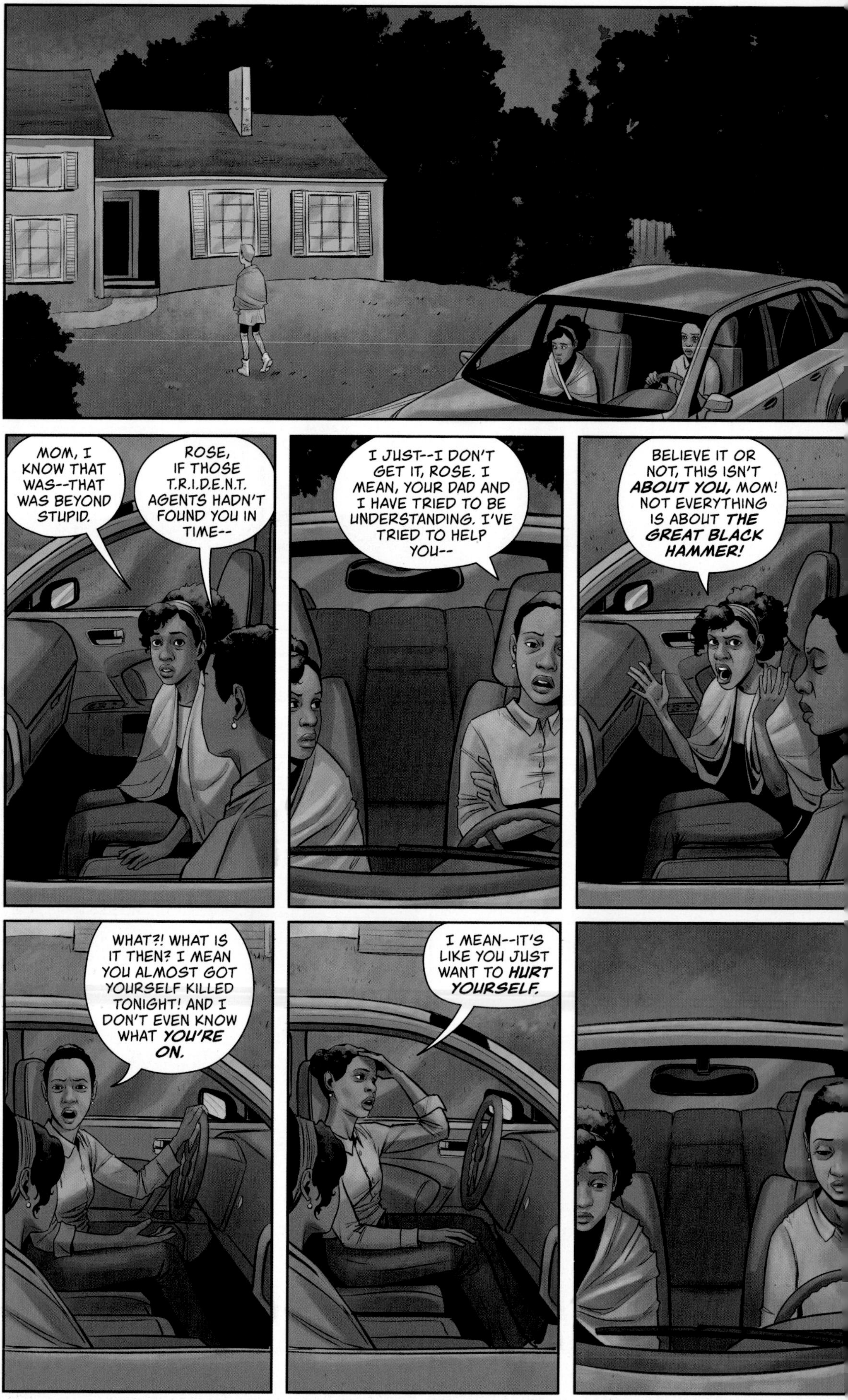
MOM, I KNOW THAT WAS--THAT WAS BEYOND STUPID.
ROSE, IF THOSE T.R.I.D.E.N.T. AGENTS HADN'T FOUND YOU IN TIME--
I JUST--I DON'T GET IT, ROSE. I MEAN, YOUR DAD AND I HAVE TRIED TO BE UNDERSTANDING. I'VE TRIED TO HELP YOU--
BELIEVE IT OR NOT, THIS ISN'T ABOUT YOU, MOM! NOT EVERYTHING IS ABOUT THE GREAT BLACK HAMMER!
WHAT?! WHAT IS IT THEN? I MEAN YOU ALMOST GOT YOURSELF KILLED TONIGHT! AND I DON'T EVEN KNOW WHAT YOU'RE ON.
I MEAN--IT'S LIKE YOU JUST WANT TO HURT YOURSELF.

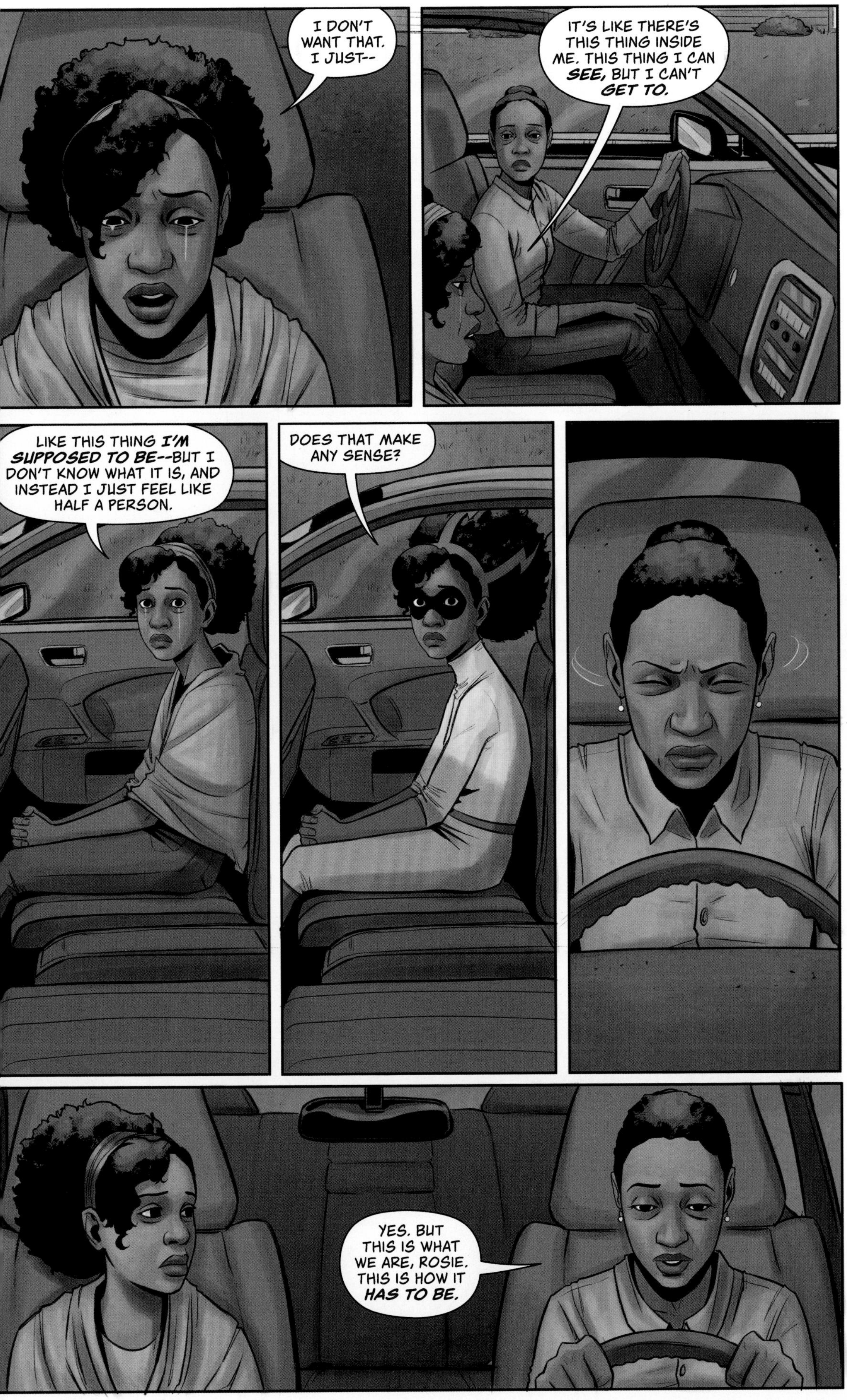
I DON'T WANT THAT. I JUST--
IT'S LIKE THERE'S THIS THING INSIDE ME. THIS THING I CAN *SEE,* BUT I CAN'T *GET TO.*
LIKE THIS THING *I'M SUPPOSED TO BE*--BUT I DON'T KNOW WHAT IT IS, AND INSTEAD I JUST FEEL LIKE HALF A PERSON.
DOES THAT MAKE ANY SENSE?
YES. BUT THIS IS WHAT WE ARE, ROSIE. THIS IS HOW IT *HAS TO BE.*

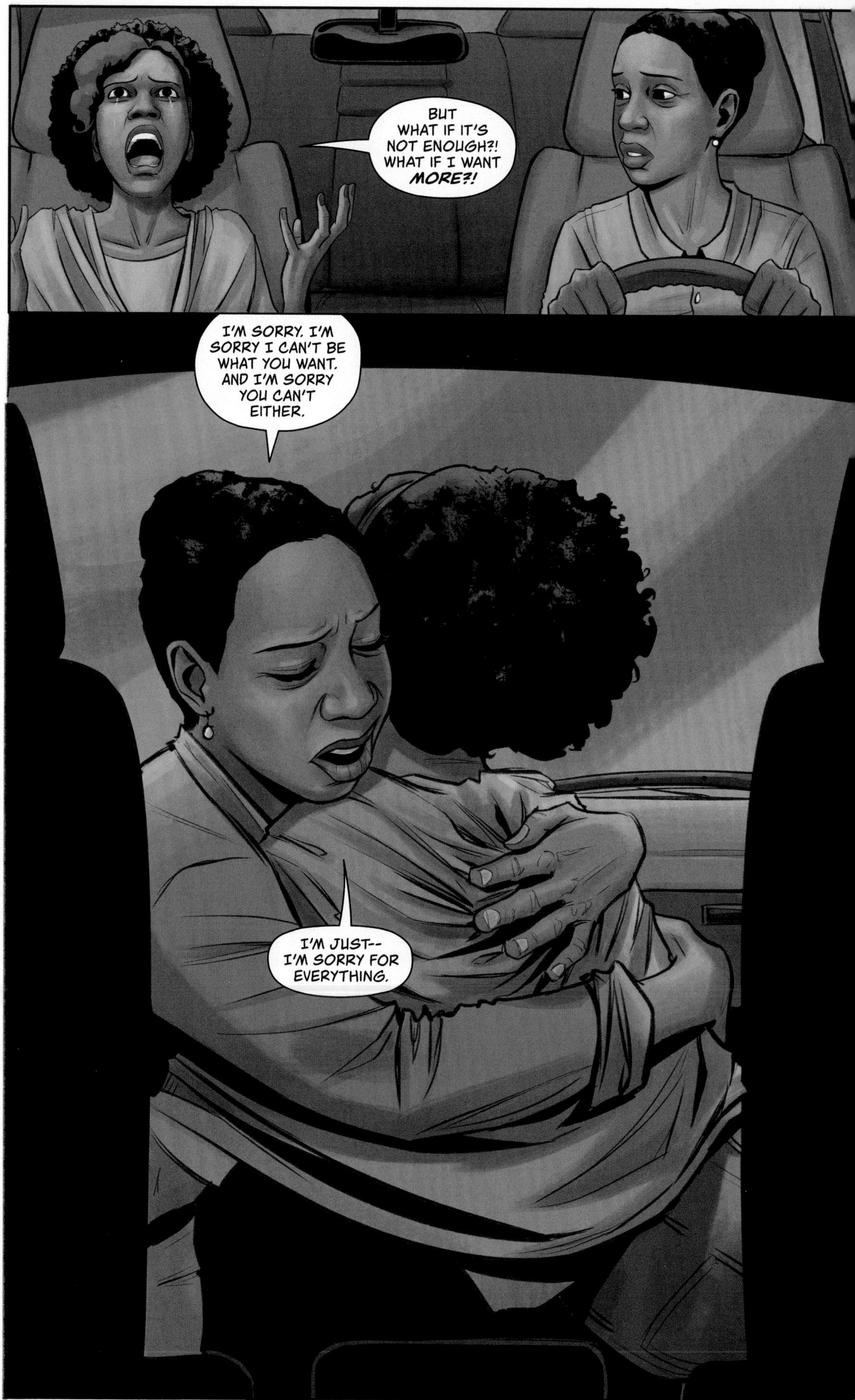
BUT WHAT IF IT'S NOT ENOUGH?! WHAT IF I WANT *MORE?!*
I'M SORRY. I'M SORRY I CAN'T BE WHAT YOU WANT. AND I'M SORRY YOU CAN'T EITHER.
I'M JUST-- I'M SORRY FOR EVERYTHING.

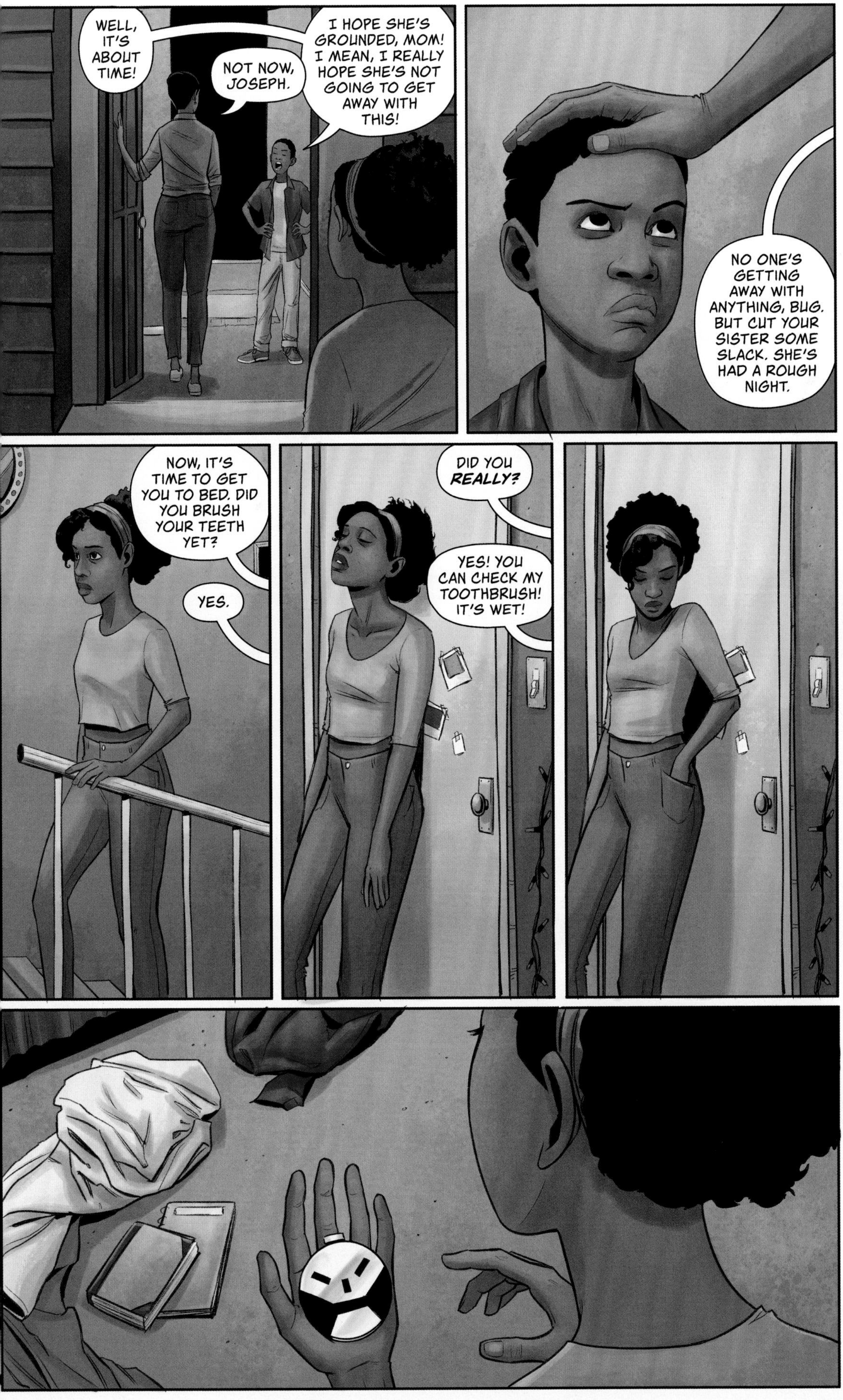

WELL, IT'S ABOUT TIME!
I HOPE SHE'S GROUNDED, MOM! I MEAN, I REALLY HOPE SHE'S NOT GOING TO GET AWAY WITH THIS!
NOT NOW, JOSEPH.
NO ONE'S GETTING AWAY WITH ANYTHING, BUG. BUT CUT YOUR SISTER SOME SLACK. SHE'S HAD A ROUGH NIGHT.
NOW, IT'S TIME TO GET YOU TO BED. DID YOU BRUSH YOUR TEETH YET?
YES.
DID YOU *REALLY?*
YES! YOU CAN CHECK MY TOOTHBRUSH! IT'S WET!

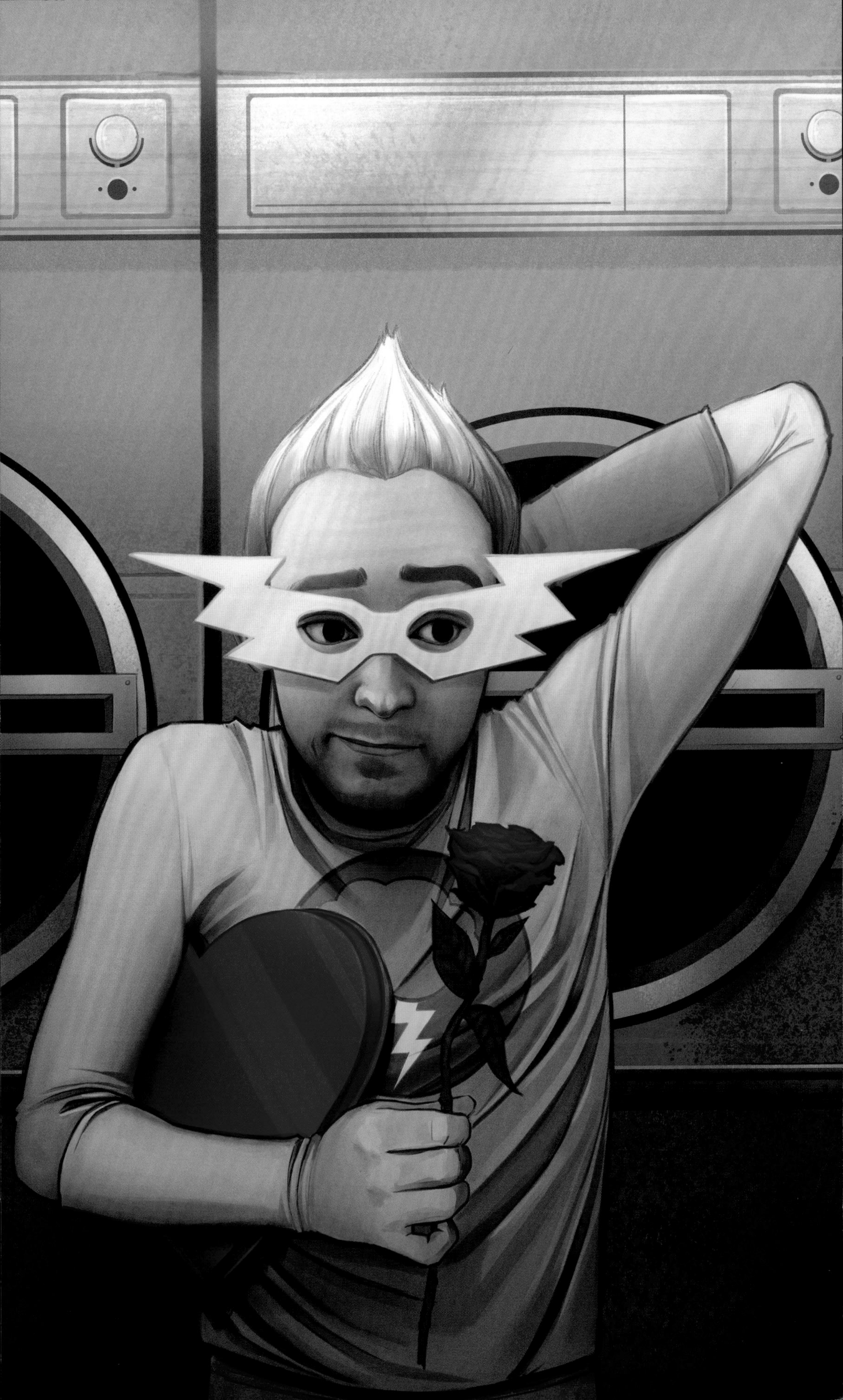

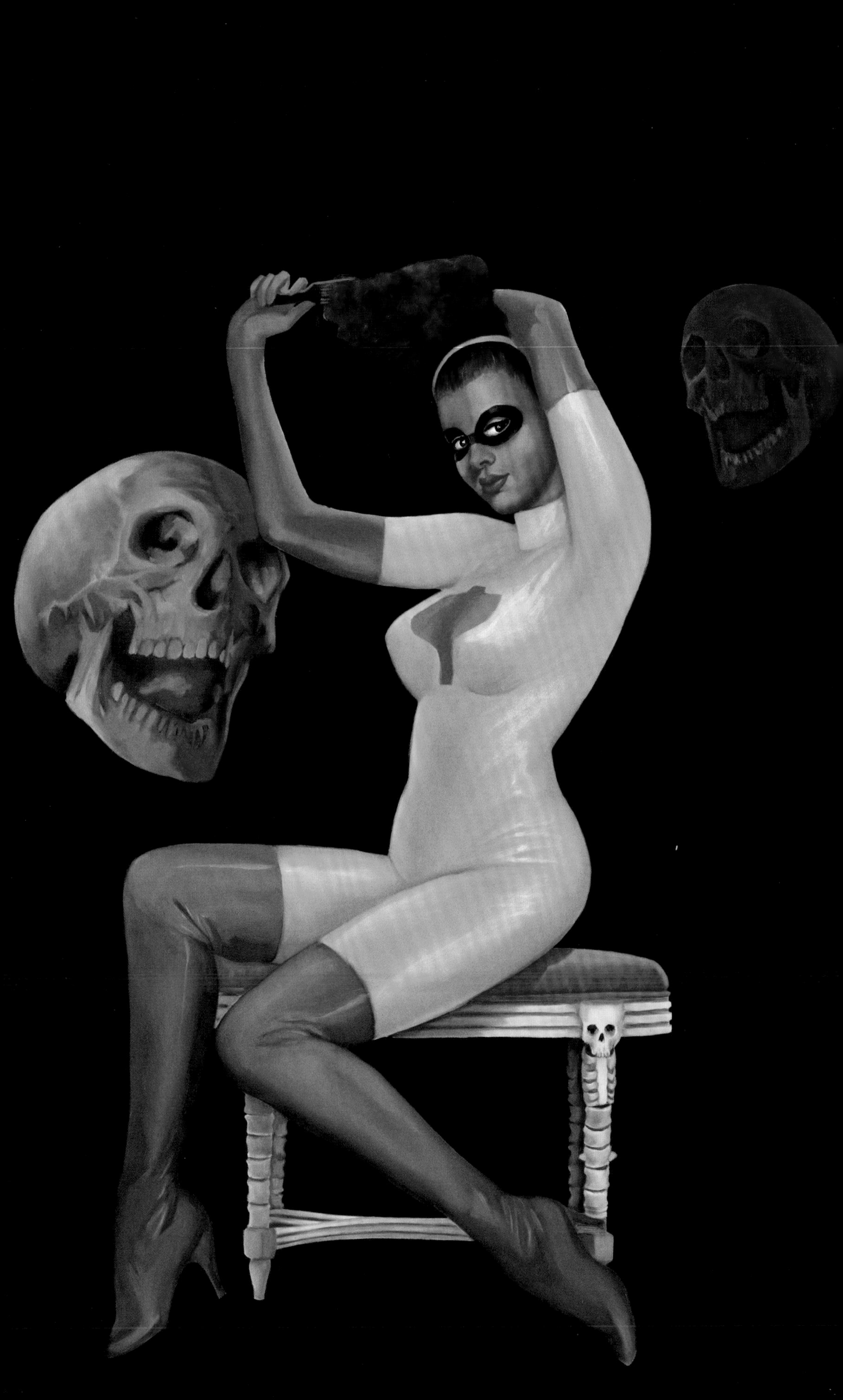

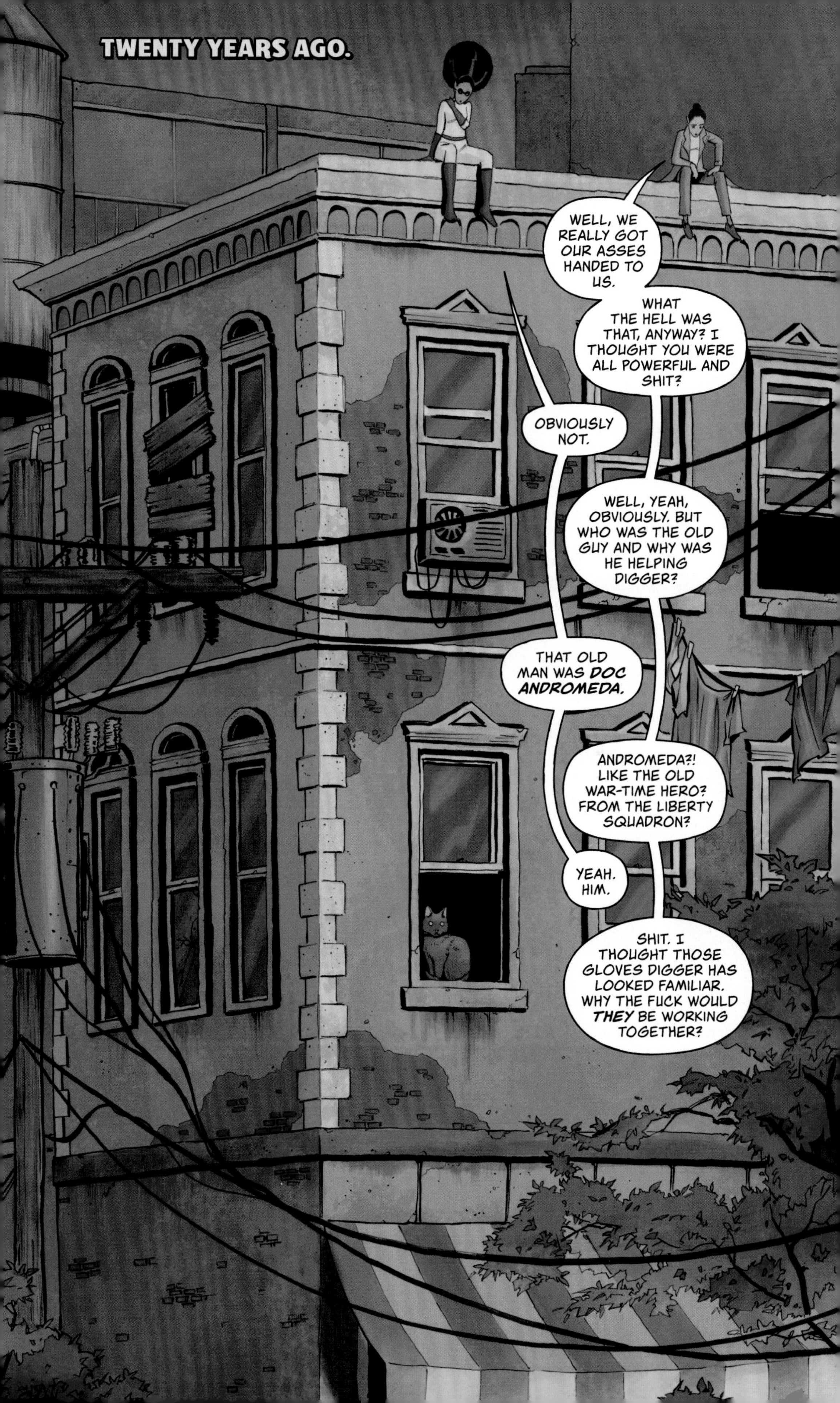

TWENTY YEARS AGO.
WELL, WE REALLY GOT OUR ASSES HANDED TO US.
WHAT THE HELL WAS THAT, ANYWAY? I THOUGHT YOU WERE ALL POWERFUL AND SHIT?
OBVIOUSLY NOT.
WELL, YEAH, OBVIOUSLY. BUT WHO WAS THE OLD GUY AND WHY WAS HE HELPING DIGGER?
THAT OLD MAN WAS ***DOC ANDROMEDA.***
ANDROMEDA?! LIKE THE OLD WAR-TIME HERO? FROM THE LIBERTY SQUADRON?
YEAH. HIM.
SHIT. I THOUGHT THOSE GLOVES DIGGER HAS LOOKED FAMILIAR. WHY THE FUCK WOULD ***THEY*** BE WORKING TOGETHER?

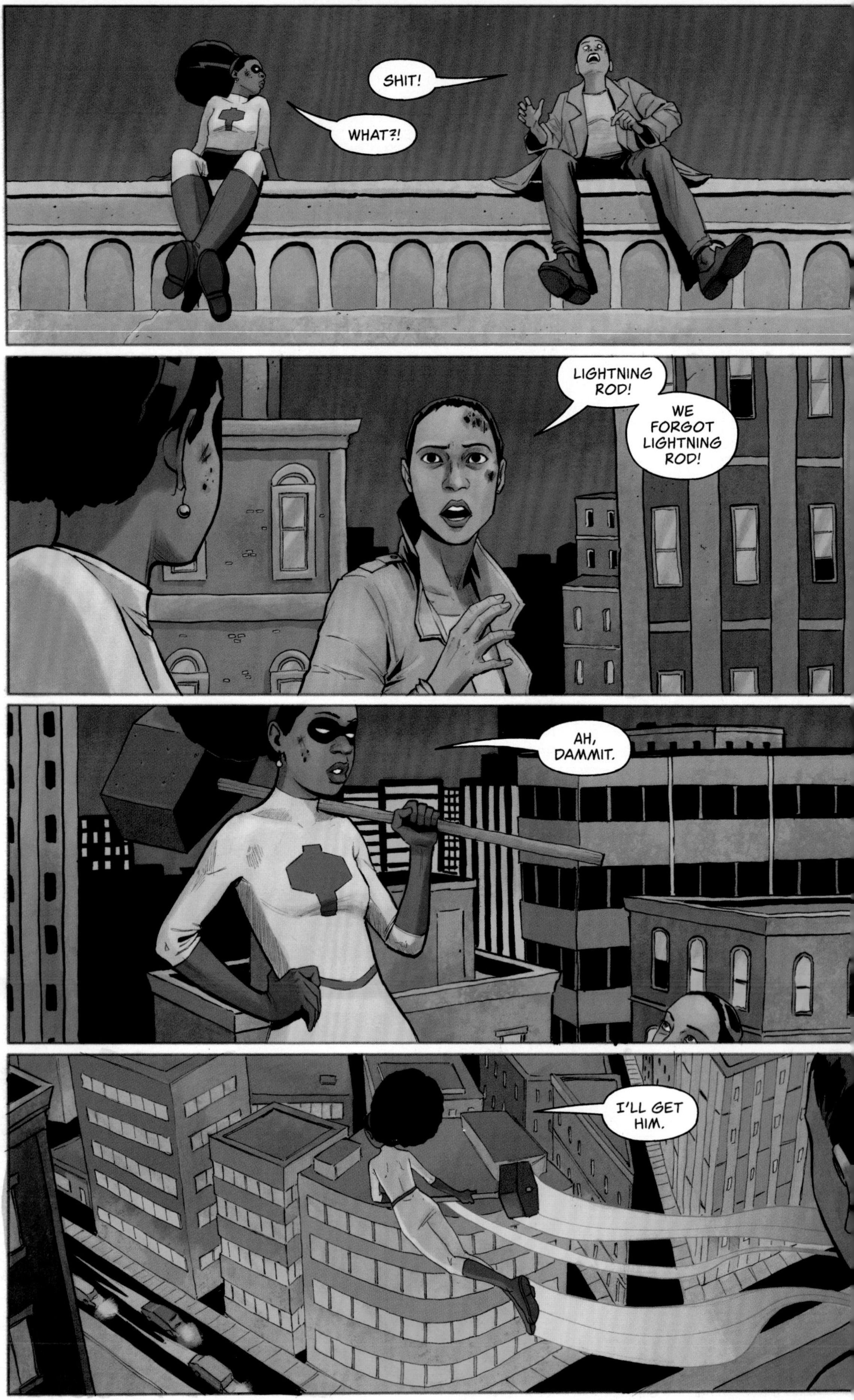
SHIT!
WHAT?!
LIGHTNING ROD!
WE FORGOT LIGHTNING ROD!
AH, DAMMIT.
I'LL GET HIM.

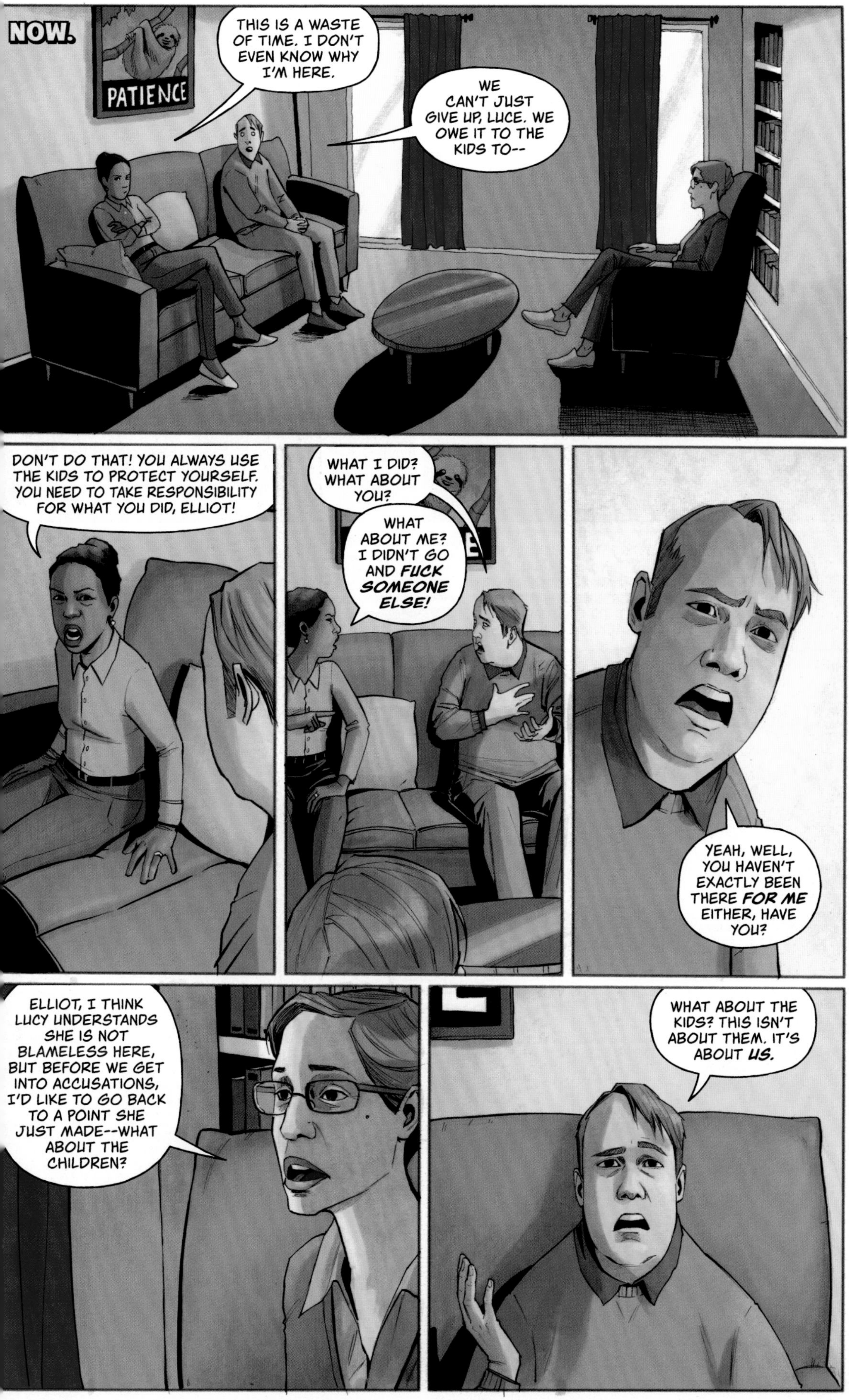
NOW.
PATIENCE
THIS IS A WASTE OF TIME. I DON'T EVEN KNOW WHY I'M HERE.
WE CAN'T JUST GIVE UP, LUCE. WE OWE IT TO THE KIDS TO--
DON'T DO THAT! YOU ALWAYS USE THE KIDS TO PROTECT YOURSELF. YOU NEED TO TAKE RESPONSIBILITY FOR WHAT YOU DID, ELLIOT!
WHAT I DID? WHAT ABOUT YOU?
WHAT ABOUT ME? I DIDN'T GO AND FUCK SOMEONE ELSE!
YEAH, WELL, YOU HAVEN'T EXACTLY BEEN THERE FOR ME EITHER, HAVE YOU?
ELLIOT, I THINK LUCY UNDERSTANDS SHE IS NOT BLAMELESS HERE, BUT BEFORE WE GET INTO ACCUSATIONS, I'D LIKE TO GO BACK TO A POINT SHE JUST MADE--WHAT ABOUT THE CHILDREN?
WHAT ABOUT THE KIDS? THIS ISN'T ABOUT THEM. IT'S ABOUT US.

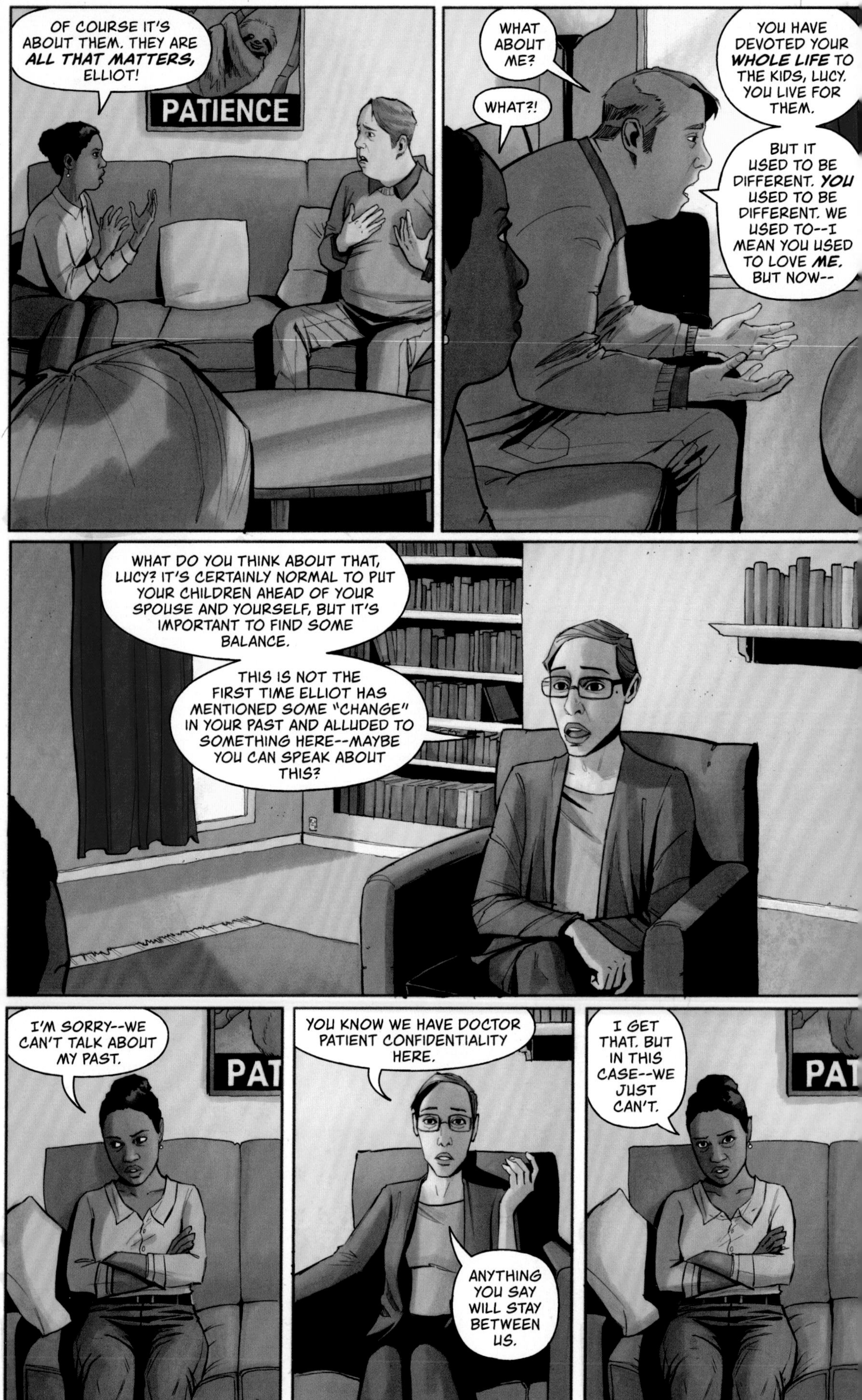
OF COURSE IT'S ABOUT THEM. THEY ARE ALL THAT MATTERS, ELLIOT!
PATIENCE
WHAT ABOUT ME?
WHAT?!
YOU HAVE DEVOTED YOUR WHOLE LIFE TO THE KIDS, LUCY. YOU LIVE FOR THEM.
BUT IT USED TO BE DIFFERENT. YOU USED TO BE DIFFERENT. WE USED TO--I MEAN YOU USED TO LOVE ME. BUT NOW--
WHAT DO YOU THINK ABOUT THAT, LUCY? IT'S CERTAINLY NORMAL TO PUT YOUR CHILDREN AHEAD OF YOUR SPOUSE AND YOURSELF, BUT IT'S IMPORTANT TO FIND SOME BALANCE.
THIS IS NOT THE FIRST TIME ELLIOT HAS MENTIONED SOME "CHANGE" IN YOUR PAST AND ALLUDED TO SOMETHING HERE--MAYBE YOU CAN SPEAK ABOUT THIS?
I'M SORRY--WE CAN'T TALK ABOUT MY PAST.
PAT
YOU KNOW WE HAVE DOCTOR PATIENT CONFIDENTIALITY HERE.
ANYTHING YOU SAY WILL STAY BETWEEN US.
I GET THAT. BUT IN THIS CASE--WE JUST CAN'T.
PAT

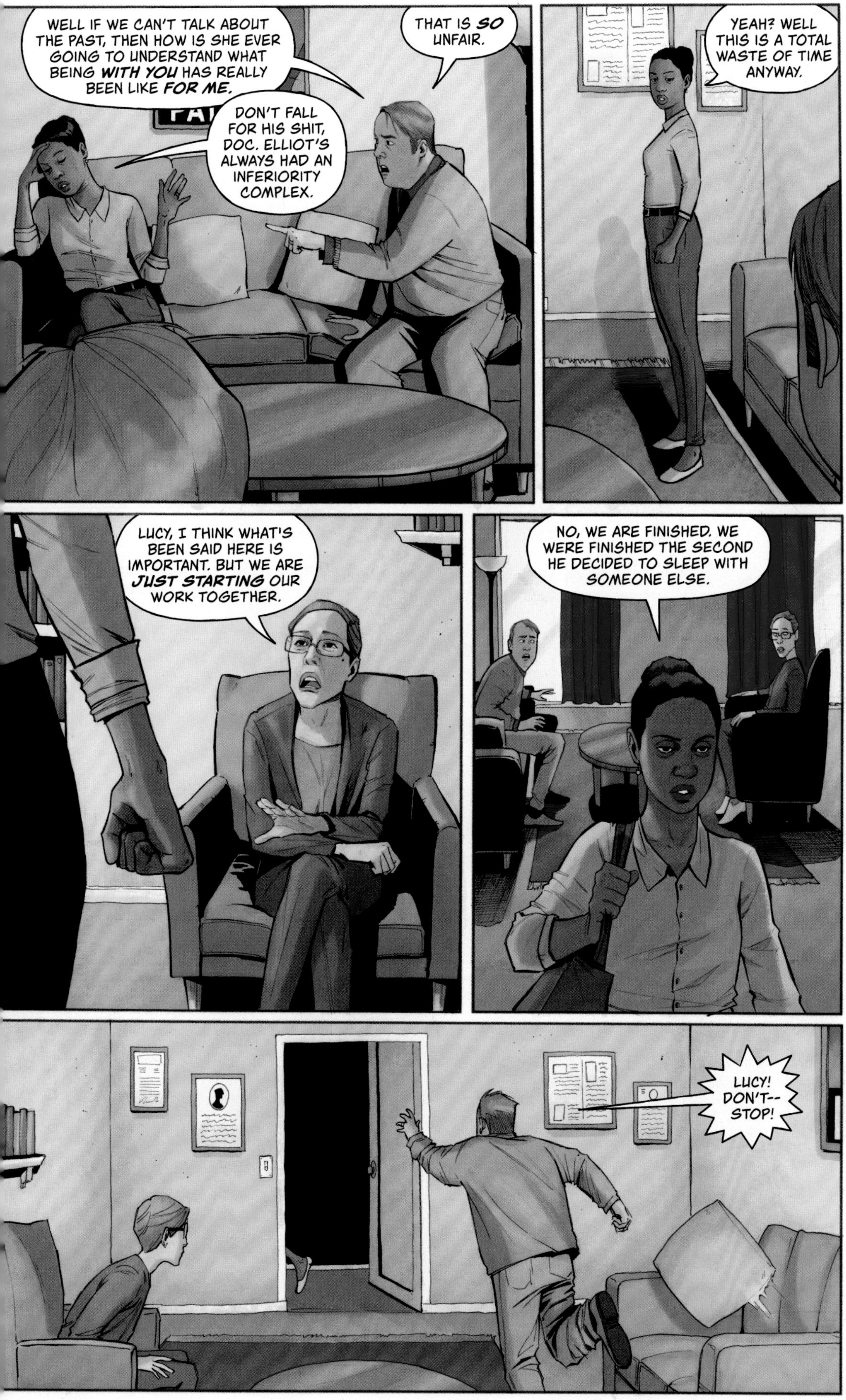
WELL IF WE CAN'T TALK ABOUT THE PAST, THEN HOW IS SHE EVER GOING TO UNDERSTAND WHAT BEING WITH YOU HAS REALLY BEEN LIKE FOR ME.
THAT IS SO UNFAIR.
DON'T FALL FOR HIS SHIT, DOC. ELLIOT'S ALWAYS HAD AN INFERIORITY COMPLEX.
YEAH? WELL THIS IS A TOTAL WASTE OF TIME ANYWAY.
LUCY, I THINK WHAT'S BEEN SAID HERE IS IMPORTANT. BUT WE ARE JUST STARTING OUR WORK TOGETHER.
NO, WE ARE FINISHED. WE WERE FINISHED THE SECOND HE DECIDED TO SLEEP WITH SOMEONE ELSE.
LUCY! DON'T-- STOP!

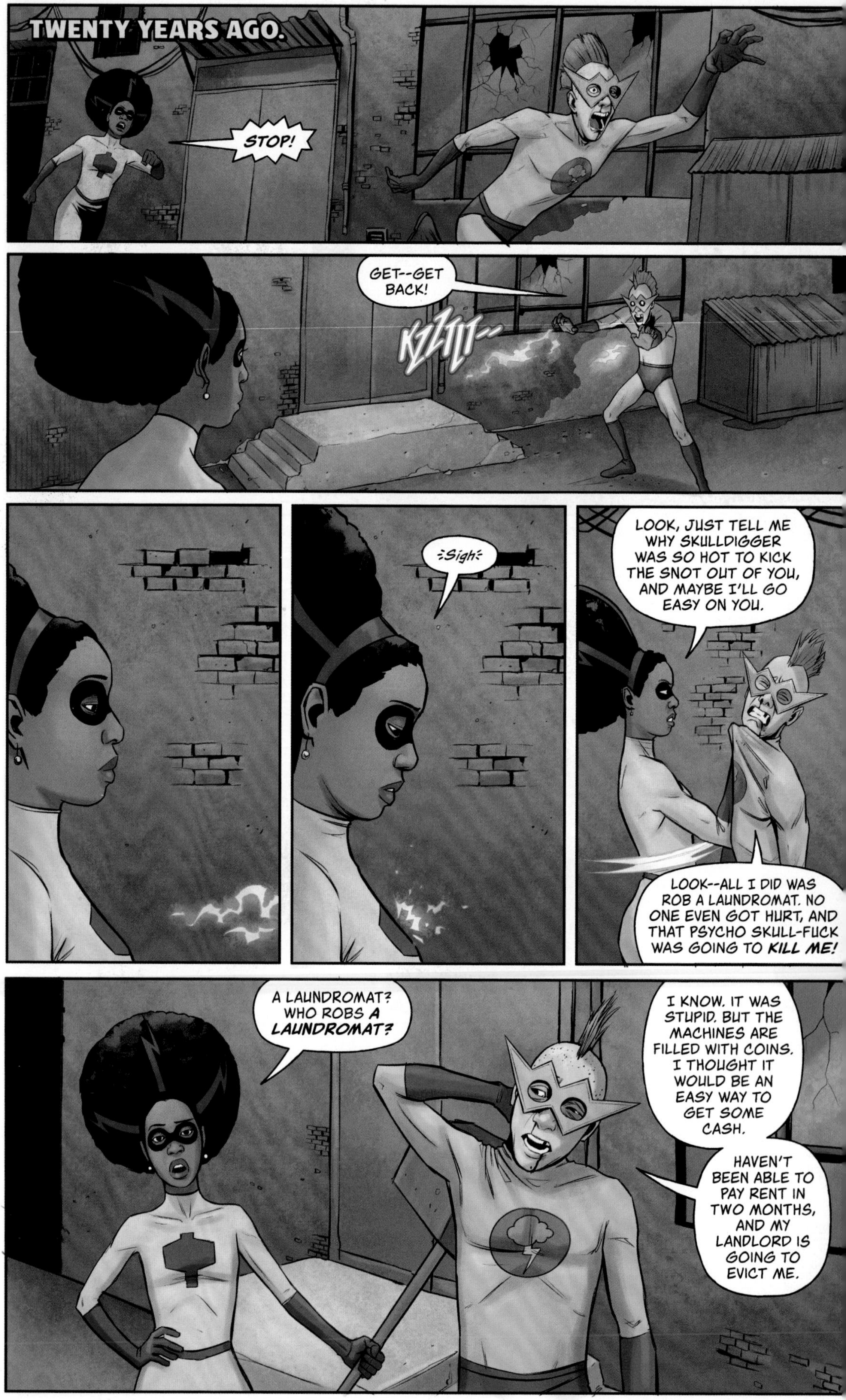
TWENTY YEARS AGO.
STOP!
GET--GET BACK!
KZZZT--
:Sigh:
LOOK, JUST TELL ME WHY SKULLDIGGER WAS SO HOT TO KICK THE SNOT OUT OF YOU, AND MAYBE I'LL GO EASY ON YOU.
LOOK--ALL I DID WAS ROB A LAUNDROMAT. NO ONE EVEN GOT HURT, AND THAT PSYCHO SKULL-FUCK WAS GOING TO KILL ME!
A LAUNDROMAT? WHO ROBS A LAUNDROMAT?
I KNOW. IT WAS STUPID. BUT THE MACHINES ARE FILLED WITH COINS. I THOUGHT IT WOULD BE AN EASY WAY TO GET SOME CASH.
HAVEN'T BEEN ABLE TO PAY RENT IN TWO MONTHS, AND MY LANDLORD IS GOING TO EVICT ME.

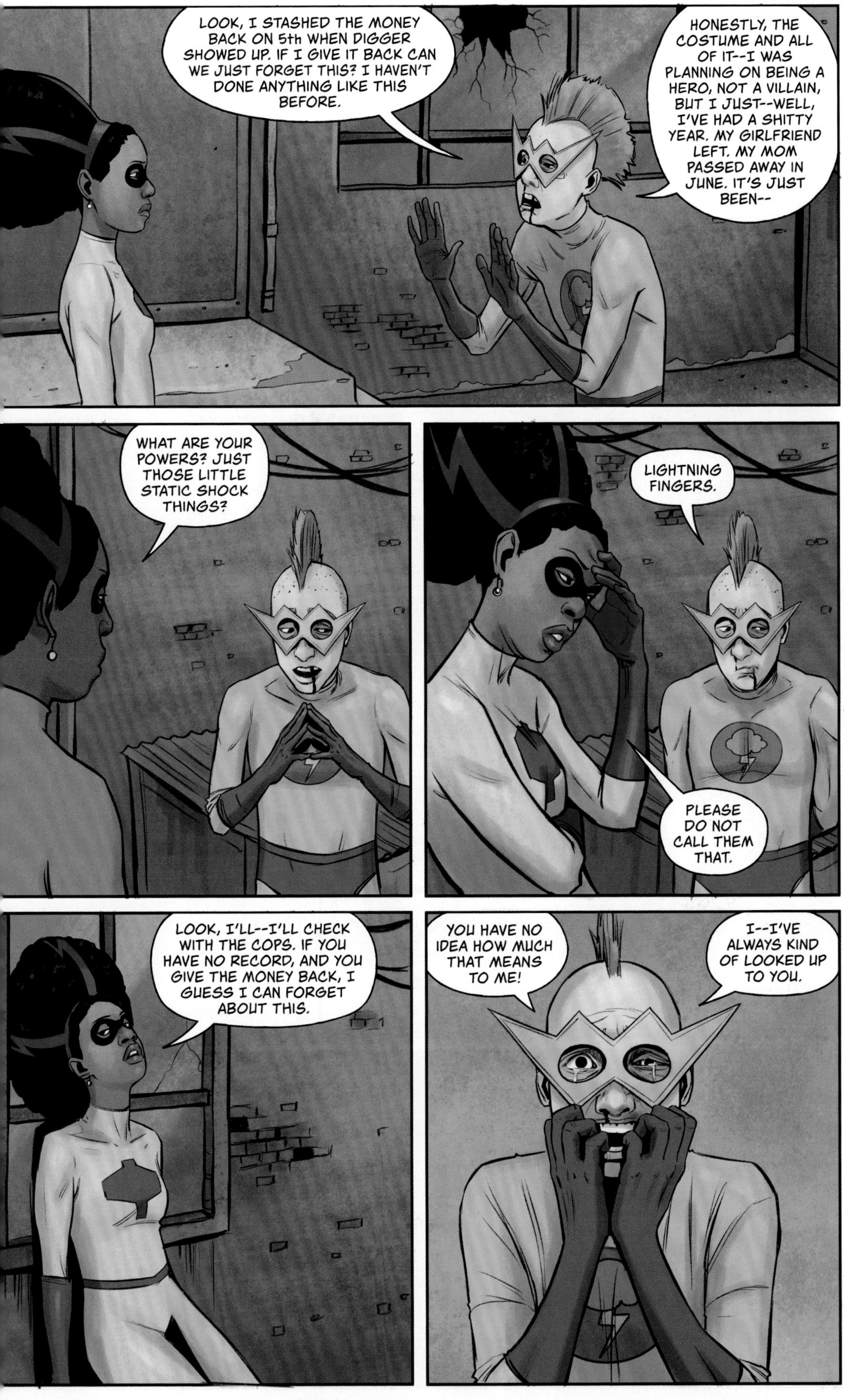

LOOK, I STASHED THE MONEY BACK ON 5th WHEN DIGGER SHOWED UP. IF I GIVE IT BACK CAN WE JUST FORGET THIS? I HAVEN'T DONE ANYTHING LIKE THIS BEFORE.
HONESTLY, THE COSTUME AND ALL OF IT--I WAS PLANNING ON BEING A HERO, NOT A VILLAIN, BUT I JUST--WELL, I'VE HAD A SHITTY YEAR. MY GIRLFRIEND LEFT. MY MOM PASSED AWAY IN JUNE. IT'S JUST BEEN--
WHAT ARE YOUR POWERS? JUST THOSE LITTLE STATIC SHOCK THINGS?
LIGHTNING FINGERS.
PLEASE DO NOT CALL THEM THAT.
LOOK, I'LL--I'LL CHECK WITH THE COPS. IF YOU HAVE NO RECORD, AND YOU GIVE THE MONEY BACK, I GUESS I CAN FORGET ABOUT THIS.
YOU HAVE NO IDEA HOW MUCH THAT MEANS TO ME!
I--I'VE ALWAYS KIND OF LOOKED UP TO YOU.

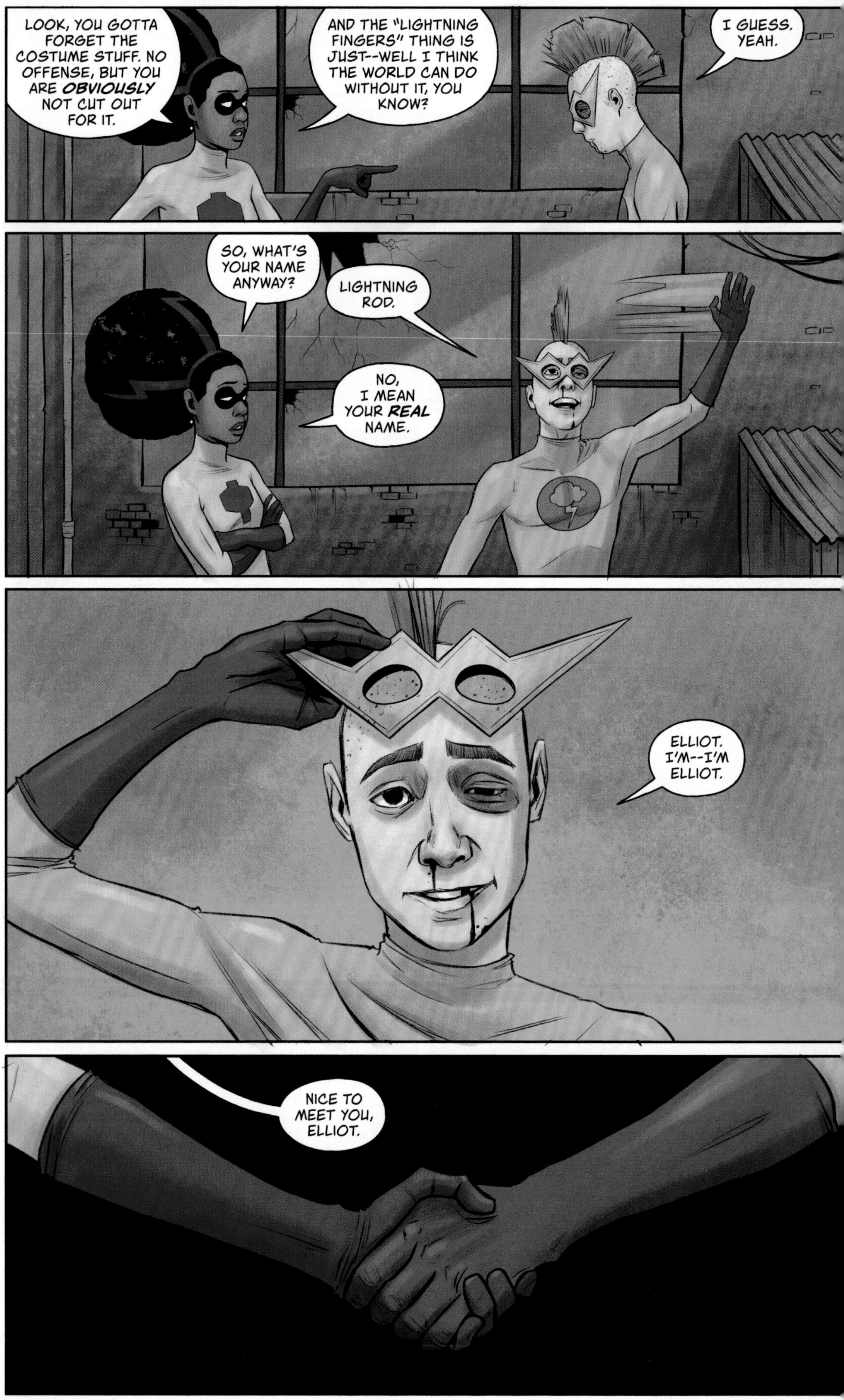

LOOK, YOU GOTTA FORGET THE COSTUME STUFF. NO OFFENSE, BUT YOU ARE ***OBVIOUSLY*** NOT CUT OUT FOR IT.
AND THE "LIGHTNING FINGERS" THING IS JUST--WELL I THINK THE WORLD CAN DO WITHOUT IT, YOU KNOW?
I GUESS. YEAH.
SO, WHAT'S YOUR NAME ANYWAY?
LIGHTNING ROD.
NO, I MEAN YOUR ***REAL*** NAME.
ELLIOT. I'M--I'M ELLIOT.
NICE TO MEET YOU, ELLIOT.

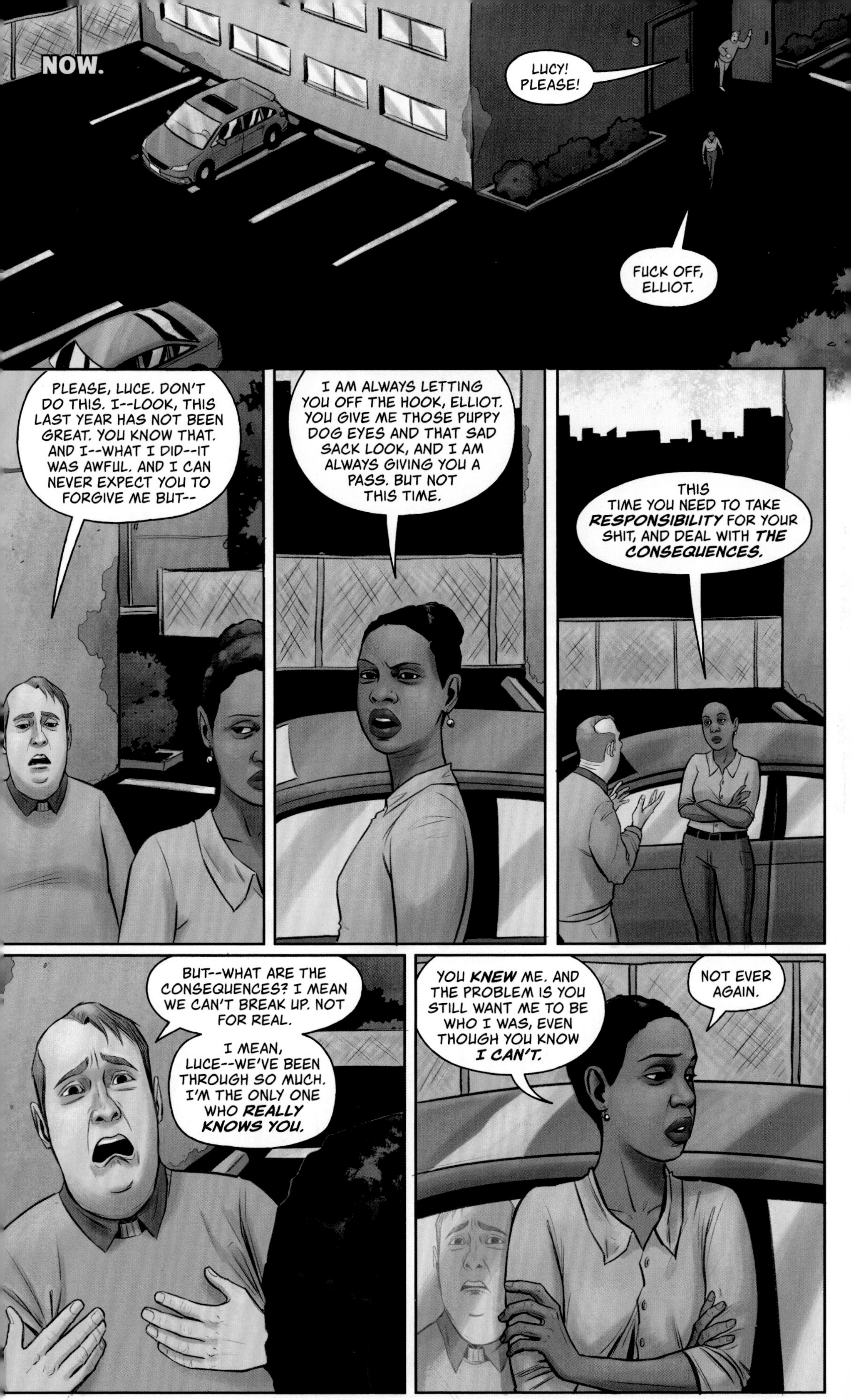
NOW.
LUCY! PLEASE!
FUCK OFF, ELLIOT.
PLEASE, LUCE. DON'T DO THIS. I--LOOK, THIS LAST YEAR HAS NOT BEEN GREAT. YOU KNOW THAT. AND I--WHAT I DID--IT WAS AWFUL. AND I CAN NEVER EXPECT YOU TO FORGIVE ME BUT--
I AM ALWAYS LETTING YOU OFF THE HOOK, ELLIOT. YOU GIVE ME THOSE PUPPY DOG EYES AND THAT SAD SACK LOOK, AND I AM ALWAYS GIVING YOU A PASS. BUT NOT THIS TIME.
THIS TIME YOU NEED TO TAKE RESPONSIBILITY FOR YOUR SHIT, AND DEAL WITH THE CONSEQUENCES.
BUT--WHAT ARE THE CONSEQUENCES? I MEAN WE CAN'T BREAK UP. NOT FOR REAL.
I MEAN, LUCE--WE'VE BEEN THROUGH SO MUCH. I'M THE ONLY ONE WHO REALLY KNOWS YOU.
YOU KNEW ME. AND THE PROBLEM IS YOU STILL WANT ME TO BE WHO I WAS, EVEN THOUGH YOU KNOW I CAN'T.
NOT EVER AGAIN.

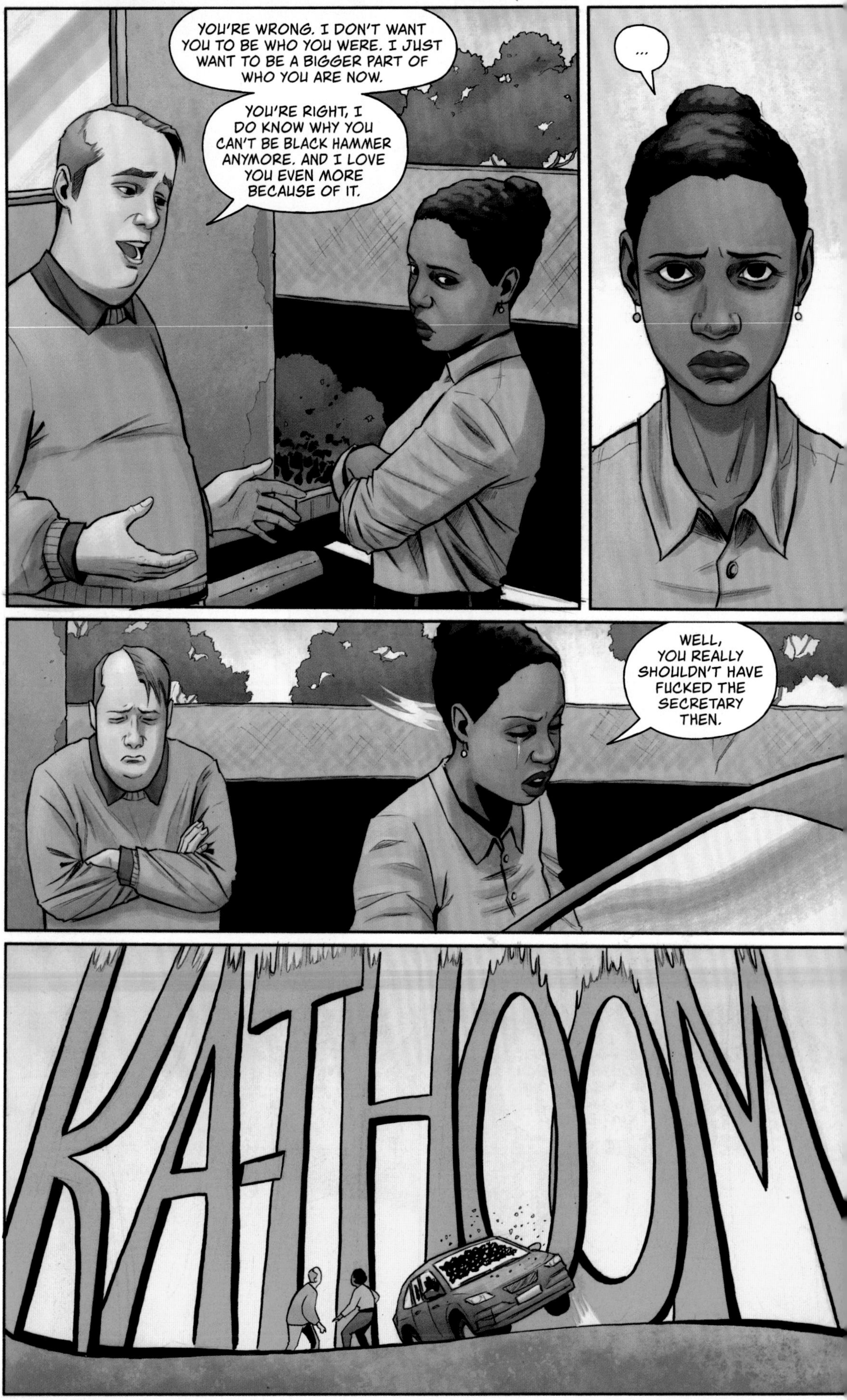
YOU'RE WRONG. I DON'T WANT YOU TO BE WHO YOU WERE. I JUST WANT TO BE A BIGGER PART OF WHO YOU ARE NOW.
YOU'RE RIGHT, I DO KNOW WHY YOU CAN'T BE BLACK HAMMER ANYMORE. AND I LOVE YOU EVEN MORE BECAUSE OF IT.
...
WELL, YOU REALLY SHOULDN'T HAVE FUCKED THE SECRETARY THEN.
KA-THOOM

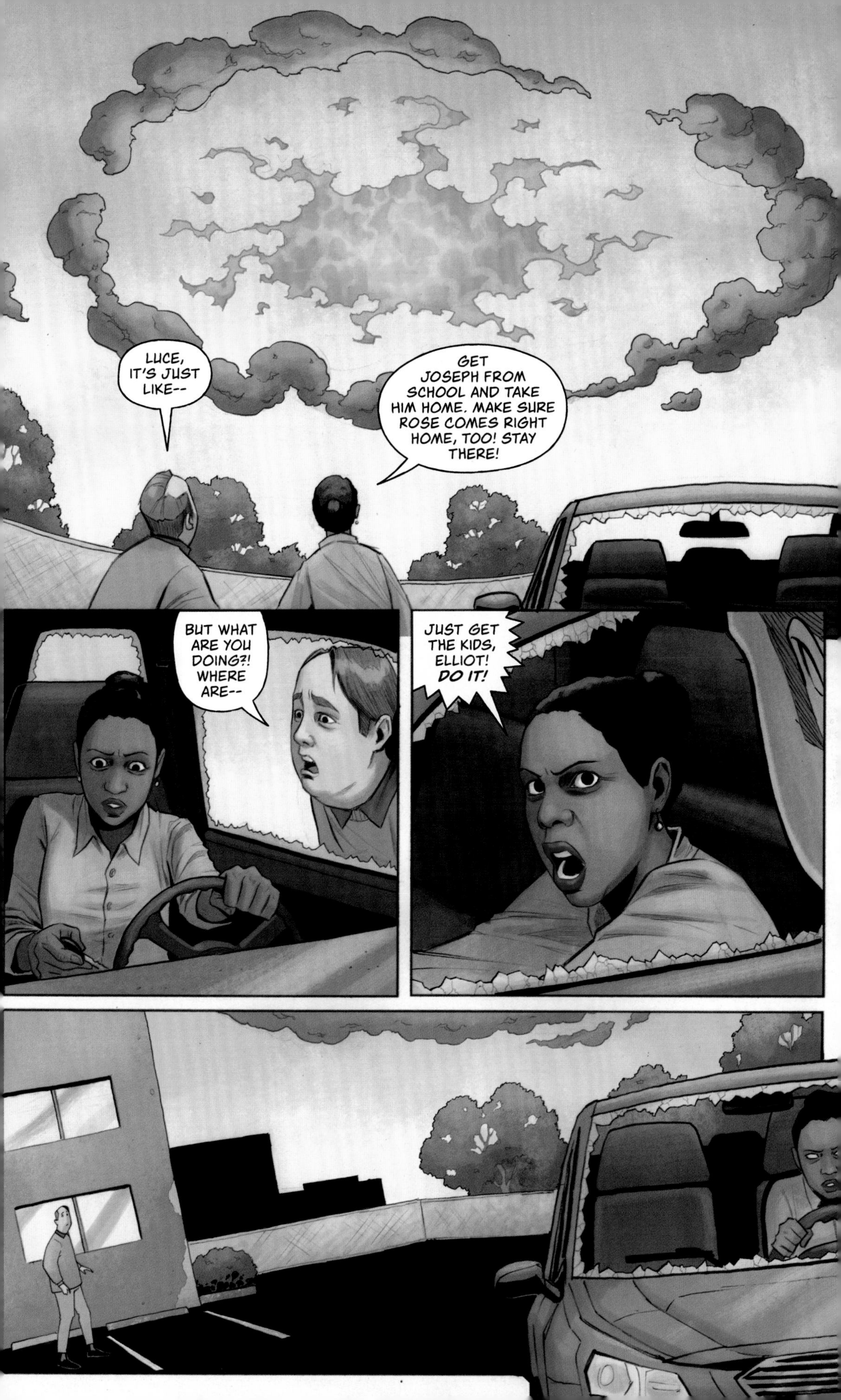
LUCE, IT'S JUST LIKE--
GET JOSEPH FROM SCHOOL AND TAKE HIM HOME. MAKE SURE ROSE COMES RIGHT HOME, TOO! STAY THERE!
BUT WHAT ARE YOU DOING?! WHERE ARE--
JUST GET THE KIDS, ELLIOT! *DO IT!*

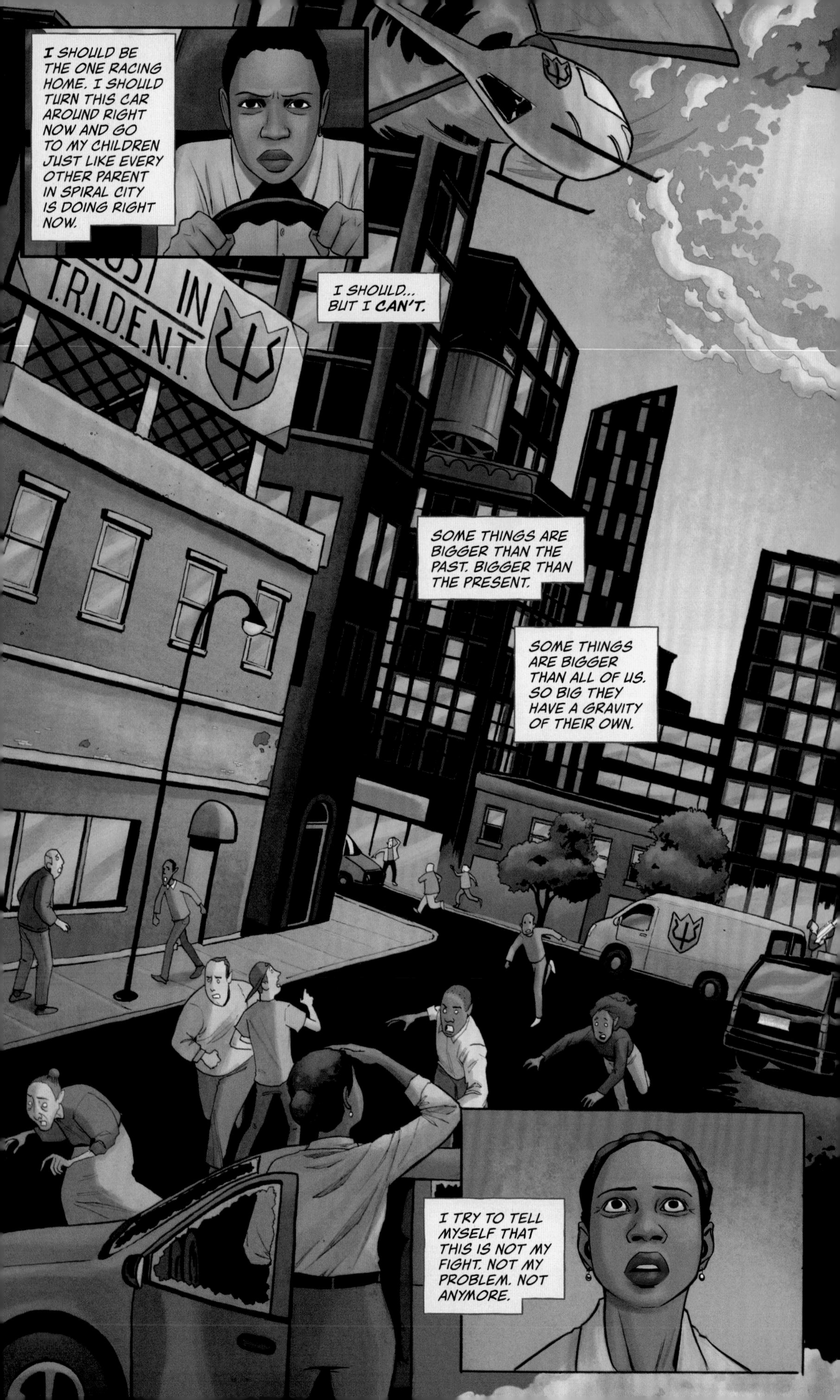
I SHOULD BE THE ONE RACING HOME. I SHOULD TURN THIS CAR AROUND RIGHT NOW AND GO TO MY CHILDREN JUST LIKE EVERY OTHER PARENT IN SPIRAL CITY IS DOING RIGHT NOW.
T.R.I.D.E.N.T.
I SHOULD... BUT I CAN'T.
SOME THINGS ARE BIGGER THAN THE PAST. BIGGER THAN THE PRESENT.
SOME THINGS ARE BIGGER THAN ALL OF US. SO BIG THEY HAVE A GRAVITY OF THEIR OWN.
I TRY TO TELL MYSELF THAT THIS IS NOT MY FIGHT. NOT MY PROBLEM. NOT ANYMORE.

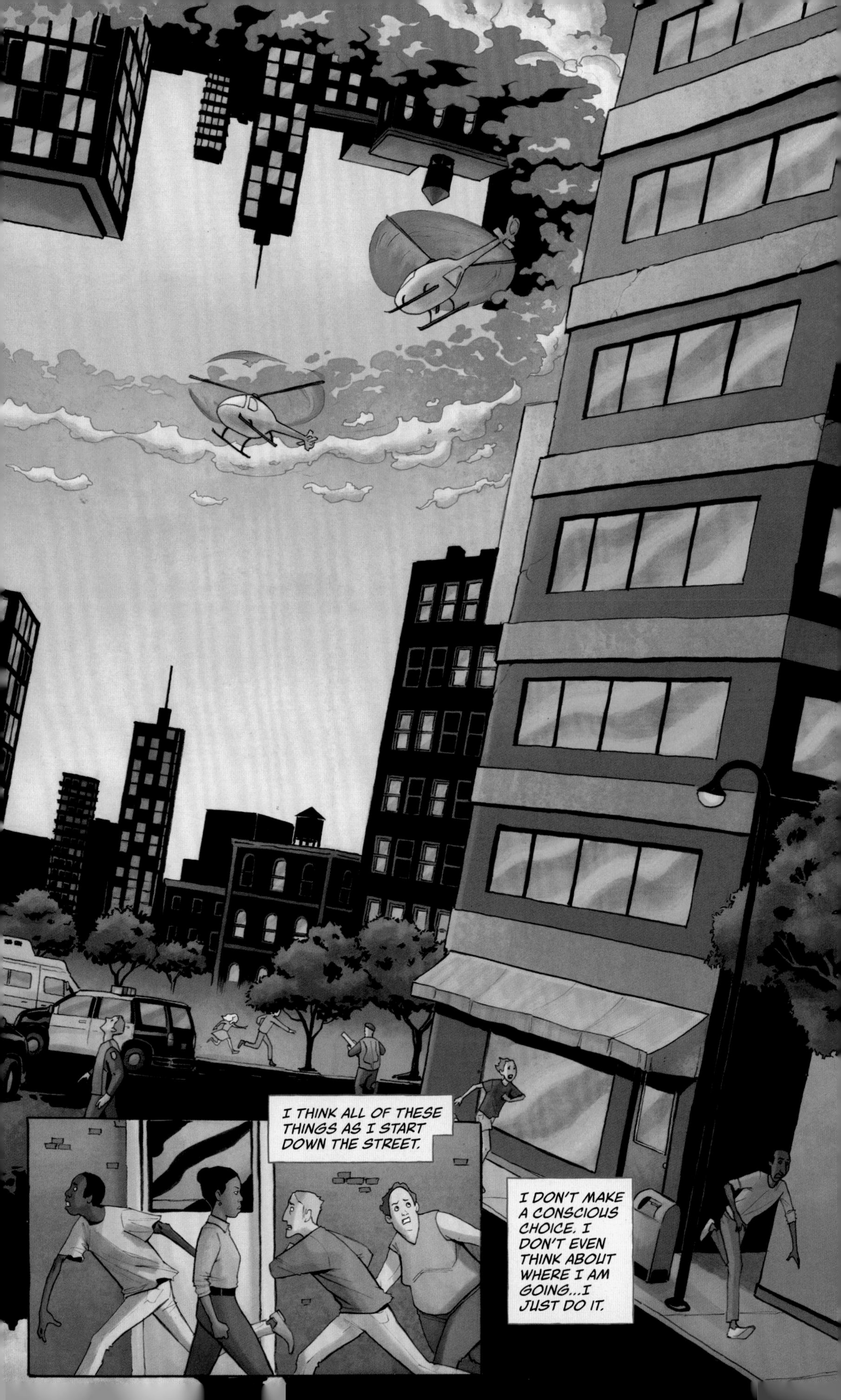

I THINK ALL OF THESE THINGS AS I START DOWN THE STREET.
I DON'T MAKE A CONSCIOUS CHOICE. I DON'T EVEN THINK ABOUT WHERE I AM GOING...I JUST DO IT.

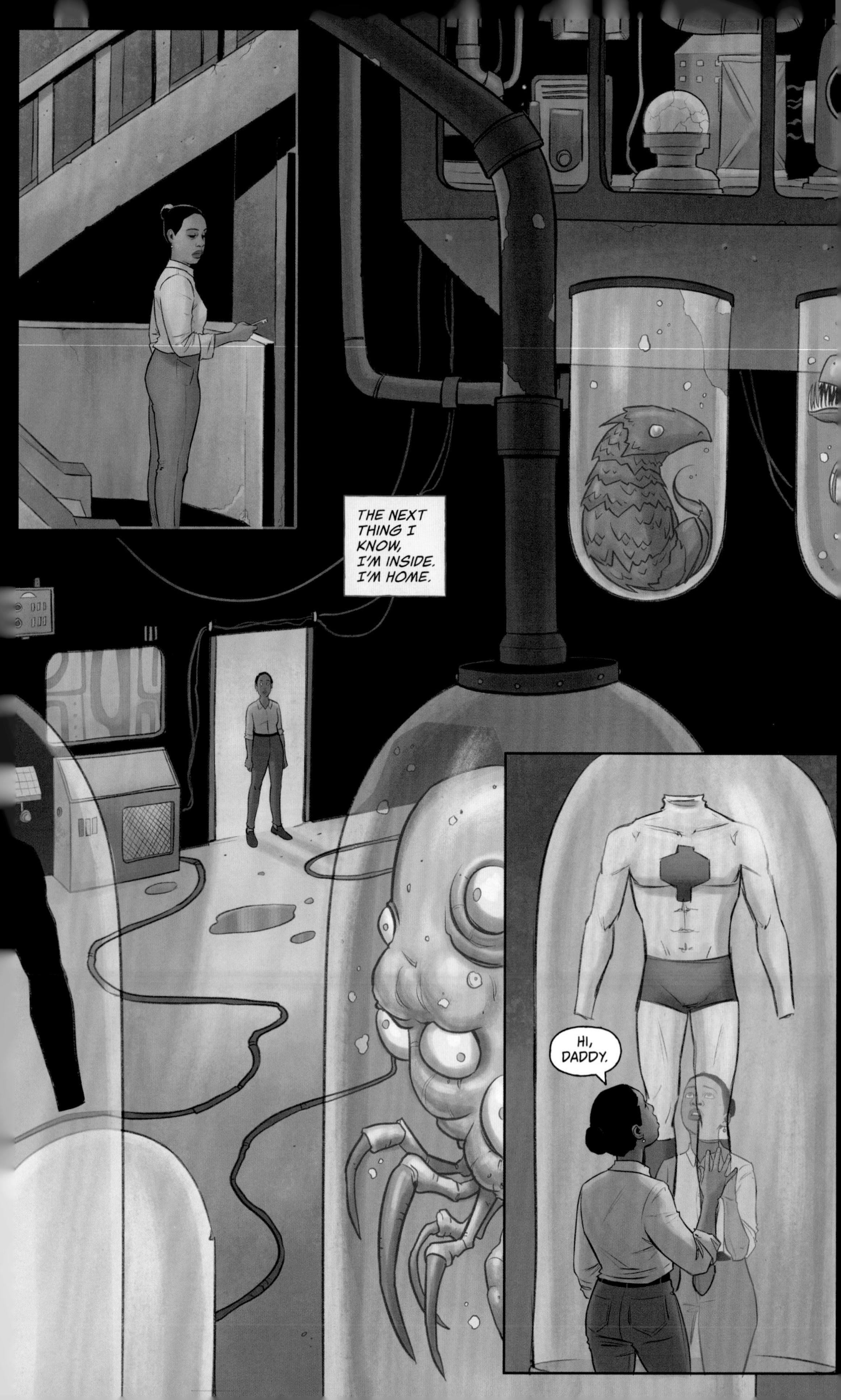
THE NEXT THING I KNOW, I'M INSIDE. I'M HOME.
HI, DADDY.

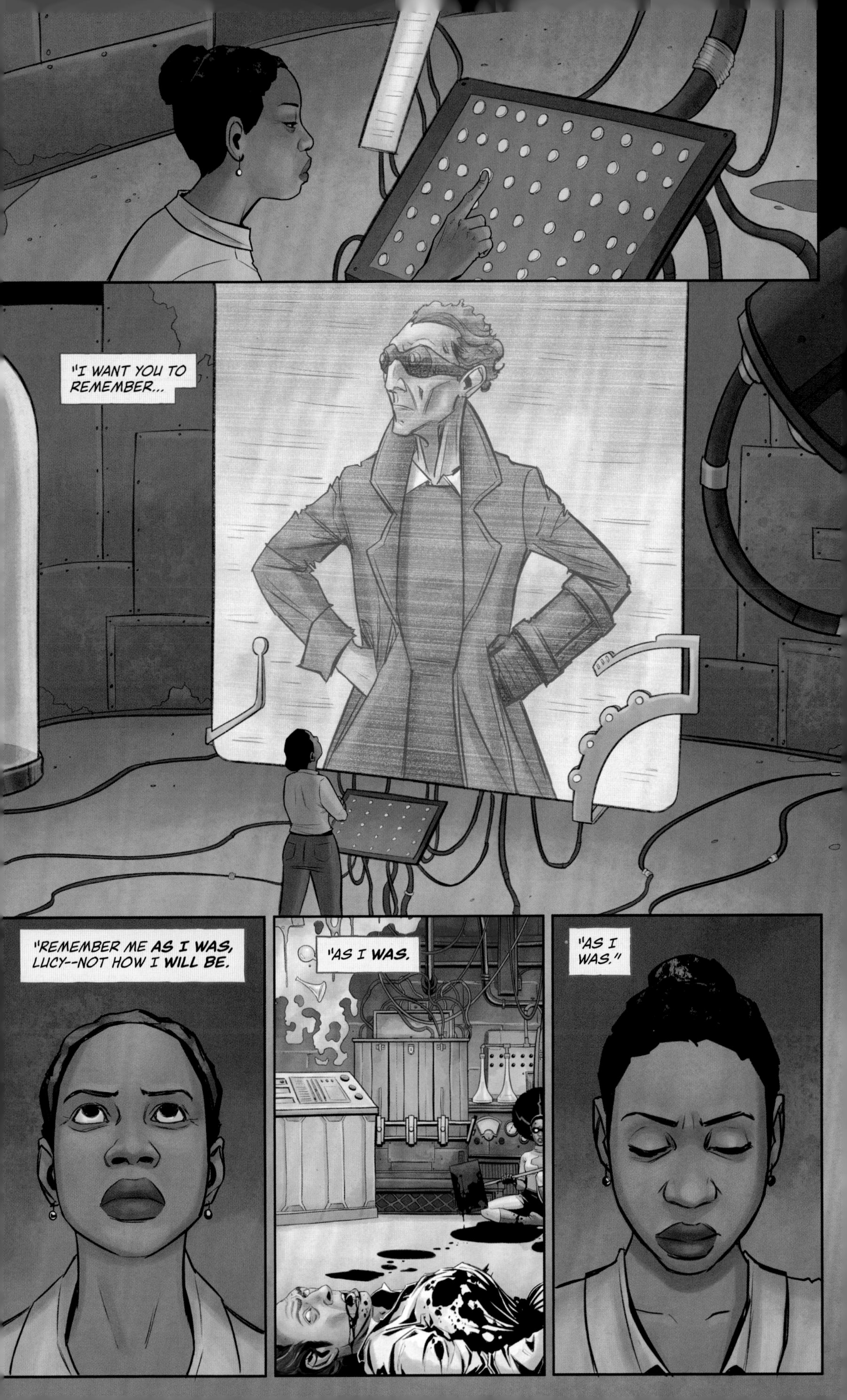
"I WANT YOU TO REMEMBER...
"REMEMBER ME AS I WAS, LUCY--NOT HOW I WILL BE.
"AS I WAS.
"AS I WAS."

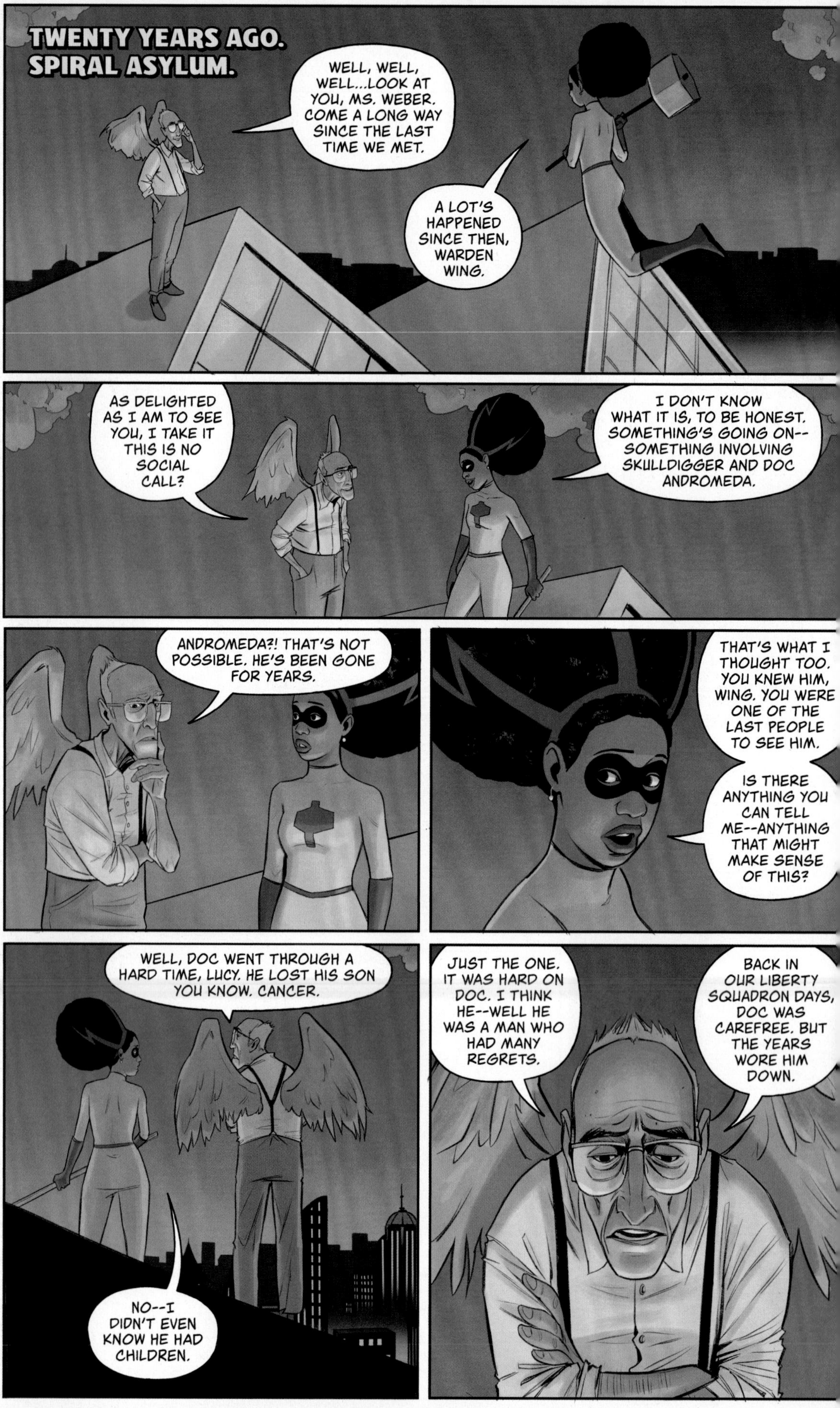
TWENTY YEARS AGO. SPIRAL ASYLUM.
WELL, WELL, WELL...LOOK AT YOU, MS. WEBER. COME A LONG WAY SINCE THE LAST TIME WE MET.
A LOT'S HAPPENED SINCE THEN, WARDEN WING.
AS DELIGHTED AS I AM TO SEE YOU, I TAKE IT THIS IS NO SOCIAL CALL?
I DON'T KNOW WHAT IT IS, TO BE HONEST. SOMETHING'S GOING ON--SOMETHING INVOLVING SKULLDIGGER AND DOC ANDROMEDA.
ANDROMEDA?! THAT'S NOT POSSIBLE. HE'S BEEN GONE FOR YEARS.
THAT'S WHAT I THOUGHT TOO. YOU KNEW HIM, WING. YOU WERE ONE OF THE LAST PEOPLE TO SEE HIM.
IS THERE ANYTHING YOU CAN TELL ME--ANYTHING THAT MIGHT MAKE SENSE OF THIS?
WELL, DOC WENT THROUGH A HARD TIME, LUCY. HE LOST HIS SON YOU KNOW. CANCER.
NO--I DIDN'T EVEN KNOW HE HAD CHILDREN.
JUST THE ONE. IT WAS HARD ON DOC. I THINK HE--WELL HE WAS A MAN WHO HAD MANY REGRETS.
BACK IN OUR LIBERTY SQUADRON DAYS, DOC WAS CAREFREE. BUT THE YEARS WORE HIM DOWN.

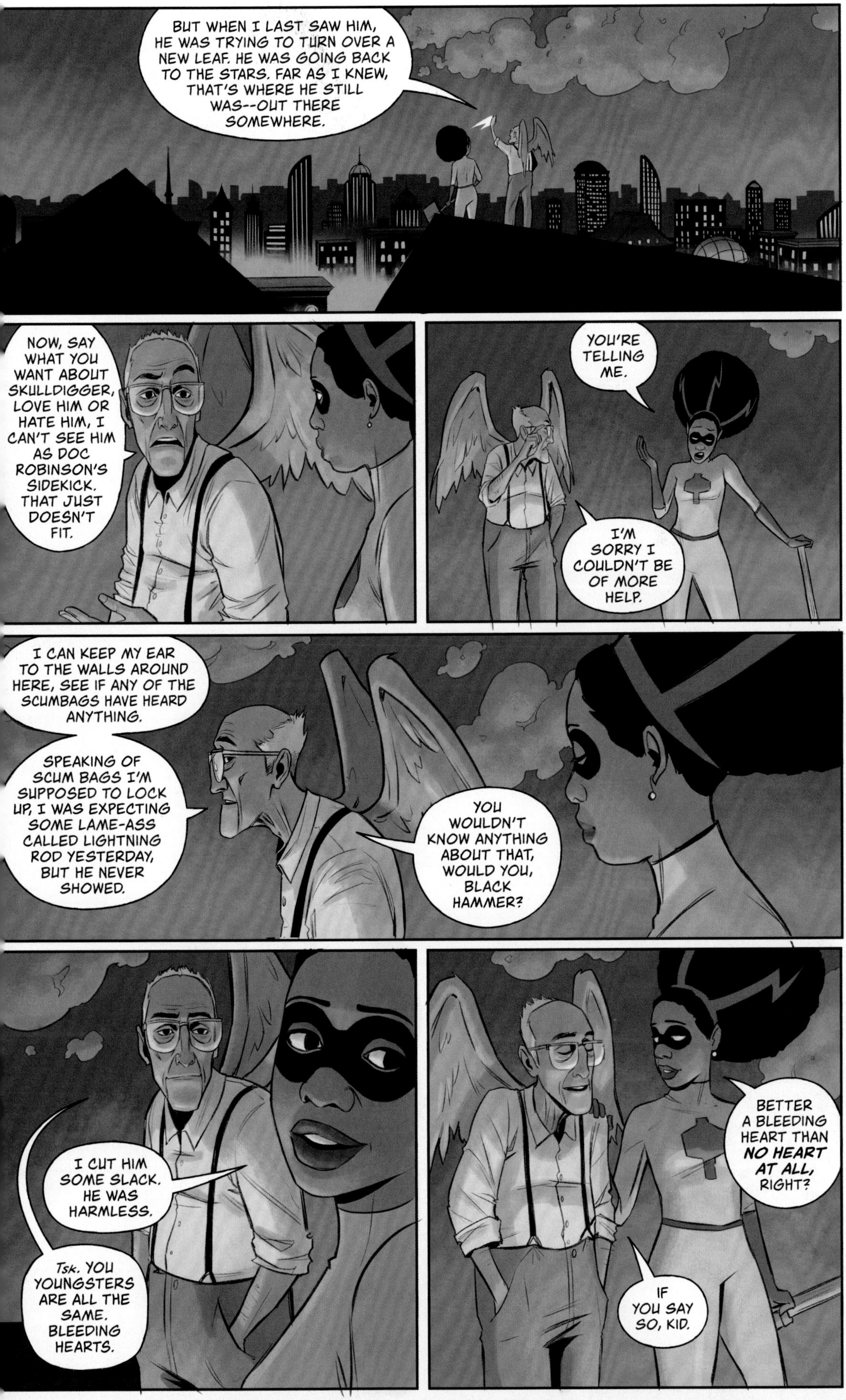

BUT WHEN I LAST SAW HIM, HE WAS TRYING TO TURN OVER A NEW LEAF. HE WAS GOING BACK TO THE STARS. FAR AS I KNEW, THAT'S WHERE HE STILL WAS--OUT THERE SOMEWHERE.
NOW, SAY WHAT YOU WANT ABOUT SKULLDIGGER, LOVE HIM OR HATE HIM, I CAN'T SEE HIM AS DOC ROBINSON'S SIDEKICK. THAT JUST DOESN'T FIT.
YOU'RE TELLING ME.
I'M SORRY I COULDN'T BE OF MORE HELP.
I CAN KEEP MY EAR TO THE WALLS AROUND HERE, SEE IF ANY OF THE SCUMBAGS HAVE HEARD ANYTHING.
SPEAKING OF SCUM BAGS I'M SUPPOSED TO LOCK UP, I WAS EXPECTING SOME LAME-ASS CALLED LIGHTNING ROD YESTERDAY, BUT HE NEVER SHOWED.
YOU WOULDN'T KNOW ANYTHING ABOUT THAT, WOULD YOU, BLACK HAMMER?
I CUT HIM SOME SLACK. HE WAS HARMLESS.
Tsk. YOU YOUNGSTERS ARE ALL THE SAME. BLEEDING HEARTS.
BETTER A BLEEDING HEART THAN ***NO HEART AT ALL,*** RIGHT?
IF YOU SAY SO, KID.

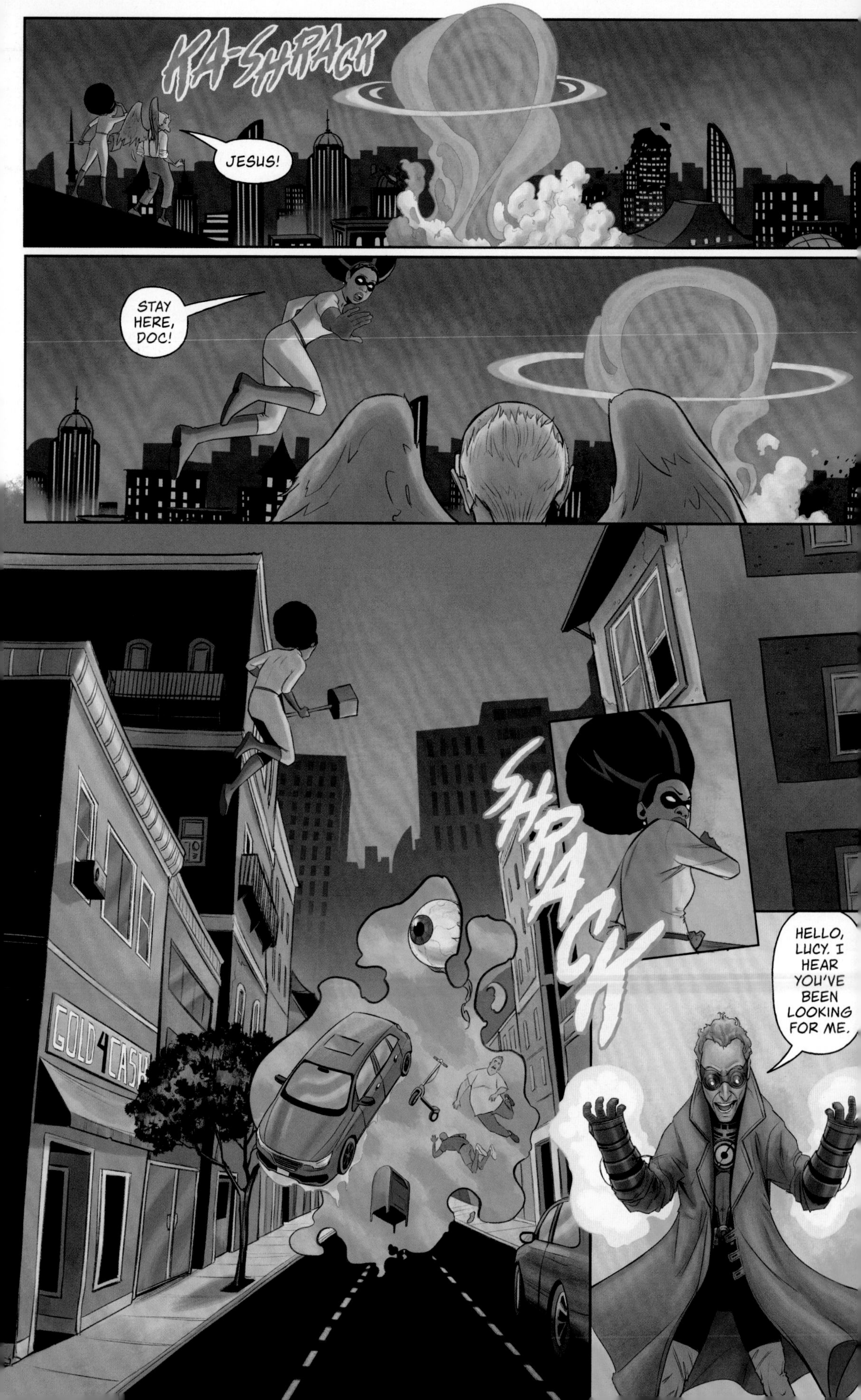
KA-SHRACK
JESUS!
STAY HERE, DOC!
GOLD 4 CASH
SHRACK
HELLO, LUCY. I HEAR YOU'VE BEEN LOOKING FOR ME.

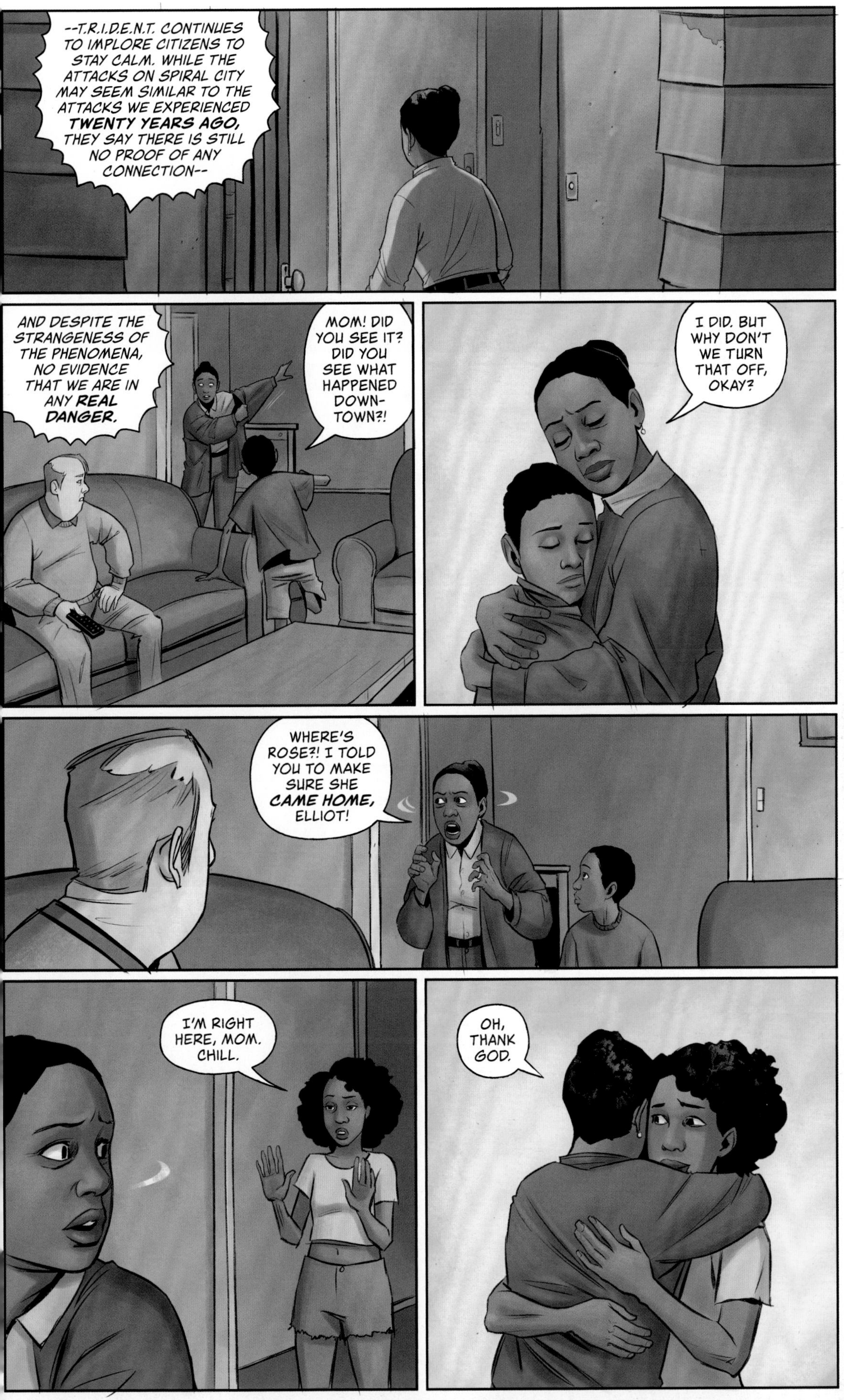
--T.R.I.D.E.N.T. CONTINUES TO IMPLORE CITIZENS TO STAY CALM. WHILE THE ATTACKS ON SPIRAL CITY MAY SEEM SIMILAR TO THE ATTACKS WE EXPERIENCED **TWENTY YEARS AGO,** THEY SAY THERE IS STILL NO PROOF OF ANY CONNECTION--
AND DESPITE THE STRANGENESS OF THE PHENOMENA, NO EVIDENCE THAT WE ARE IN ANY **REAL DANGER.**
MOM! DID YOU SEE IT? DID YOU SEE WHAT HAPPENED DOWN-TOWN?!
I DID. BUT WHY DON'T WE TURN THAT OFF, OKAY?
WHERE'S ROSE?! I TOLD YOU TO MAKE SURE SHE **CAME HOME,** ELLIOT!
I'M RIGHT HERE, MOM. CHILL.
OH, THANK GOD.

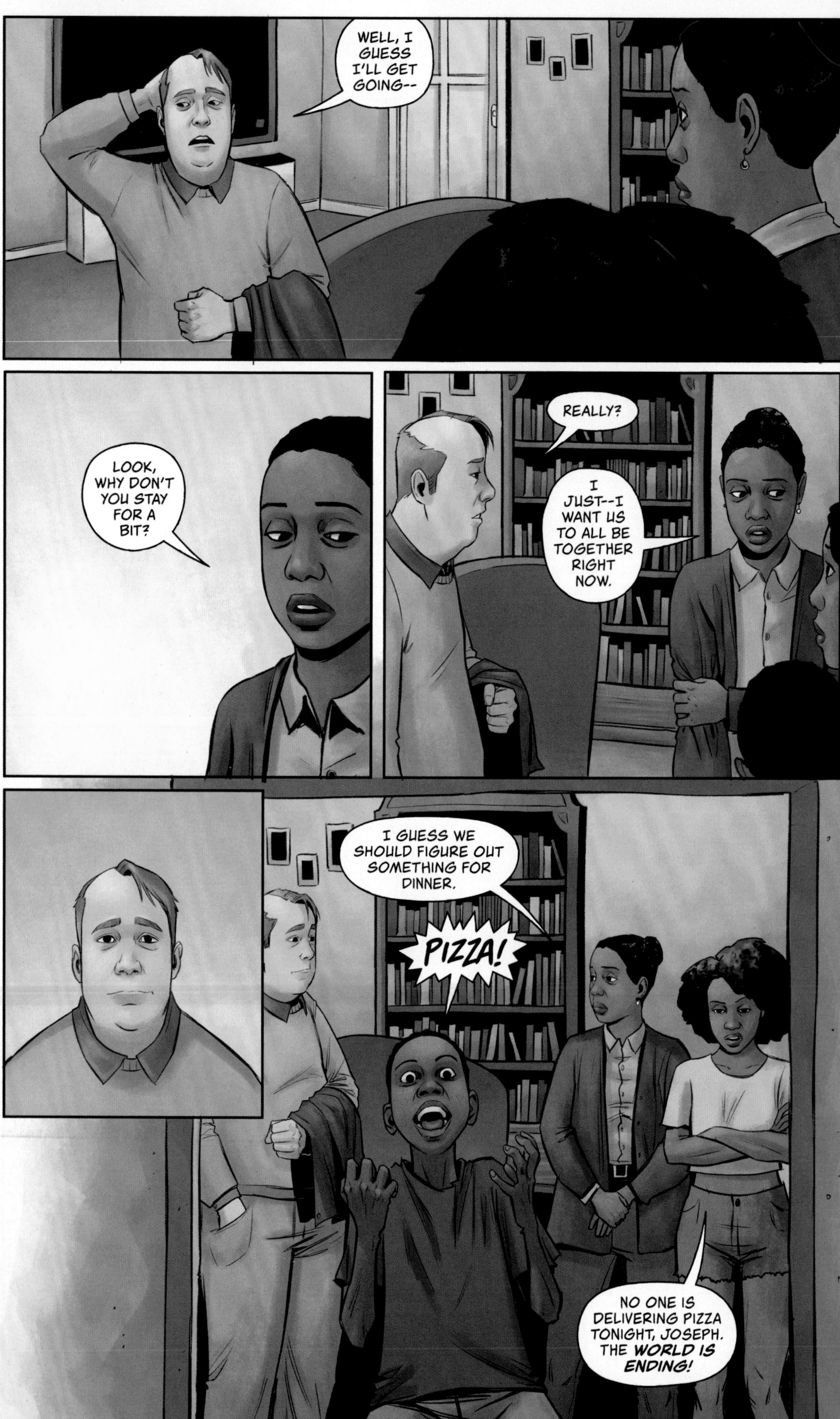

WELL, I GUESS I'LL GET GOING--
LOOK, WHY DON'T YOU STAY FOR A BIT?
REALLY?
I JUST--I WANT US TO ALL BE TOGETHER RIGHT NOW.
I GUESS WE SHOULD FIGURE OUT SOMETHING FOR DINNER.
PIZZA!
NO ONE IS DELIVERING PIZZA TONIGHT, JOSEPH. THE WORLD IS ENDING!

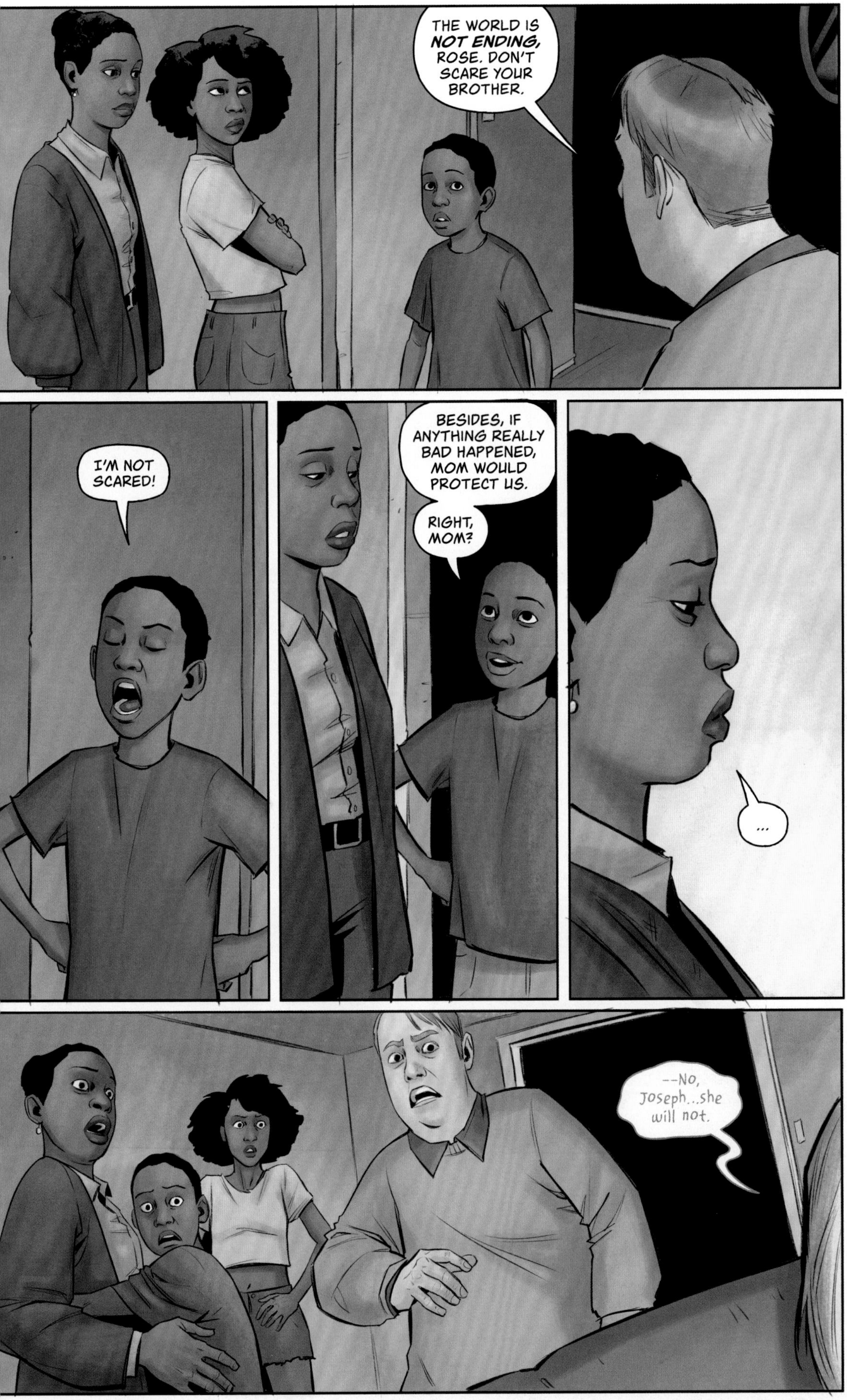
THE WORLD IS ***NOT ENDING,*** ROSE. DON'T SCARE YOUR BROTHER.
I'M NOT SCARED!
BESIDES, IF ANYTHING REALLY BAD HAPPENED, MOM WOULD PROTECT US.
RIGHT, MOM?
...
--No, Joseph...she will not.

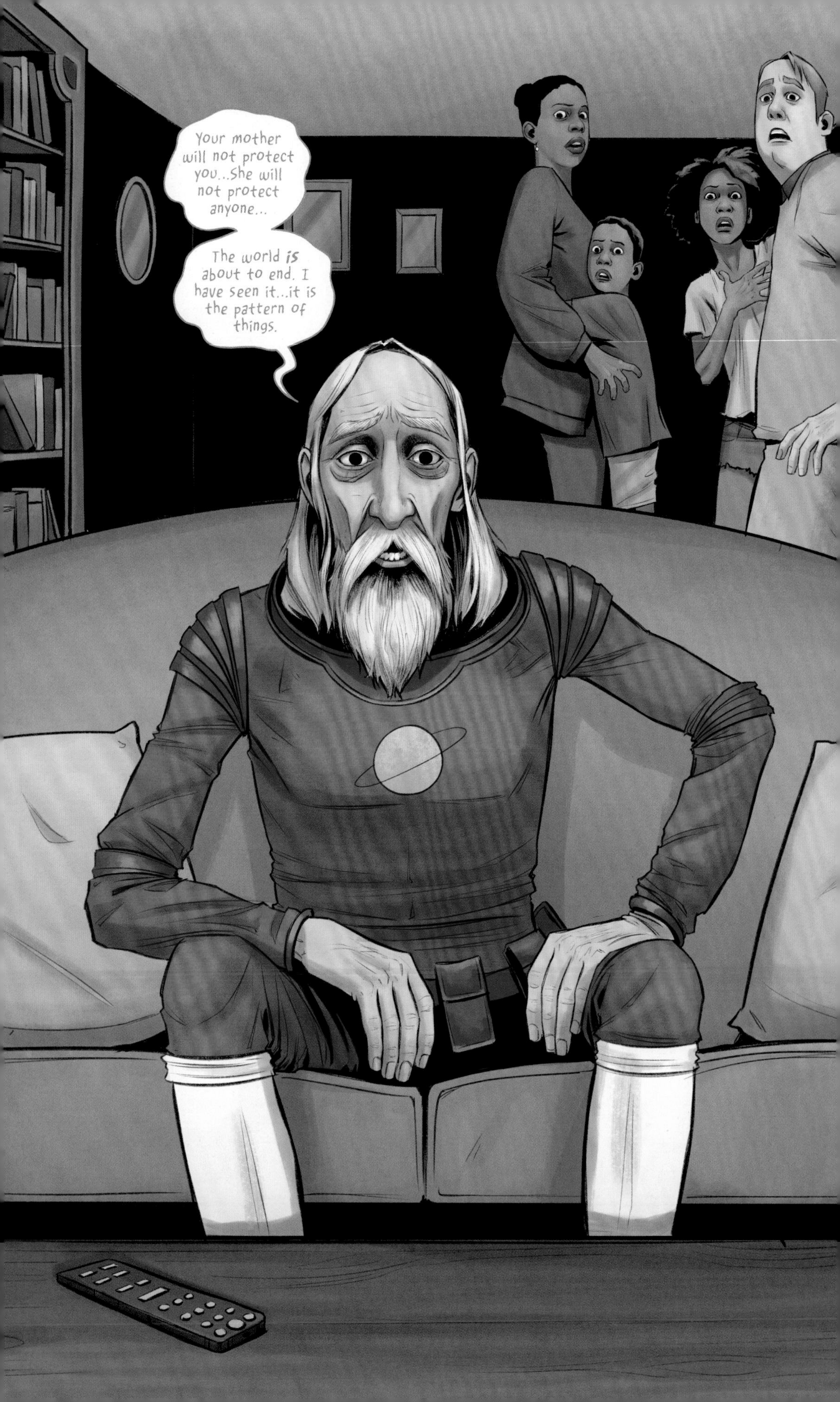
Your mother will not protect you...She will not protect anyone...
The world *is* about to end. I have seen it...it is the pattern of things.

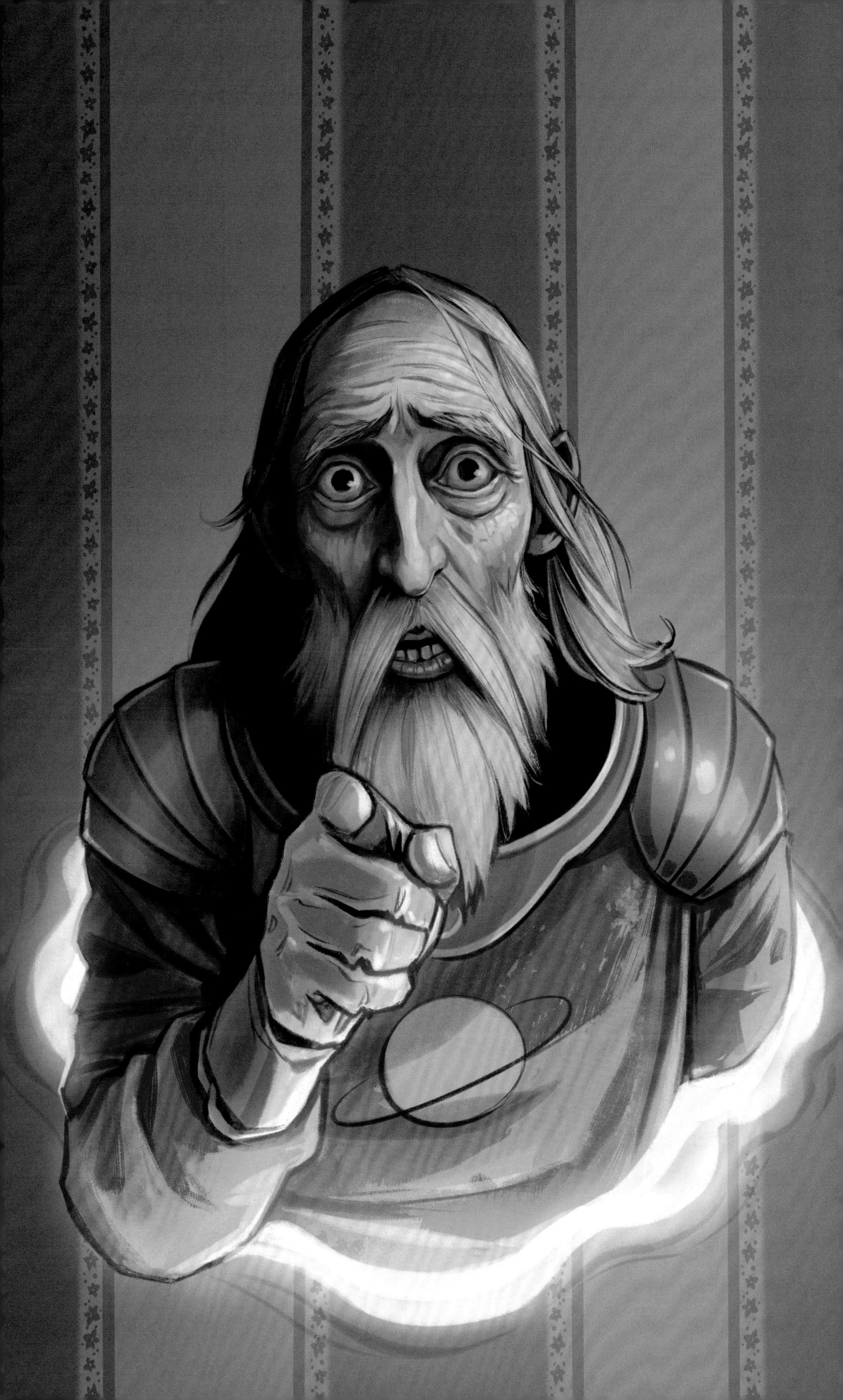

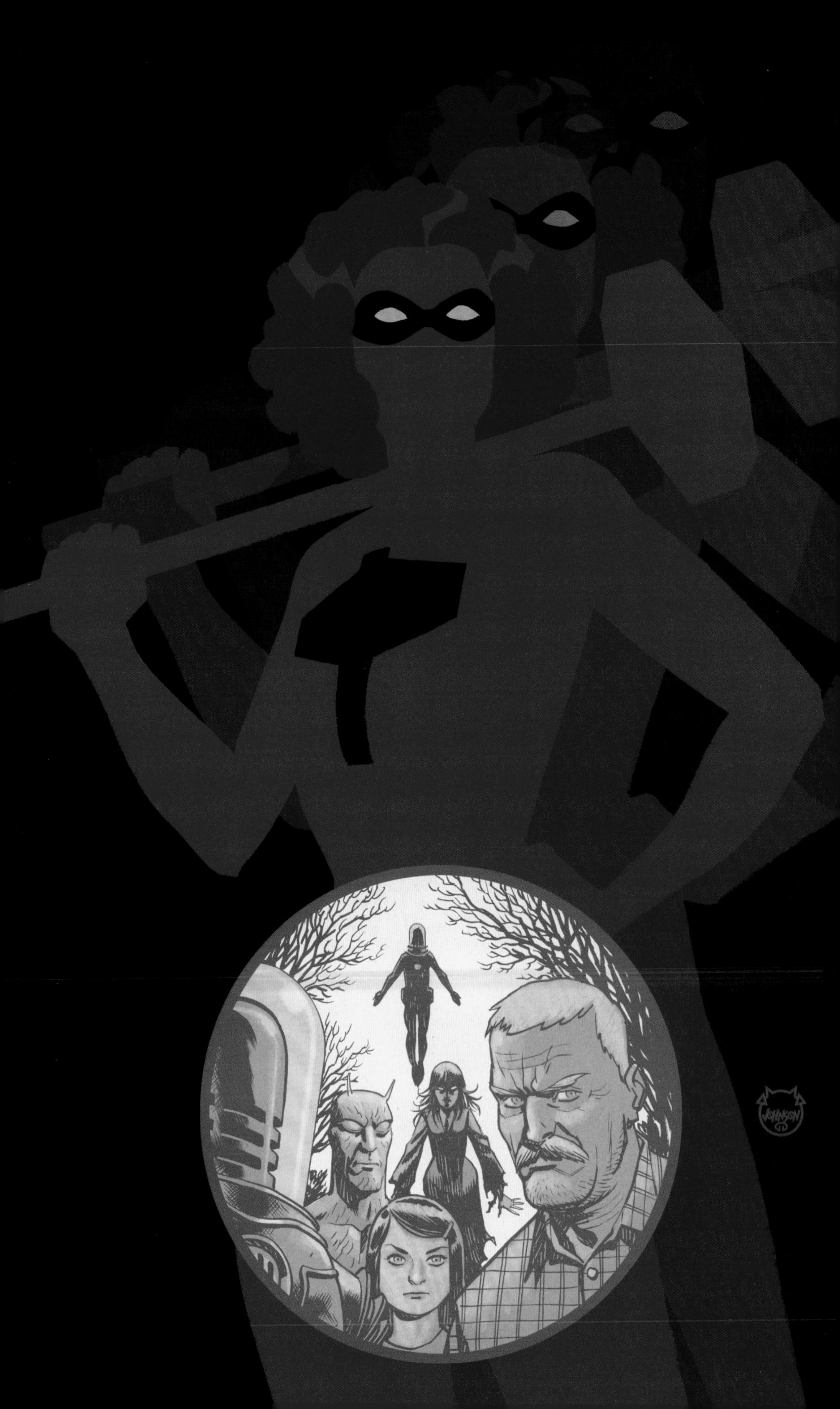

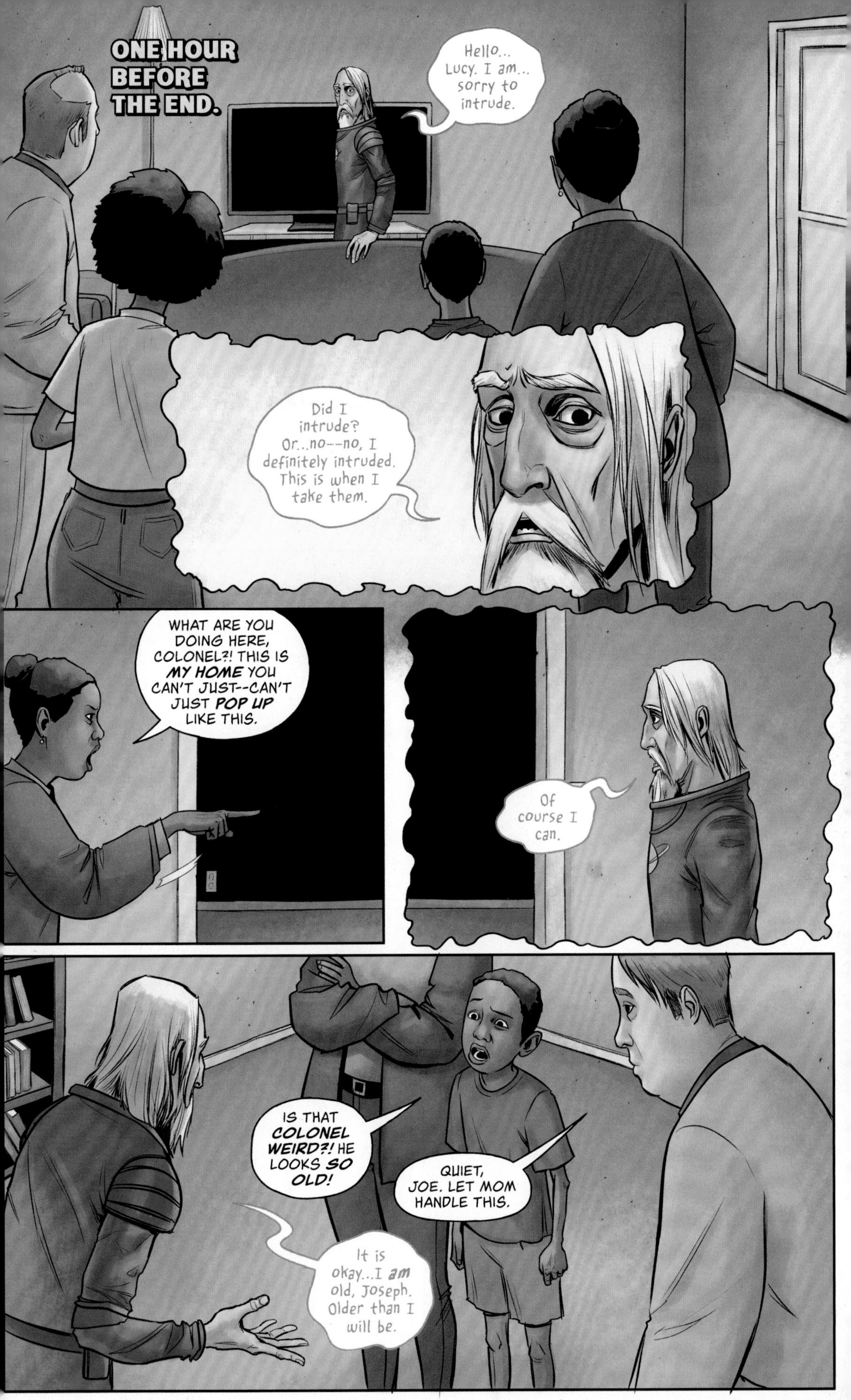
ONE HOUR BEFORE THE END.
Hello... Lucy. I am... sorry to intrude.
Did I intrude? Or...no--no, I definitely intruded. This is when I take them.
WHAT ARE YOU DOING HERE, COLONEL?! THIS IS MY HOME YOU CAN'T JUST--CAN'T JUST POP UP LIKE THIS.
Of course I can.
IS THAT COLONEL WEIRD?! HE LOOKS SO OLD!
QUIET, JOE. LET MOM HANDLE THIS.
It is okay...I am old, Joseph. Older than I will be.

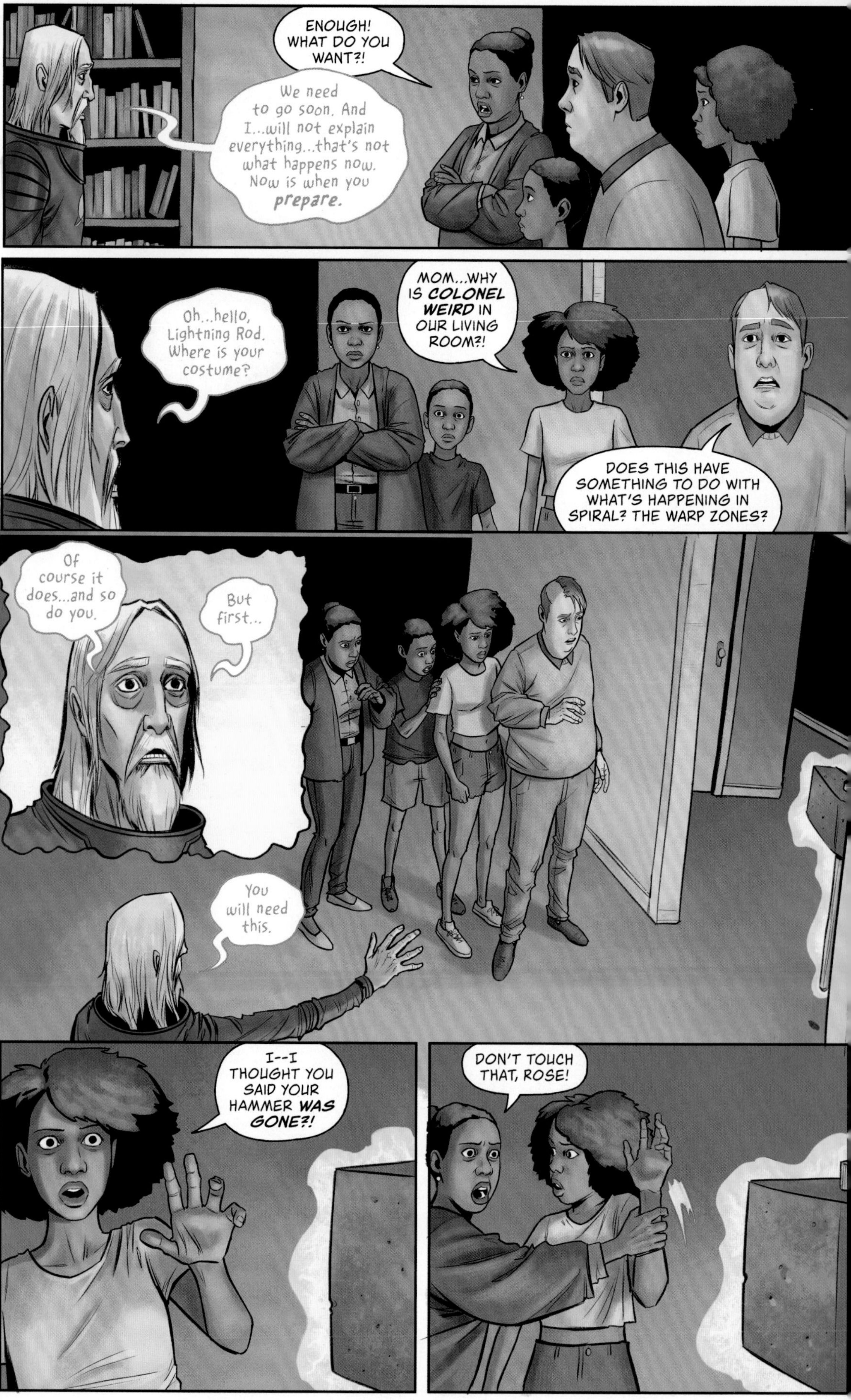
ENOUGH! WHAT DO YOU WANT?!
We need to go soon. And I...will not explain everything...that's not what happens now. Now is when you prepare.
Oh...hello, Lightning Rod. Where is your costume?
MOM...WHY IS COLONEL WEIRD IN OUR LIVING ROOM?!
DOES THIS HAVE SOMETHING TO DO WITH WHAT'S HAPPENING IN SPIRAL? THE WARP ZONES?
Of course it does...and so do you.
But first...
You will need this.
I--I THOUGHT YOU SAID YOUR HAMMER WAS GONE?!
DON'T TOUCH THAT, ROSE!

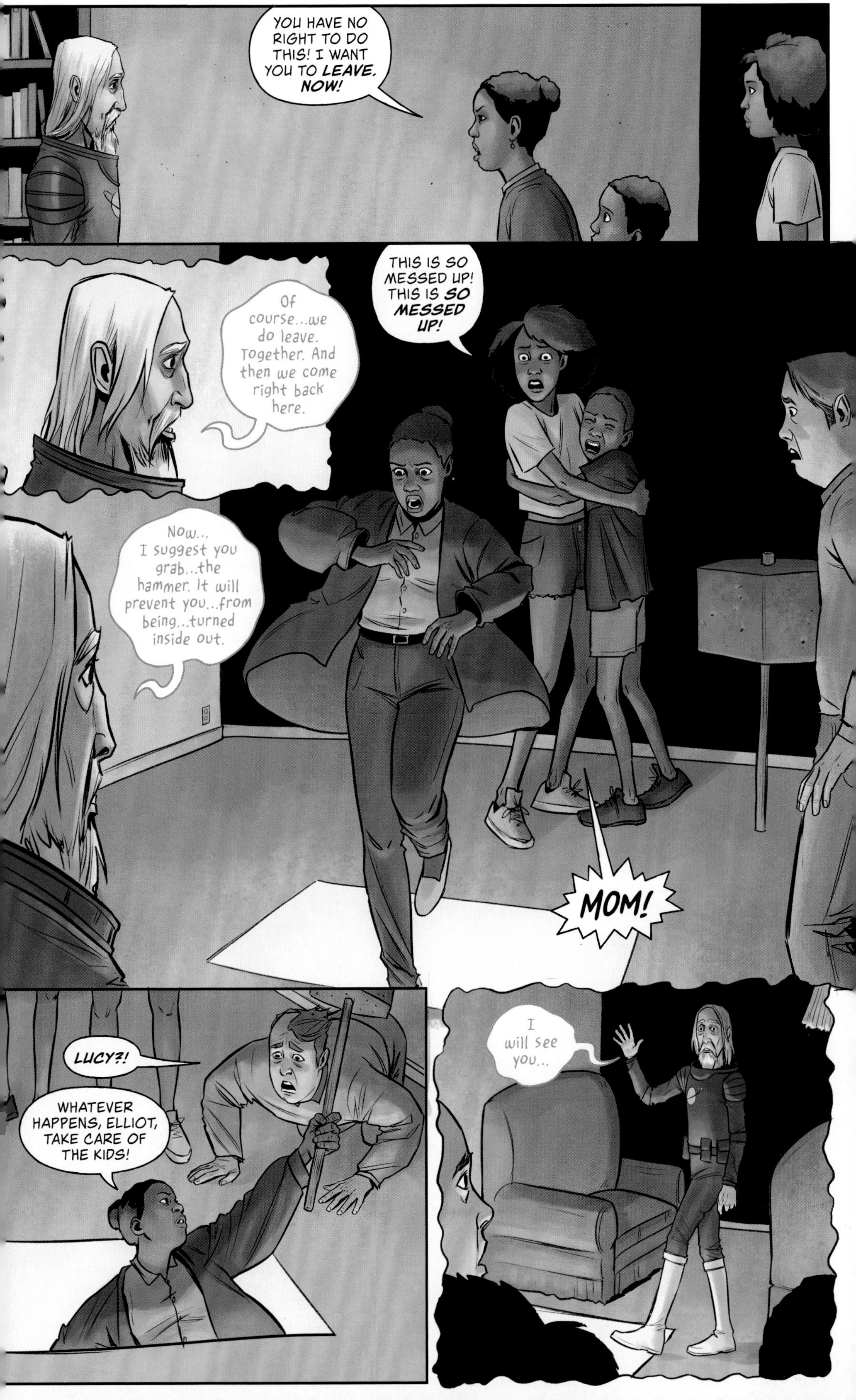
YOU HAVE NO RIGHT TO DO THIS! I WANT YOU TO **LEAVE. NOW!**
Of course...we do leave. Together. And then we come right back here.
THIS IS SO MESSED UP! THIS IS **SO MESSED UP!**
Now... I suggest you grab...the hammer. It will prevent you...from being...turned inside out.
MOM!
LUCY?!
WHATEVER HAPPENS, ELLIOT, TAKE CARE OF THE KIDS!
I will see you...

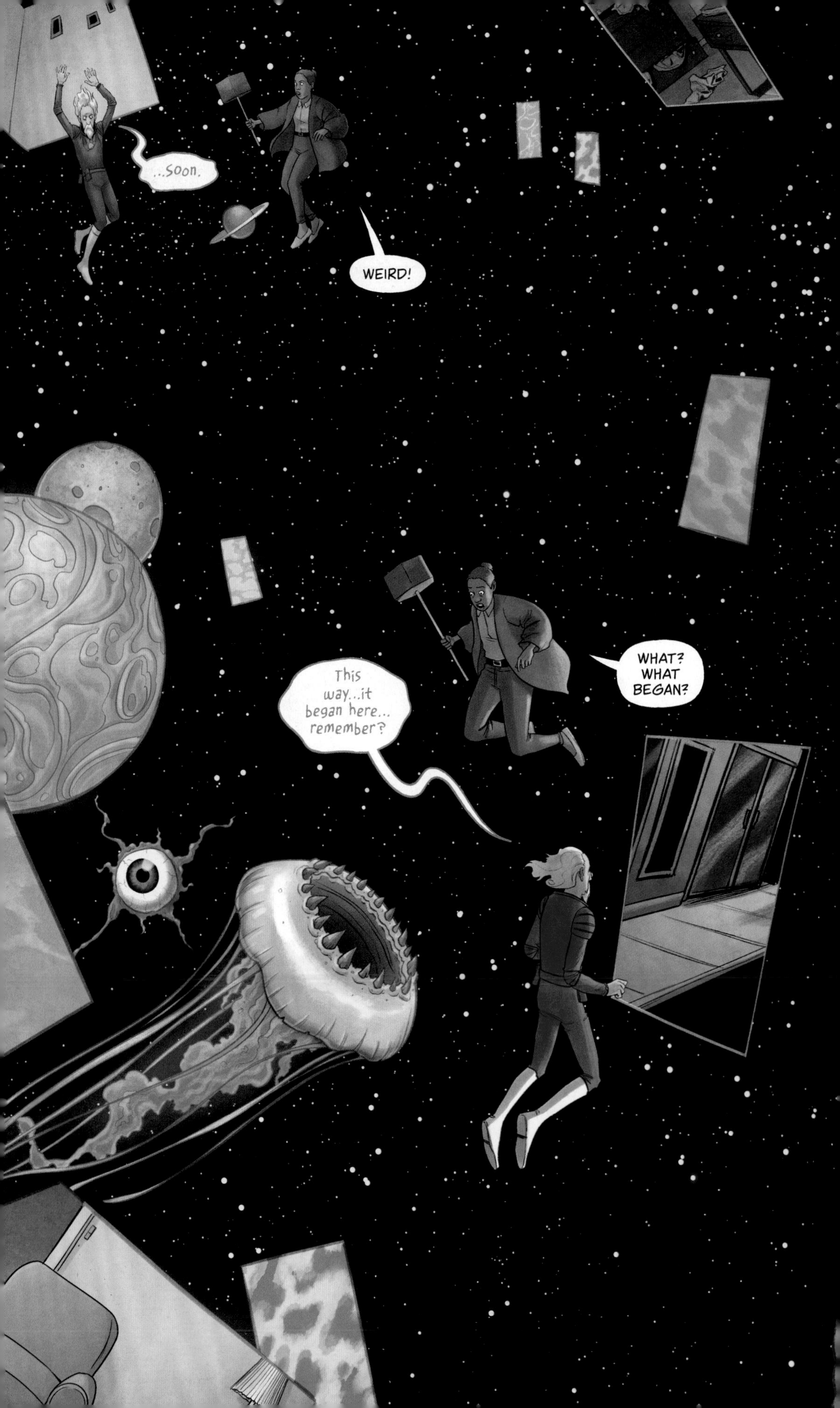

...Soon.
WEIRD!
This way...it began here... remember?
WHAT? WHAT BEGAN?

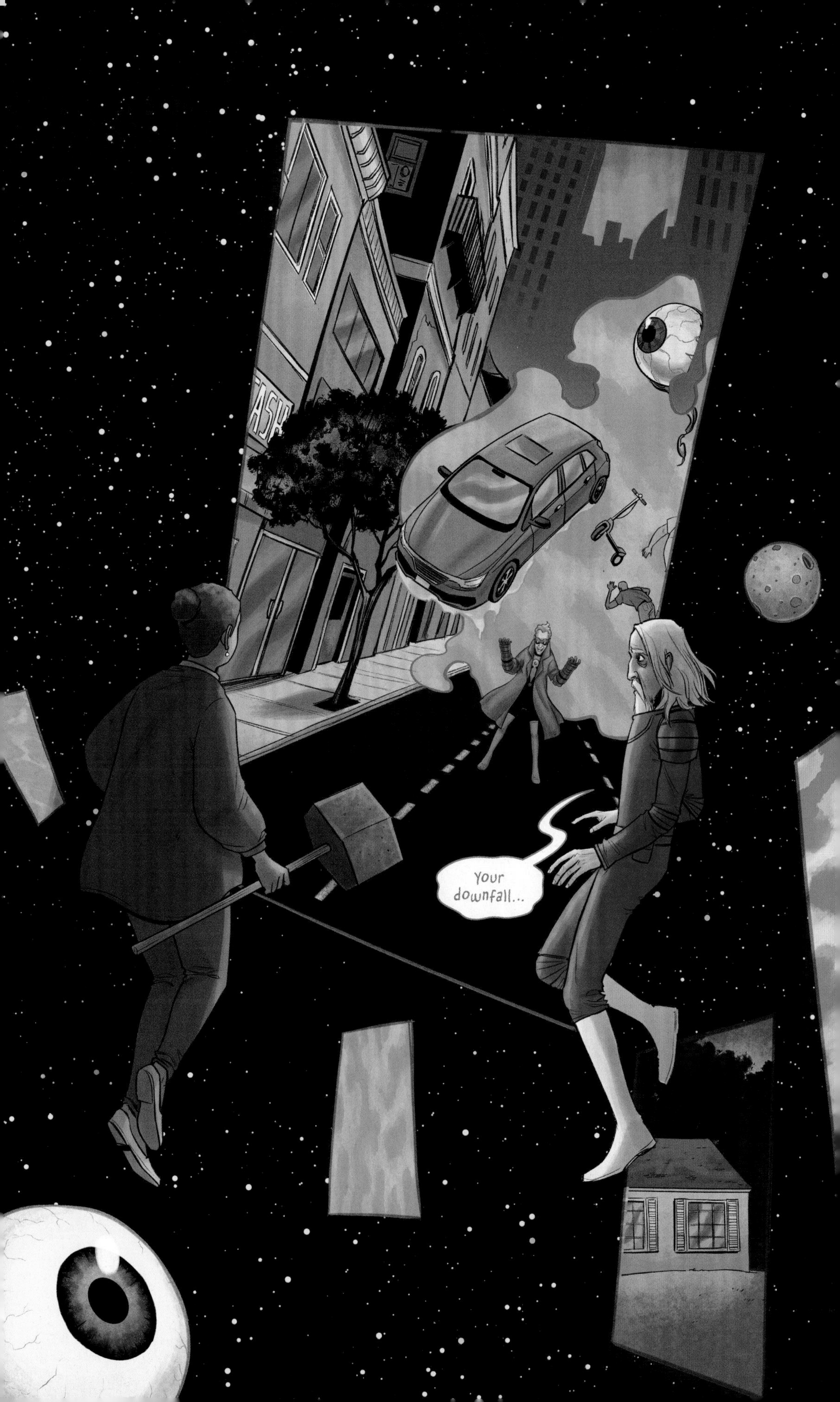
Your downfall...

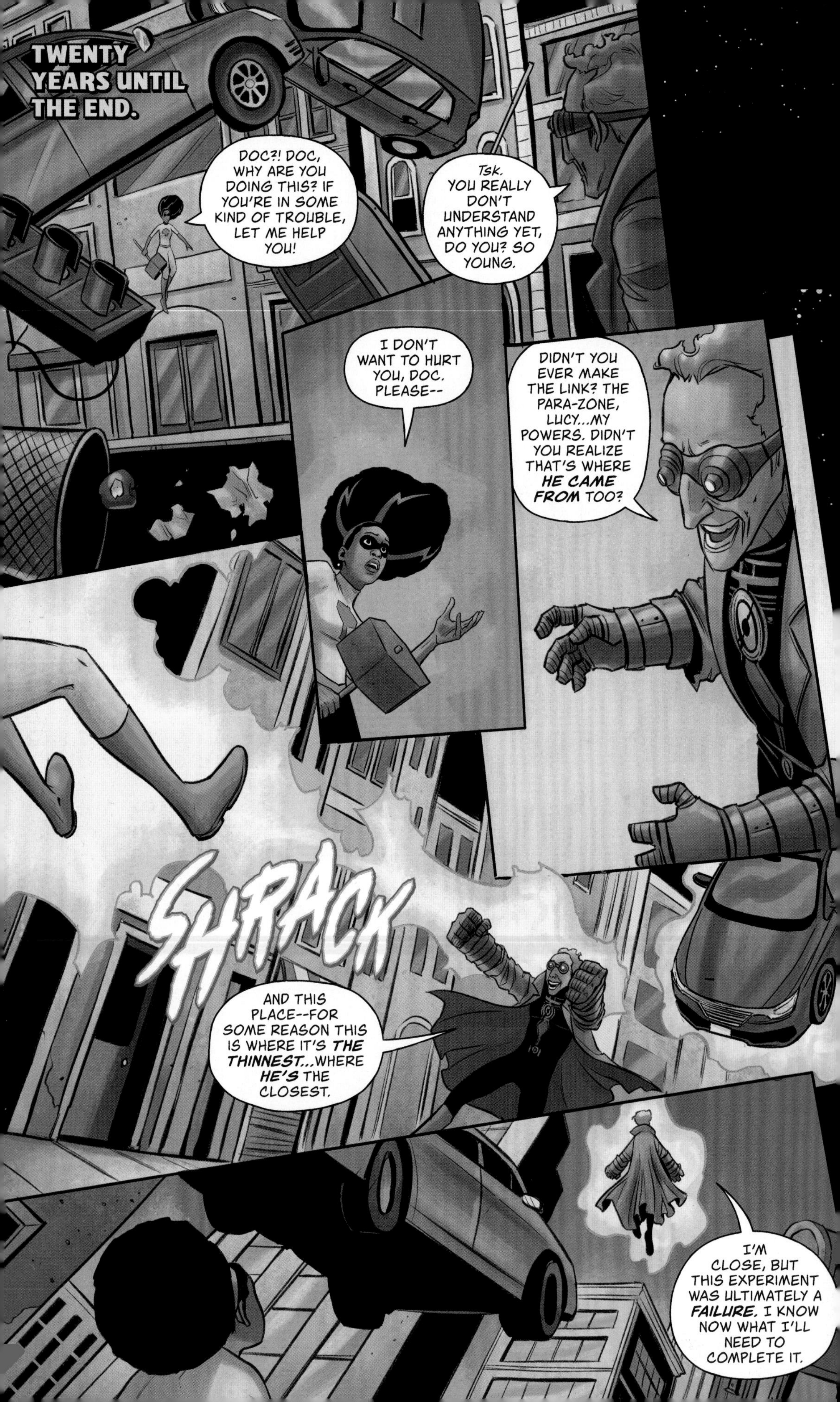
TWENTY YEARS UNTIL THE END.
DOC?! DOC, WHY ARE YOU DOING THIS? IF YOU'RE IN SOME KIND OF TROUBLE, LET ME HELP YOU!
Tsk. YOU REALLY DON'T UNDERSTAND ANYTHING YET, DO YOU? SO YOUNG.
I DON'T WANT TO HURT YOU, DOC. PLEASE--
DIDN'T YOU EVER MAKE THE LINK? THE PARA-ZONE, LUCY...MY POWERS. DIDN'T YOU REALIZE THAT'S WHERE HE CAME FROM TOO?
SHRACK
AND THIS PLACE--FOR SOME REASON THIS IS WHERE IT'S THE THINNEST...WHERE HE'S THE CLOSEST.
I'M CLOSE, BUT THIS EXPERIMENT WAS ULTIMATELY A FAILURE. I KNOW NOW WHAT I'LL NEED TO COMPLETE IT.

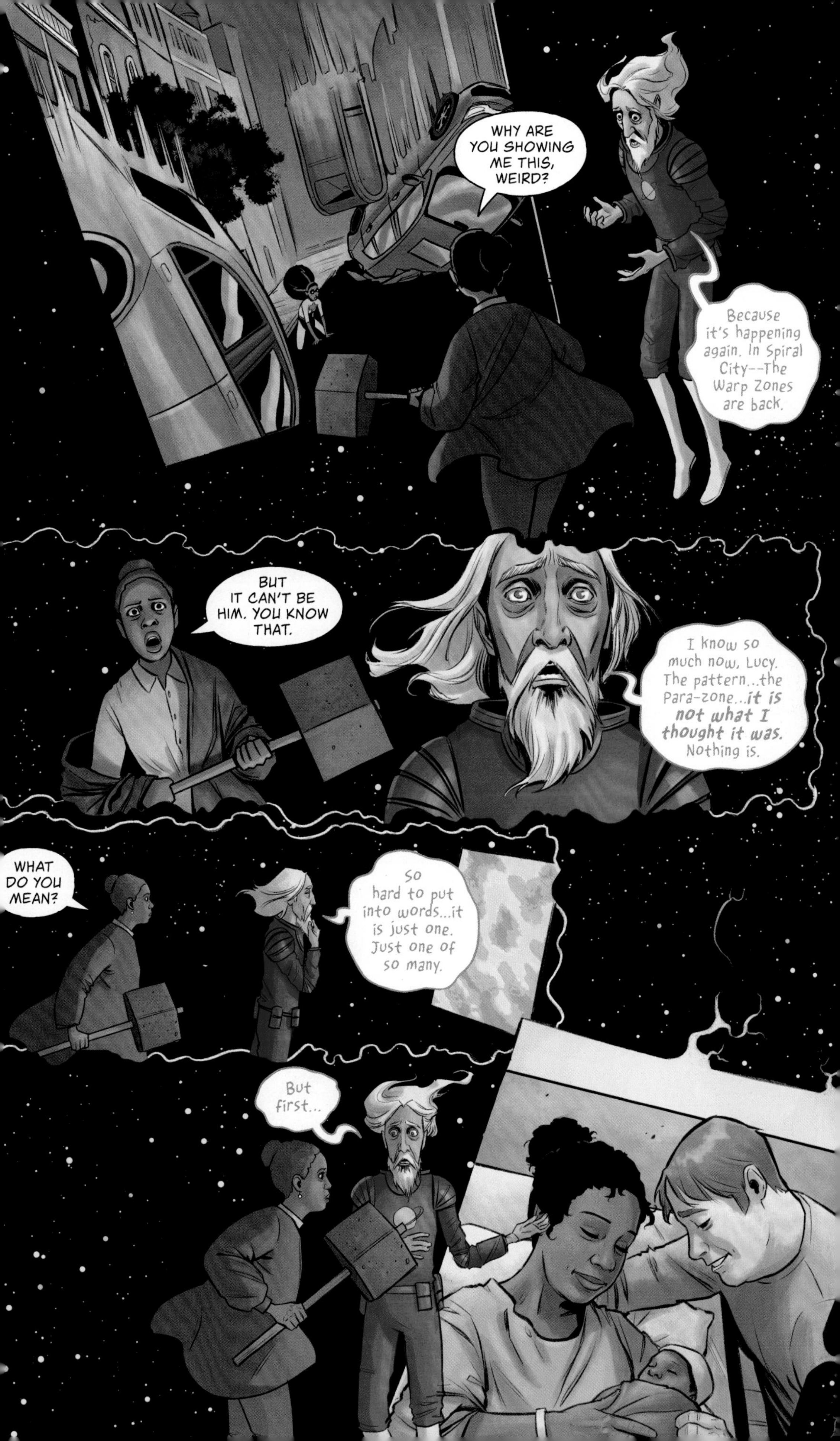
WHY ARE YOU SHOWING ME THIS, WEIRD?
Because it's happening again. In Spiral City--The Warp Zones are back.
BUT IT CAN'T BE HIM. YOU KNOW THAT.
I know so much now, Lucy. The pattern...the Para-zone...*it is not what I thought it was.* Nothing is.
WHAT DO YOU MEAN?
So hard to put into words...it is just one. Just one of so many.
But first...

NINE YEARS BEFORE THE END.

JOSEPH... LIKE MY DAD.

IT'S PERFECT. HE'S PERFECT.

MOMMY!

HEY, BABY...COME HERE.

ROSIE, MEET JOSEPH.

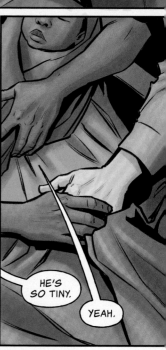

HE'S SO TINY.

YEAH.

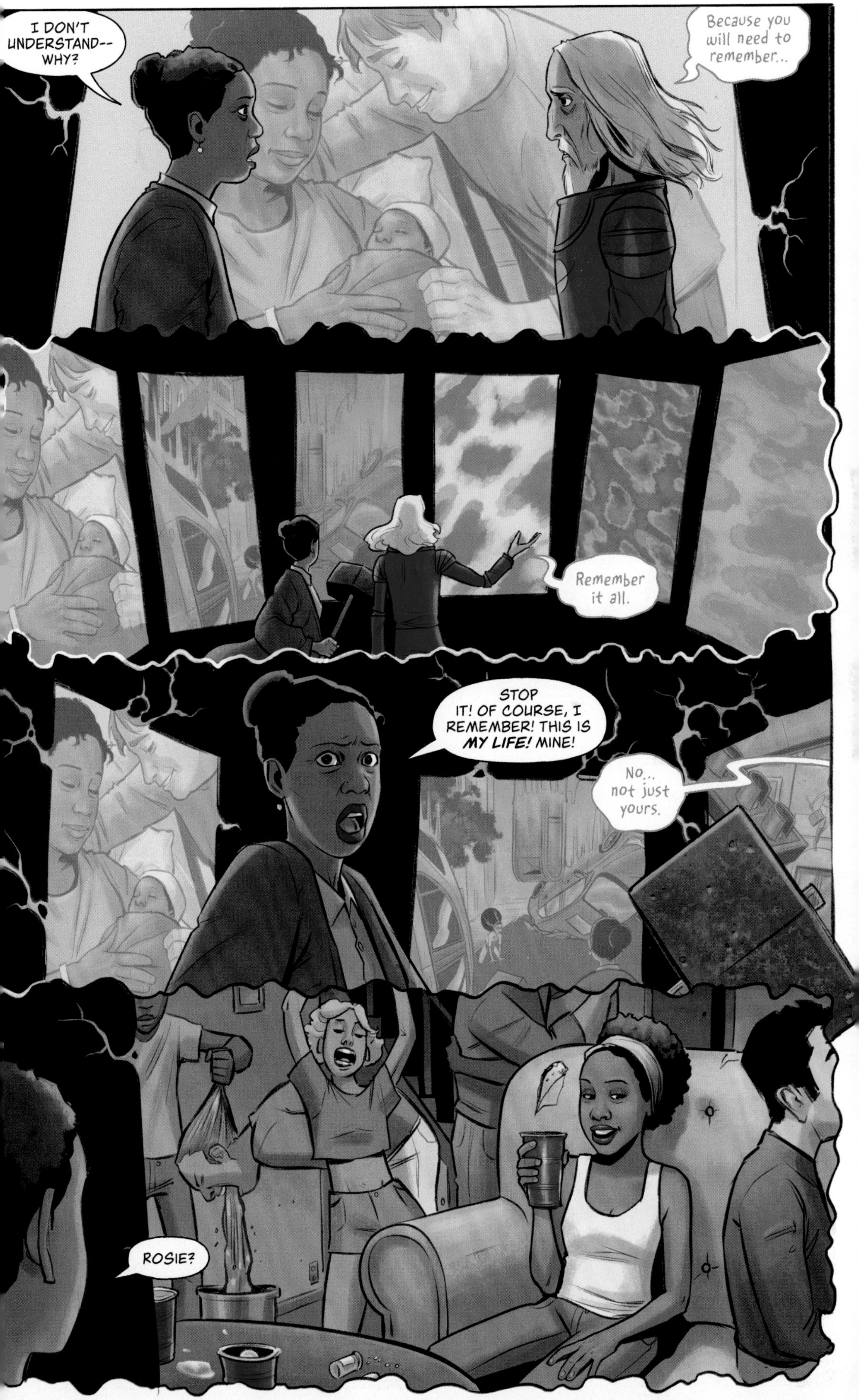
I DON'T UNDERSTAND-- WHY?
Because you will need to remember...
Remember it all.
STOP IT! OF COURSE, I REMEMBER! THIS IS *MY LIFE!* MINE!
No... not just yours.
ROSIE?

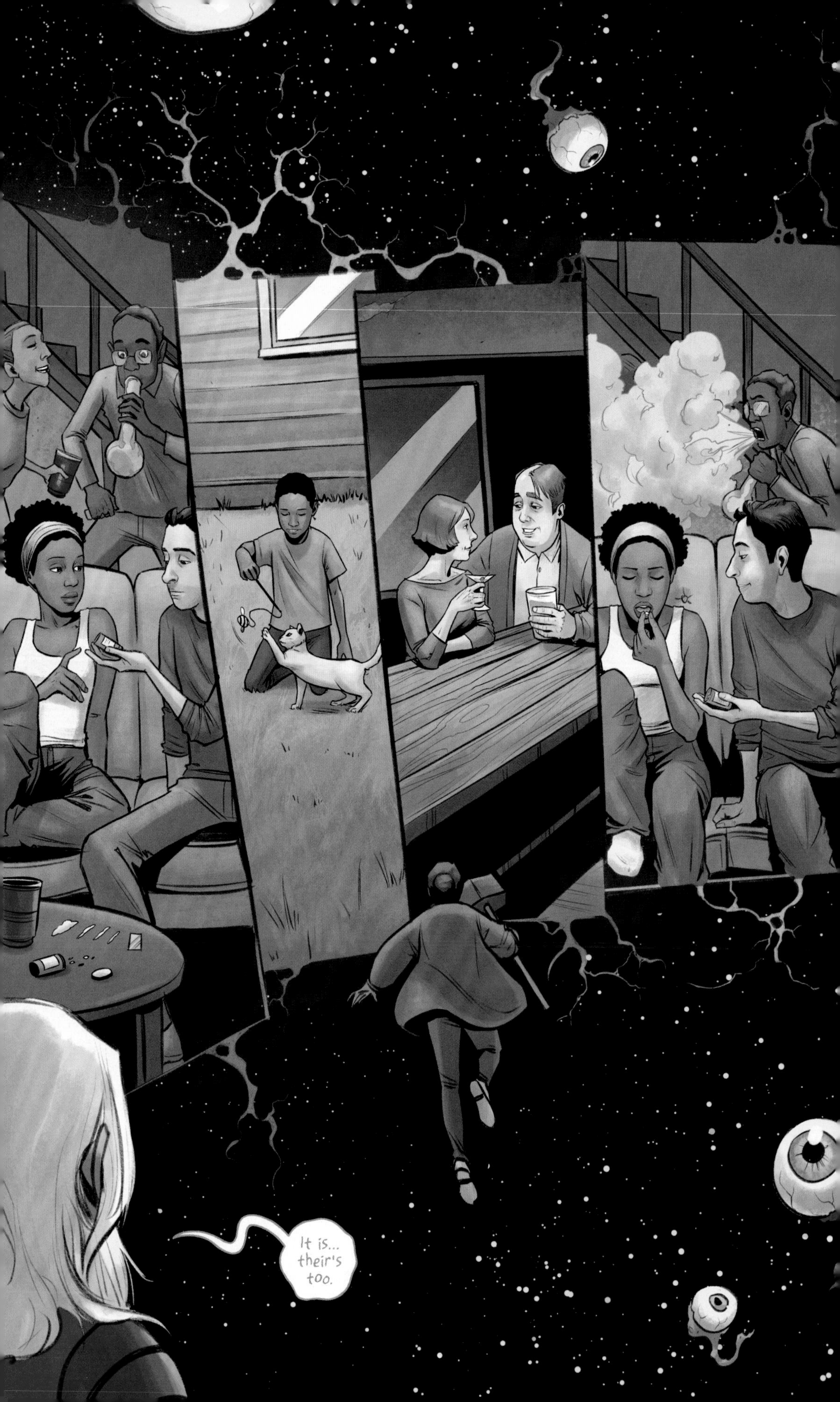
It is... their's too.

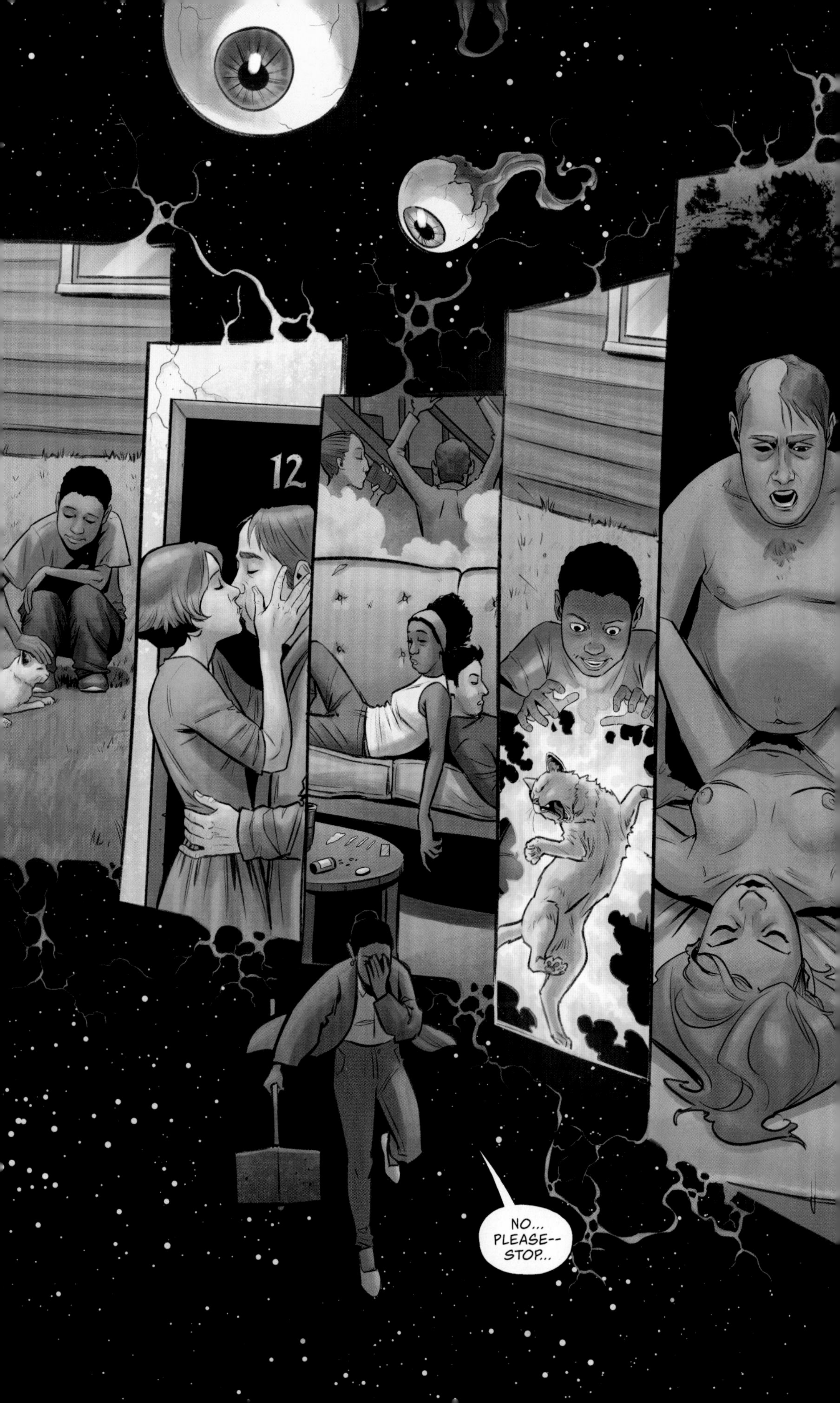
12
NO... PLEASE-- STOP...

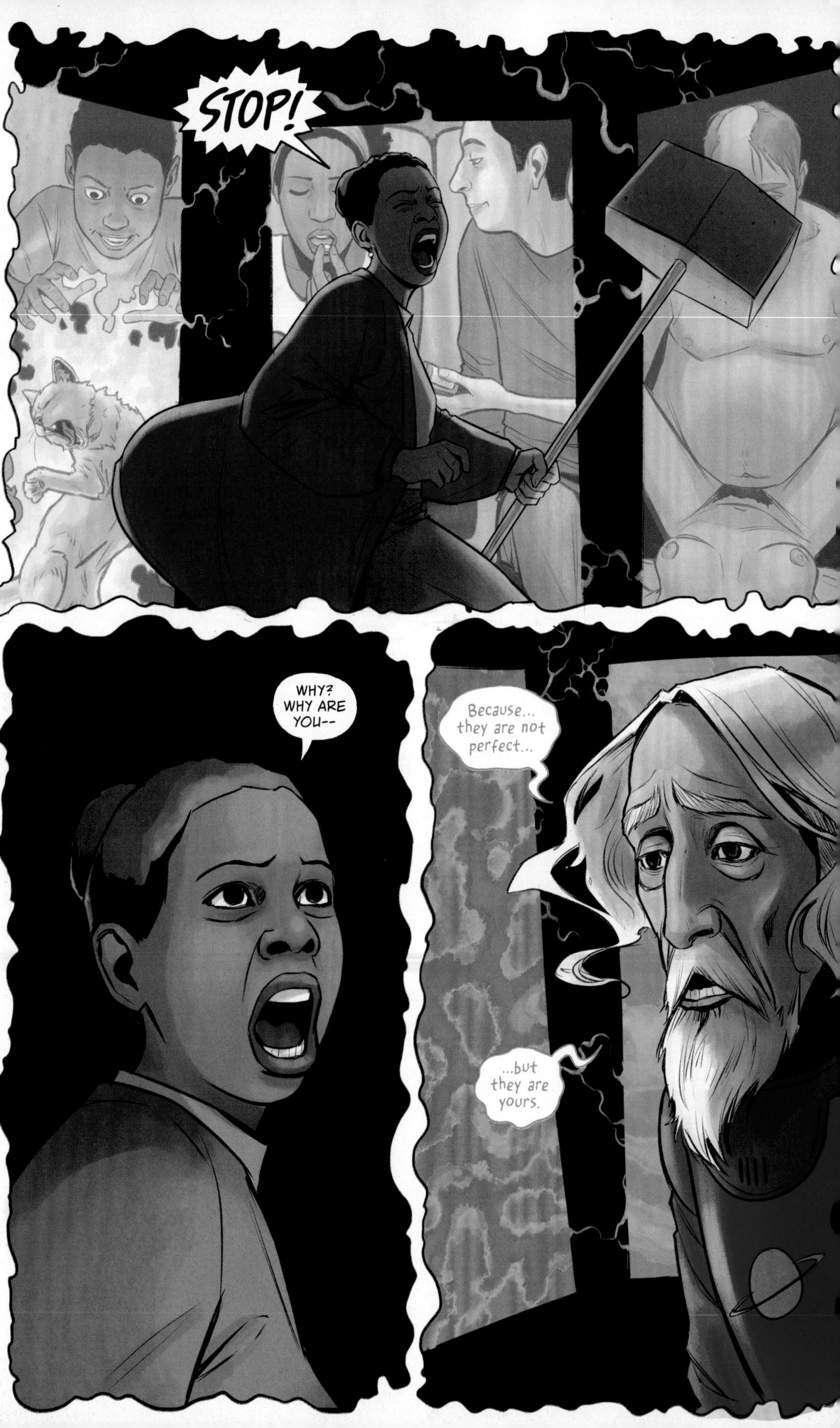
STOP!
WHY? WHY ARE YOU--
Because... they are not perfect...
...but they are yours.

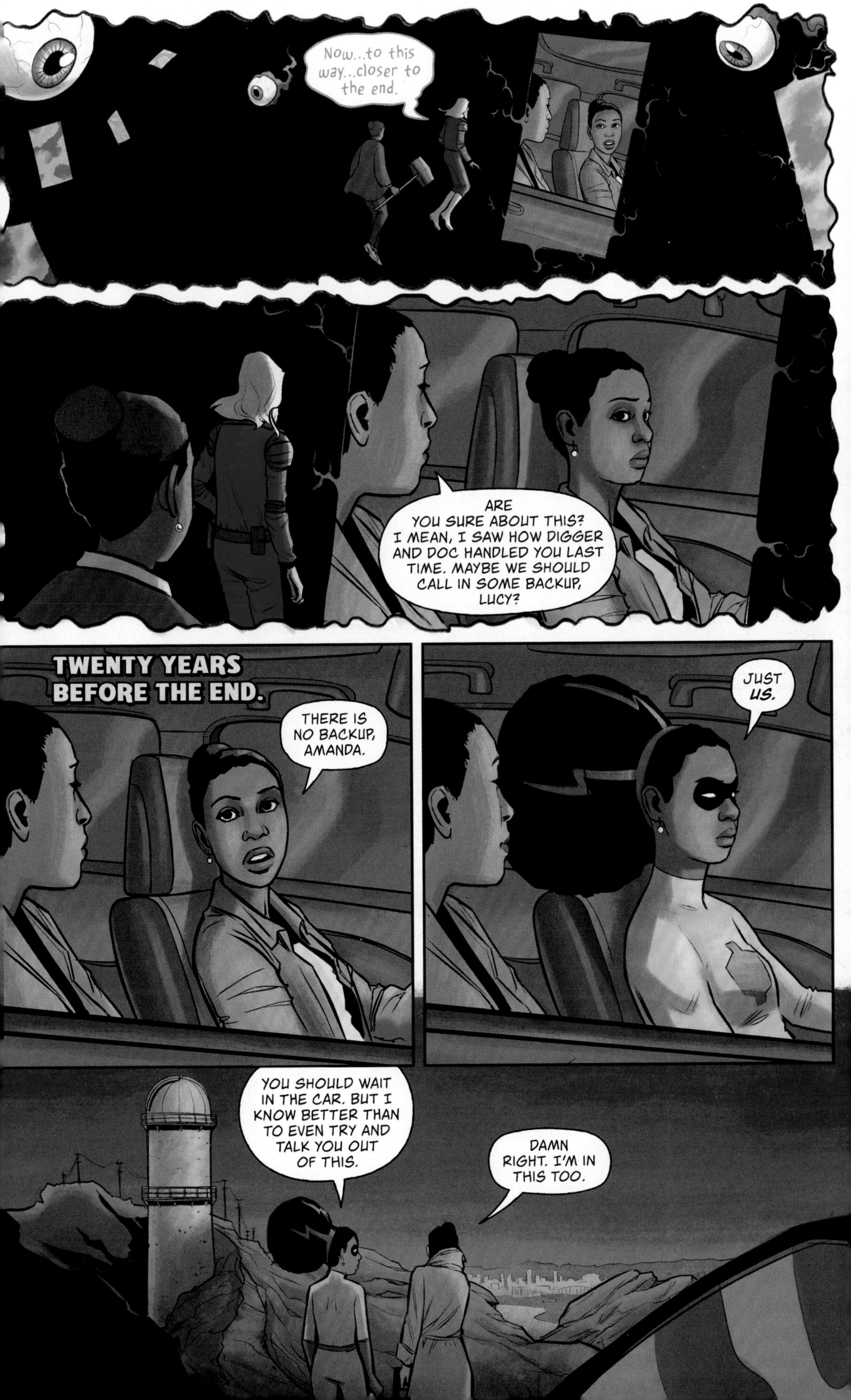
Now...to this way...closer to the end.
ARE YOU SURE ABOUT THIS? I MEAN, I SAW HOW DIGGER AND DOC HANDLED YOU LAST TIME. MAYBE WE SHOULD CALL IN SOME BACKUP, LUCY?
TWENTY YEARS BEFORE THE END.
THERE IS NO BACKUP, AMANDA.
JUST US.
YOU SHOULD WAIT IN THE CAR. BUT I KNOW BETTER THAN TO EVEN TRY AND TALK YOU OUT OF THIS.
DAMN RIGHT. I'M IN THIS TOO.

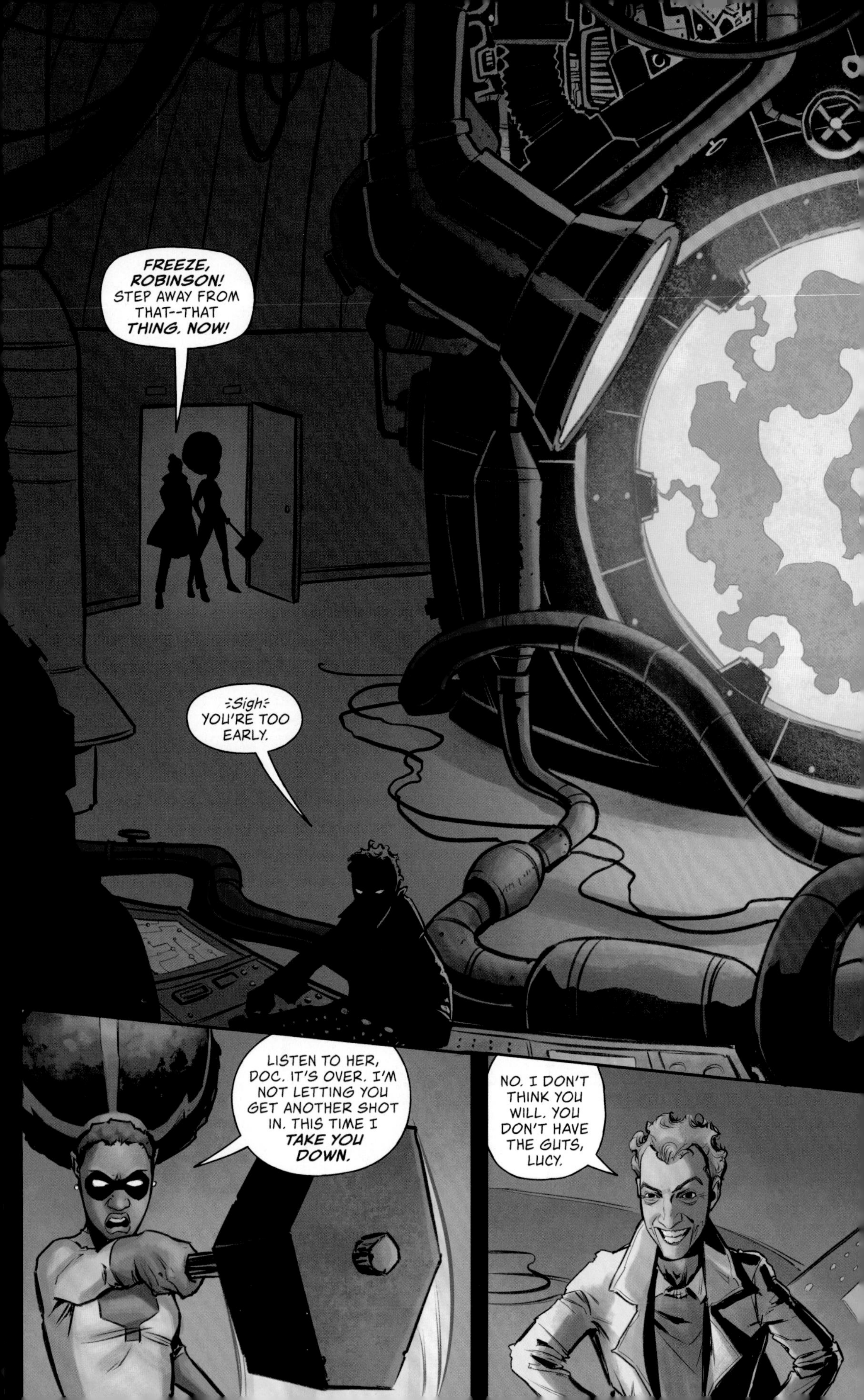
FREEZE, ROBINSON! STEP AWAY FROM THAT--THAT THING. NOW!
=Sigh= YOU'RE TOO EARLY.
LISTEN TO HER, DOC. IT'S OVER. I'M NOT LETTING YOU GET ANOTHER SHOT IN. THIS TIME I TAKE YOU DOWN.
NO. I DON'T THINK YOU WILL. YOU DON'T HAVE THE GUTS, LUCY.

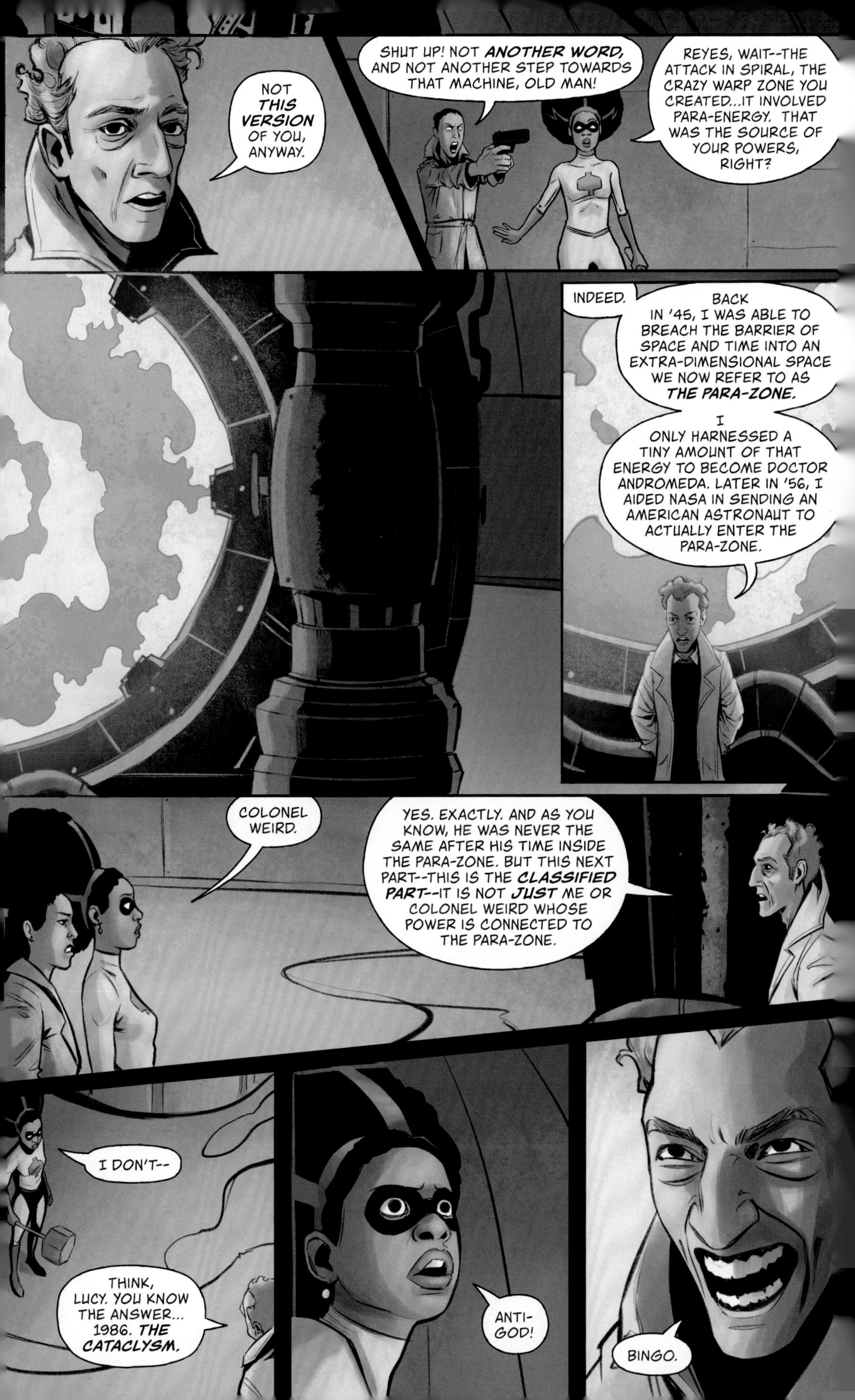
NOT THIS VERSION OF YOU, ANYWAY.
SHUT UP! NOT ANOTHER WORD, AND NOT ANOTHER STEP TOWARDS THAT MACHINE, OLD MAN!
REYES, WAIT--THE ATTACK IN SPIRAL, THE CRAZY WARP ZONE YOU CREATED...IT INVOLVED PARA-ENERGY. THAT WAS THE SOURCE OF YOUR POWERS, RIGHT?
INDEED.
BACK IN '45, I WAS ABLE TO BREACH THE BARRIER OF SPACE AND TIME INTO AN EXTRA-DIMENSIONAL SPACE WE NOW REFER TO AS THE PARA-ZONE.
I ONLY HARNESSED A TINY AMOUNT OF THAT ENERGY TO BECOME DOCTOR ANDROMEDA. LATER IN '56, I AIDED NASA IN SENDING AN AMERICAN ASTRONAUT TO ACTUALLY ENTER THE PARA-ZONE.
COLONEL WEIRD.
YES. EXACTLY. AND AS YOU KNOW, HE WAS NEVER THE SAME AFTER HIS TIME INSIDE THE PARA-ZONE. BUT THIS NEXT PART--THIS IS THE CLASSIFIED PART--IT IS NOT JUST ME OR COLONEL WEIRD WHOSE POWER IS CONNECTED TO THE PARA-ZONE.
I DON'T--
THINK, LUCY. YOU KNOW THE ANSWER... 1986. THE CATACLYSM.
ANTI-GOD!
BINGO.

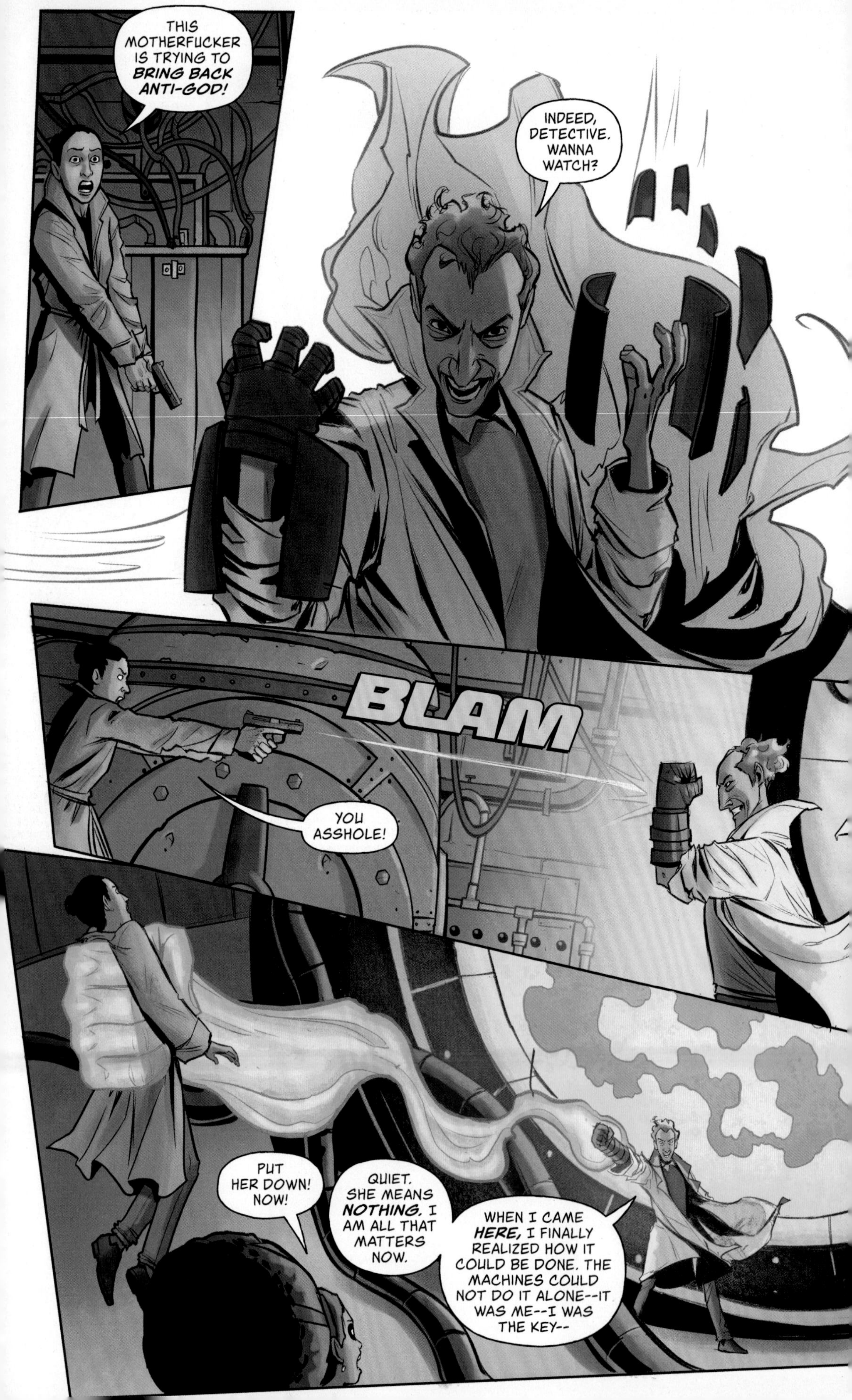
THIS MOTHERFUCKER IS TRYING TO **BRING BACK ANTI-GOD!**
INDEED, DETECTIVE. WANNA WATCH?
BLAM
YOU ASSHOLE!
PUT HER DOWN! NOW!
QUIET. SHE MEANS **NOTHING.** I AM ALL THAT MATTERS NOW.
WHEN I CAME **HERE,** I FINALLY REALIZED HOW IT COULD BE DONE. THE MACHINES COULD NOT DO IT ALONE--IT WAS ME--I WAS THE KEY--

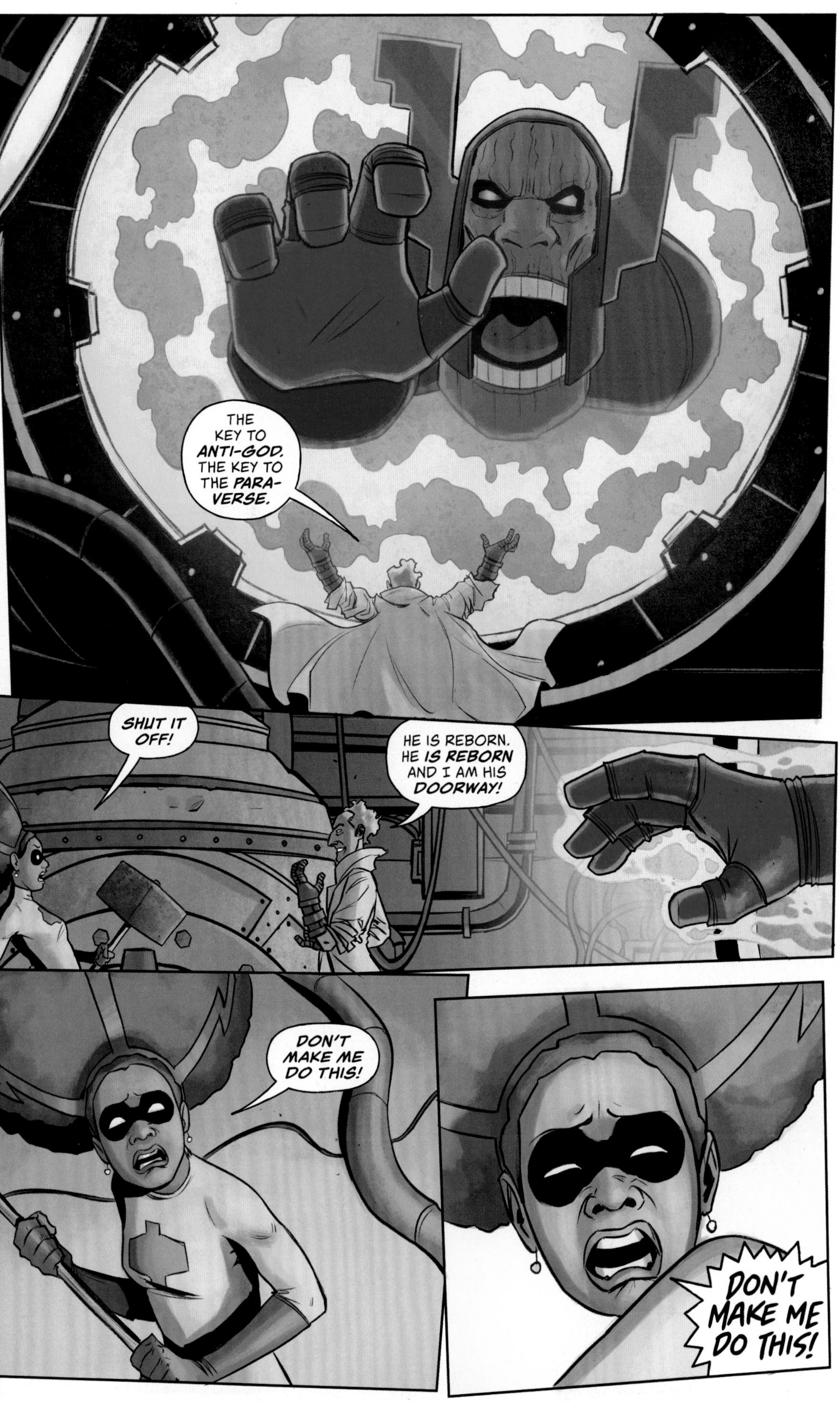
THE KEY TO ANTI-GOD. THE KEY TO THE PARA-VERSE.
SHUT IT OFF!
HE IS REBORN. HE IS REBORN AND I AM HIS DOORWAY!
DON'T MAKE ME DO THIS!
DON'T MAKE ME DO THIS!

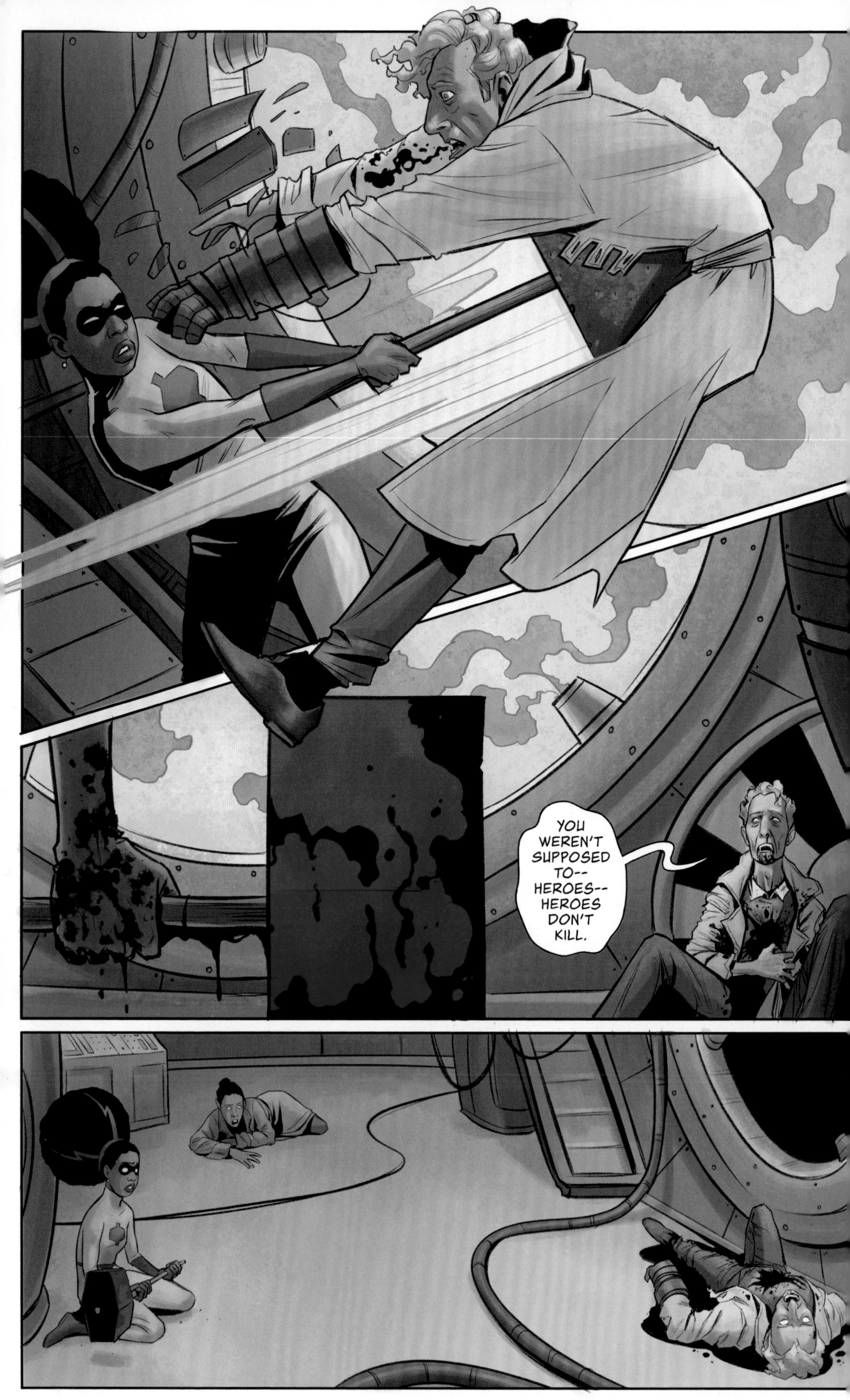
YOU WEREN'T SUPPOSED TO-- HEROES-- HEROES DON'T KILL.

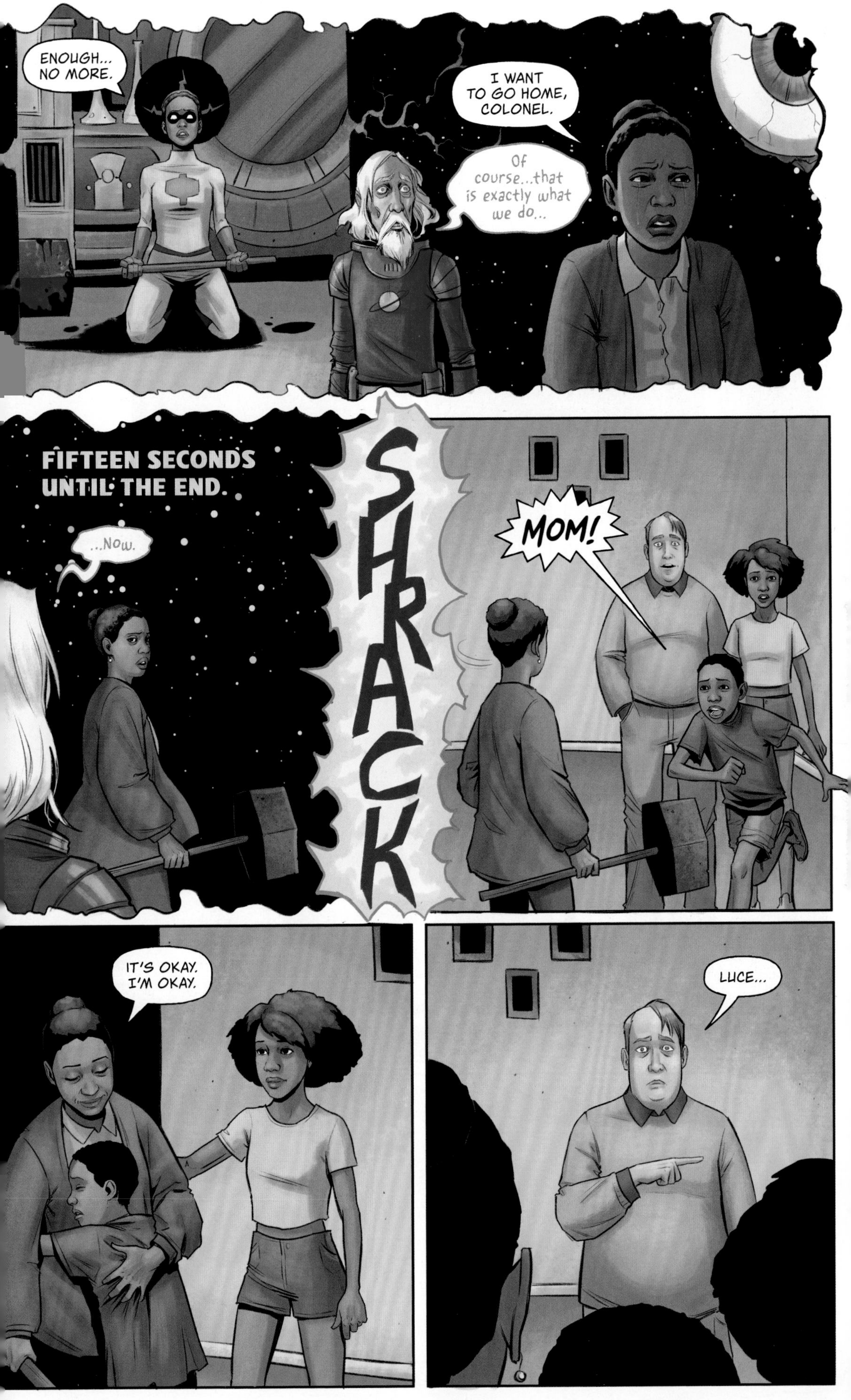
ENOUGH... NO MORE.
I WANT TO GO HOME, COLONEL.
Of course...that is exactly what we do...
FIFTEEN SECONDS UNTIL THE END.
...Now.
SHRACK
MOM!
IT'S OKAY. I'M OKAY.
LUCE...

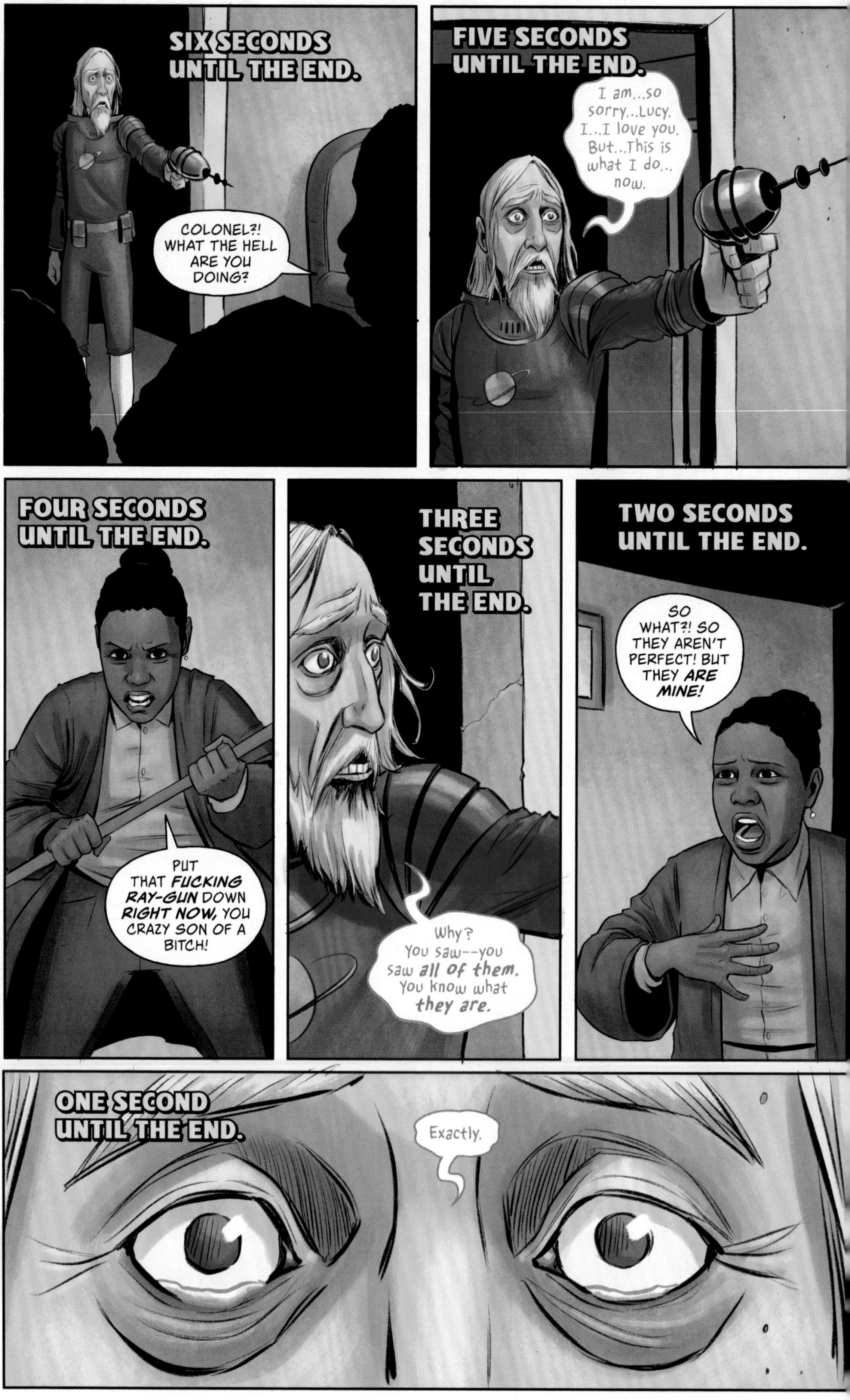
SIX SECONDS UNTIL THE END.
COLONEL?! WHAT THE HELL ARE YOU DOING?
FIVE SECONDS UNTIL THE END.
I am...so sorry...Lucy. I...I love you. But...This is what I do... now.
FOUR SECONDS UNTIL THE END.
PUT THAT FUCKING RAY-GUN DOWN RIGHT NOW, YOU CRAZY SON OF A BITCH!
THREE SECONDS UNTIL THE END.
Why? You saw--you saw all of them. You know what they are.
TWO SECONDS UNTIL THE END.
SO WHAT?! SO THEY AREN'T PERFECT! BUT THEY ARE MINE!
ONE SECOND UNTIL THE END.
Exactly.

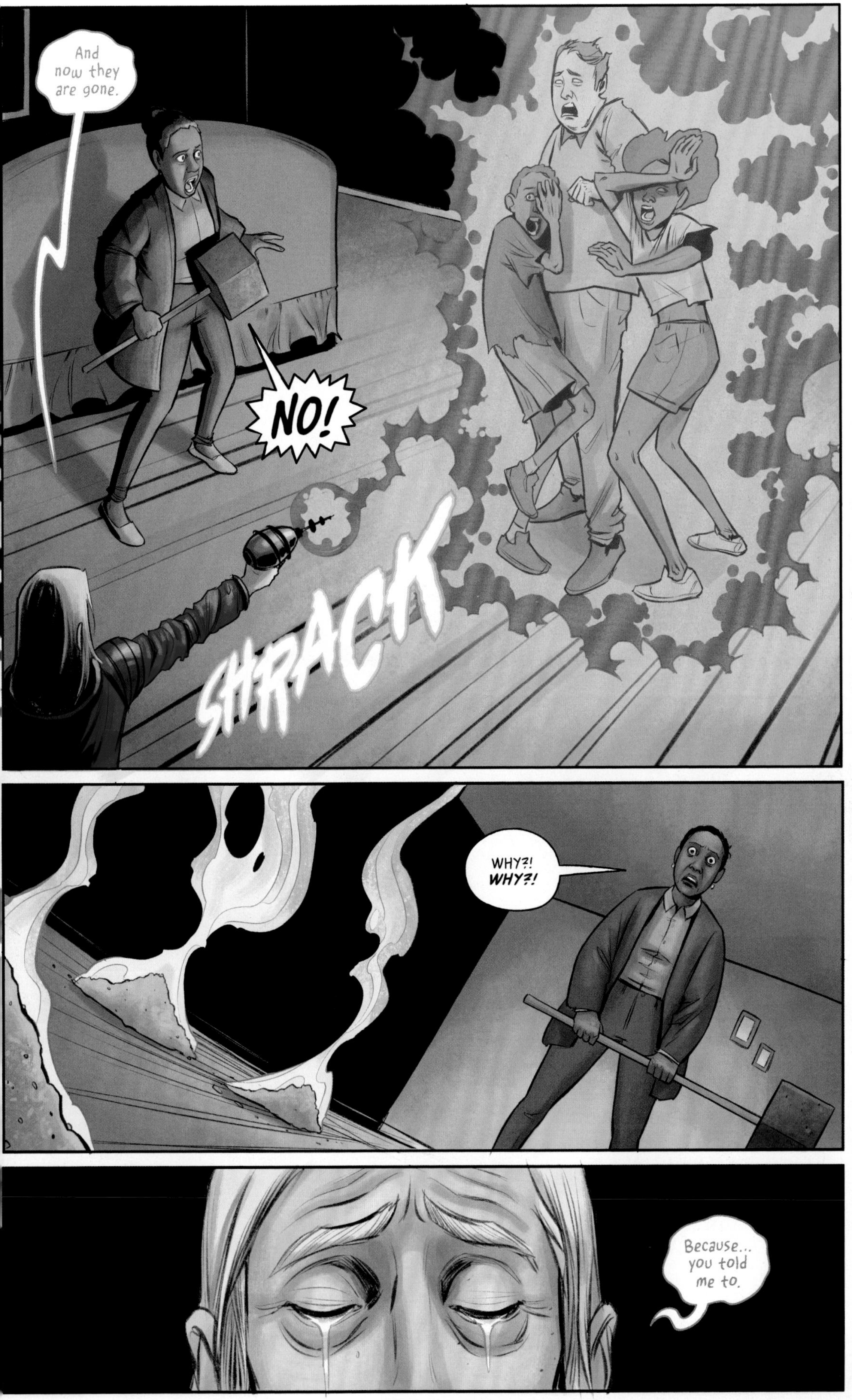
And now they are gone.
NO!
SHRACK
WHY?! WHY?!
Because... you told me to.

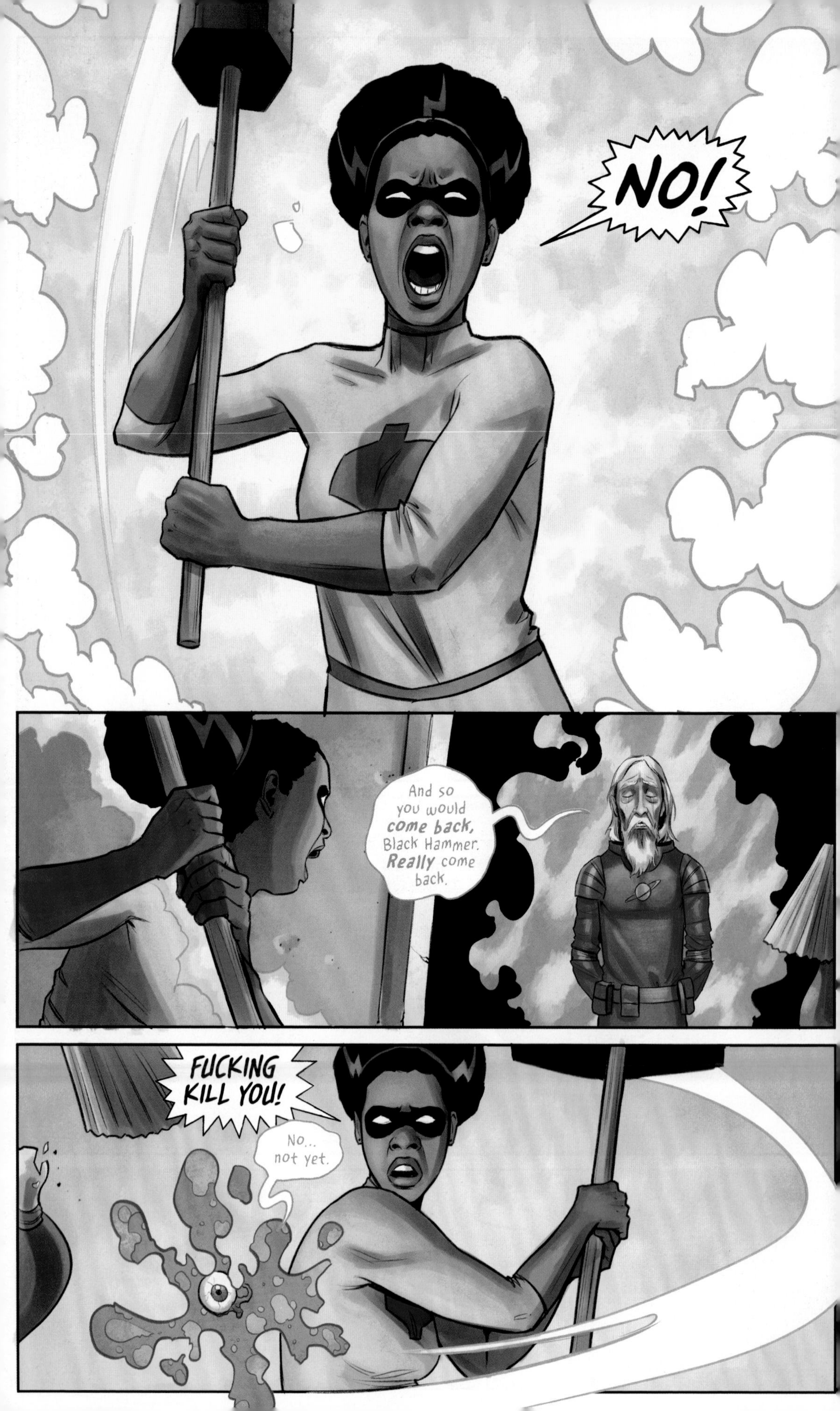
NO!
And so you would come back, Black Hammer. Really come back.
FUCKING KILL YOU!
No... not yet.

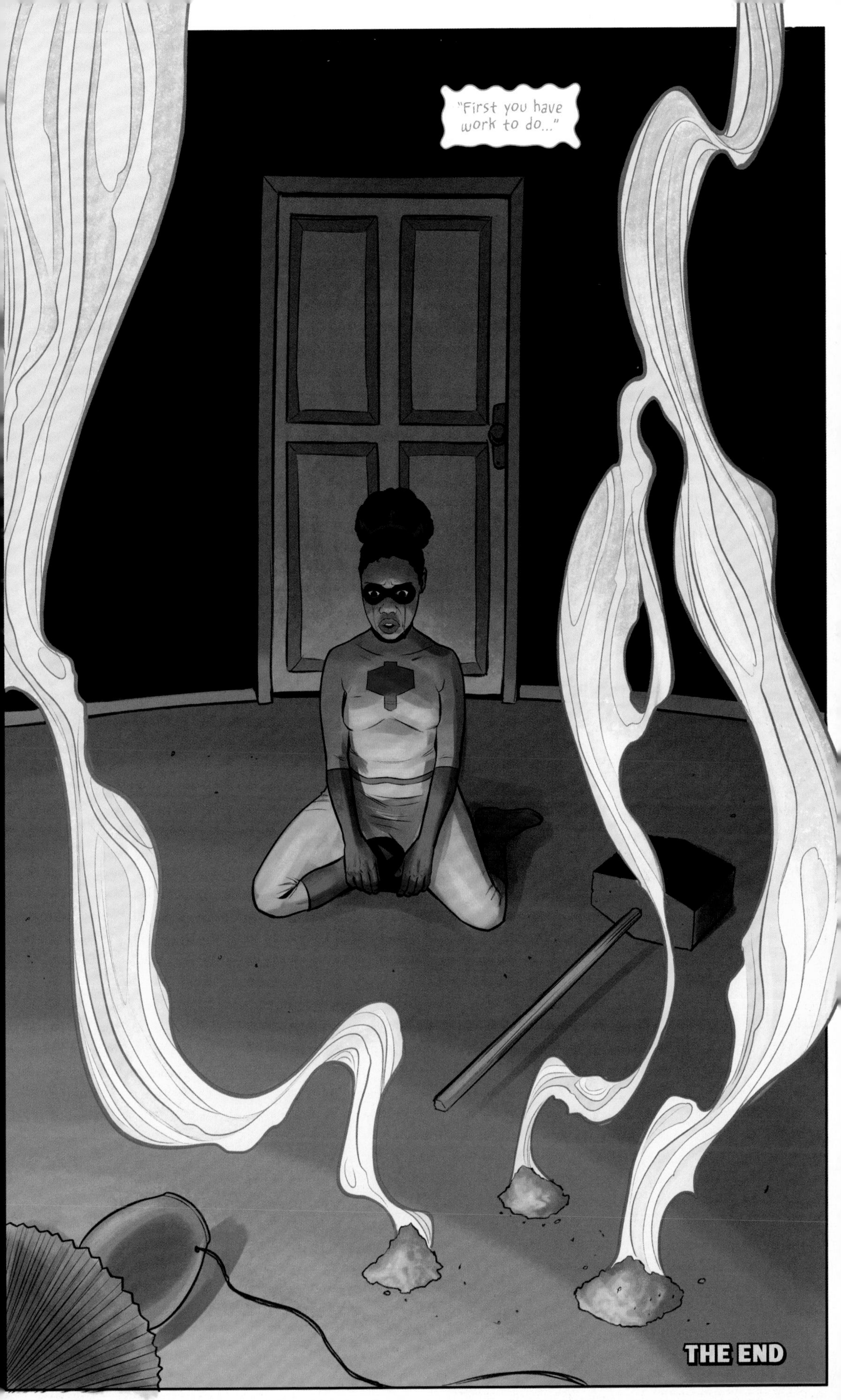
"First you have work to do..."
THE END

BLACK HAMMER™ REBORN SKETCHBOOK

NOTES BY CAITLIN YARSKY

I started drawing in order, so page one was really nerve wracking. It was the moment when the project became real, and I realized what big shoes I had to fill after Dean Ormston. That said, it was really a blast drawing Anti-God, a character that was delightfully out of my wheelhouse.

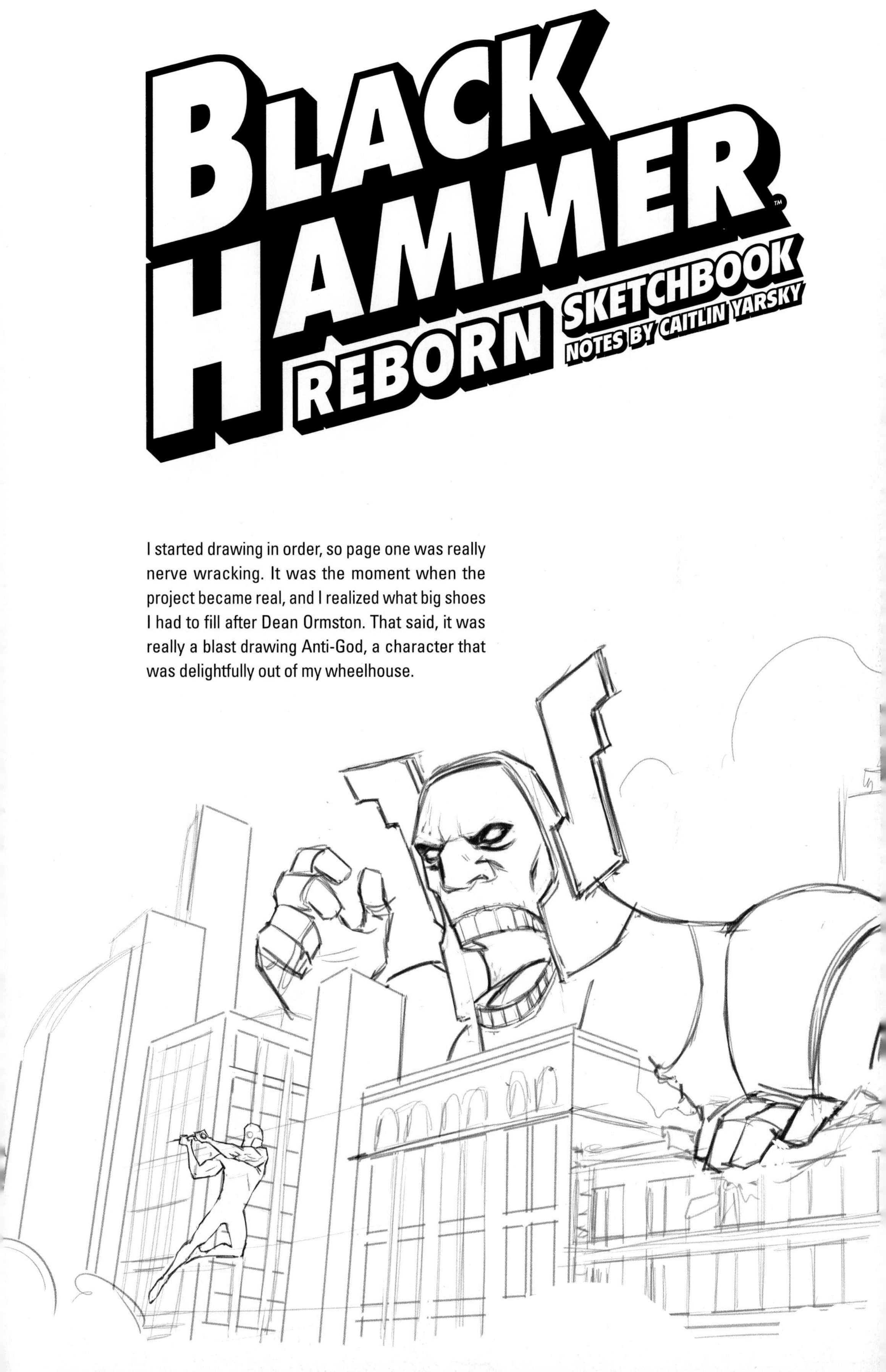

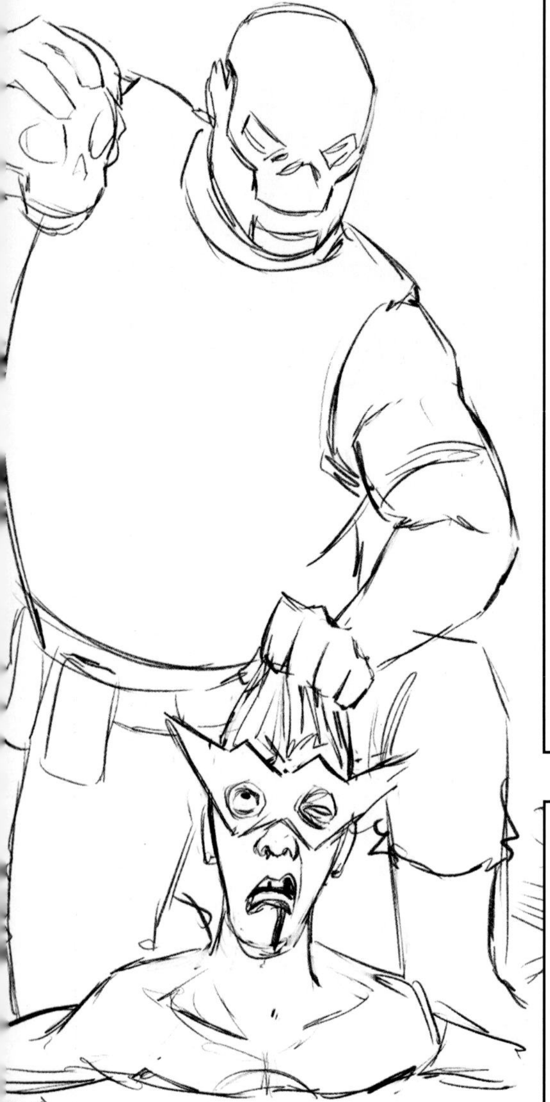

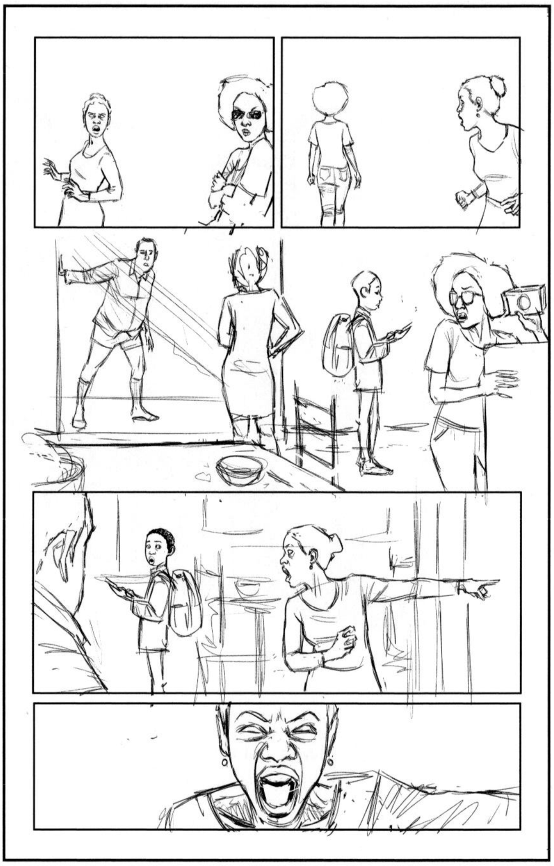

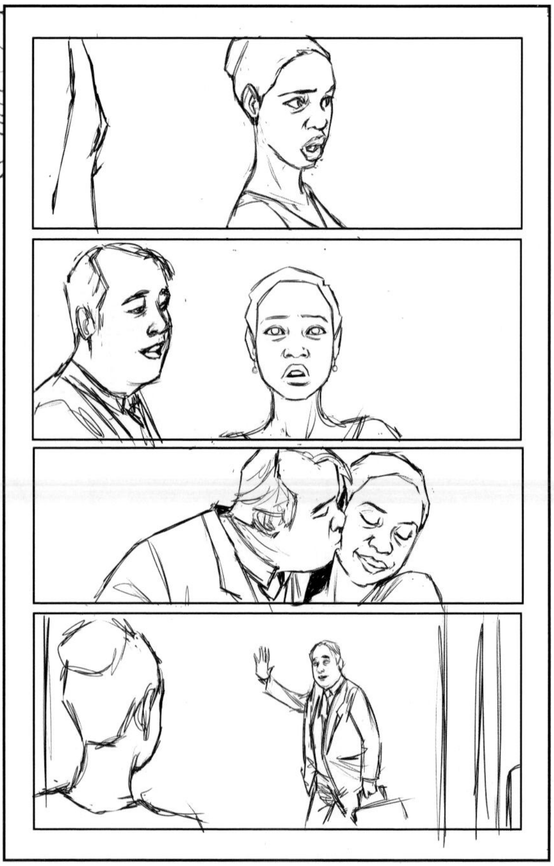

I remember taking some inspiration from Philip Seymour Hoffman for Elliot's "suburban dad" look, and pushing the feeling that he was weak (in the past and present).

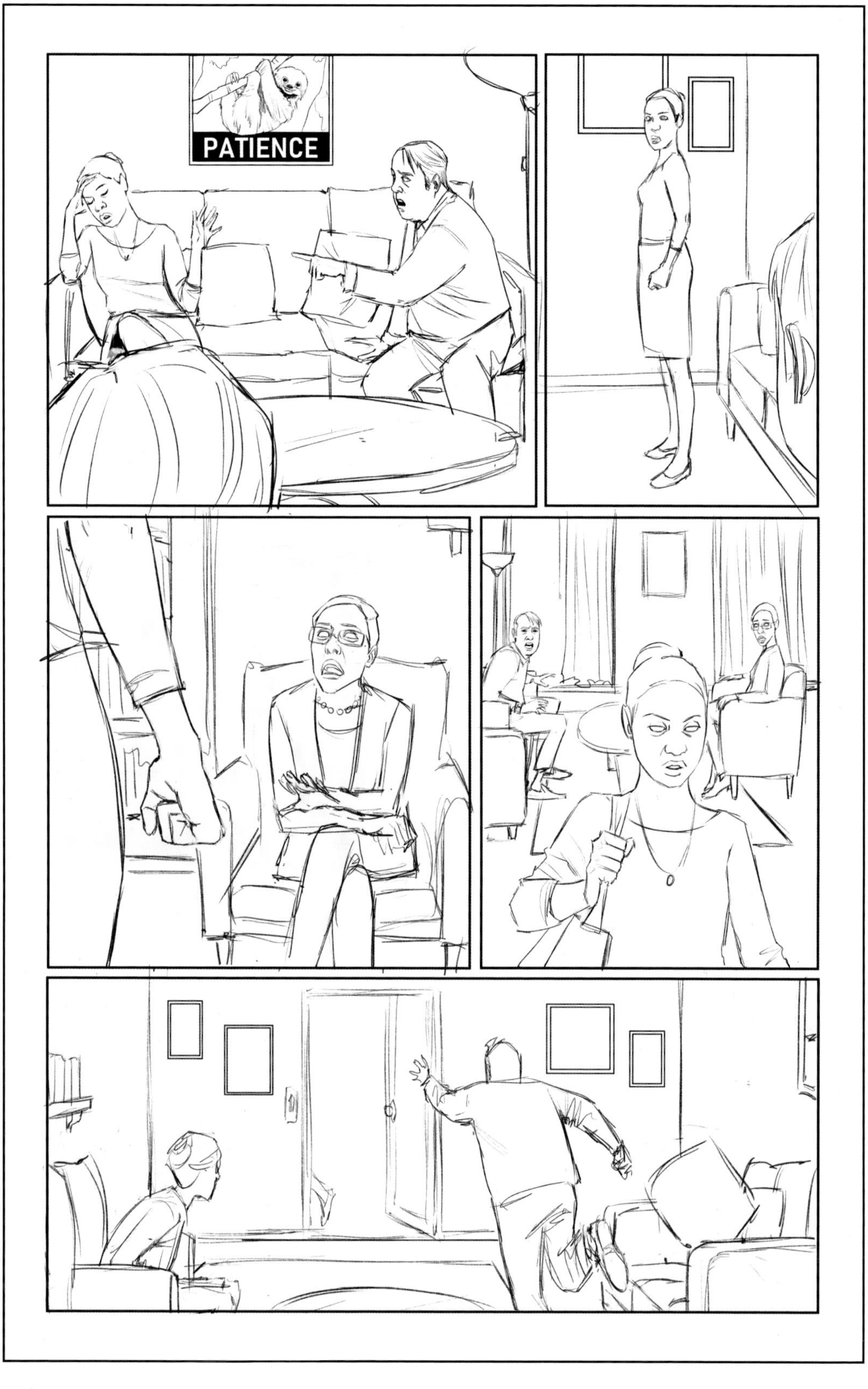
PATIENCE

The therapy scene dialogue infuriated me and was where I saw how self-centered Elliot was (and it was fun adding little Easter eggs like the "patience" sloth motivational poster).

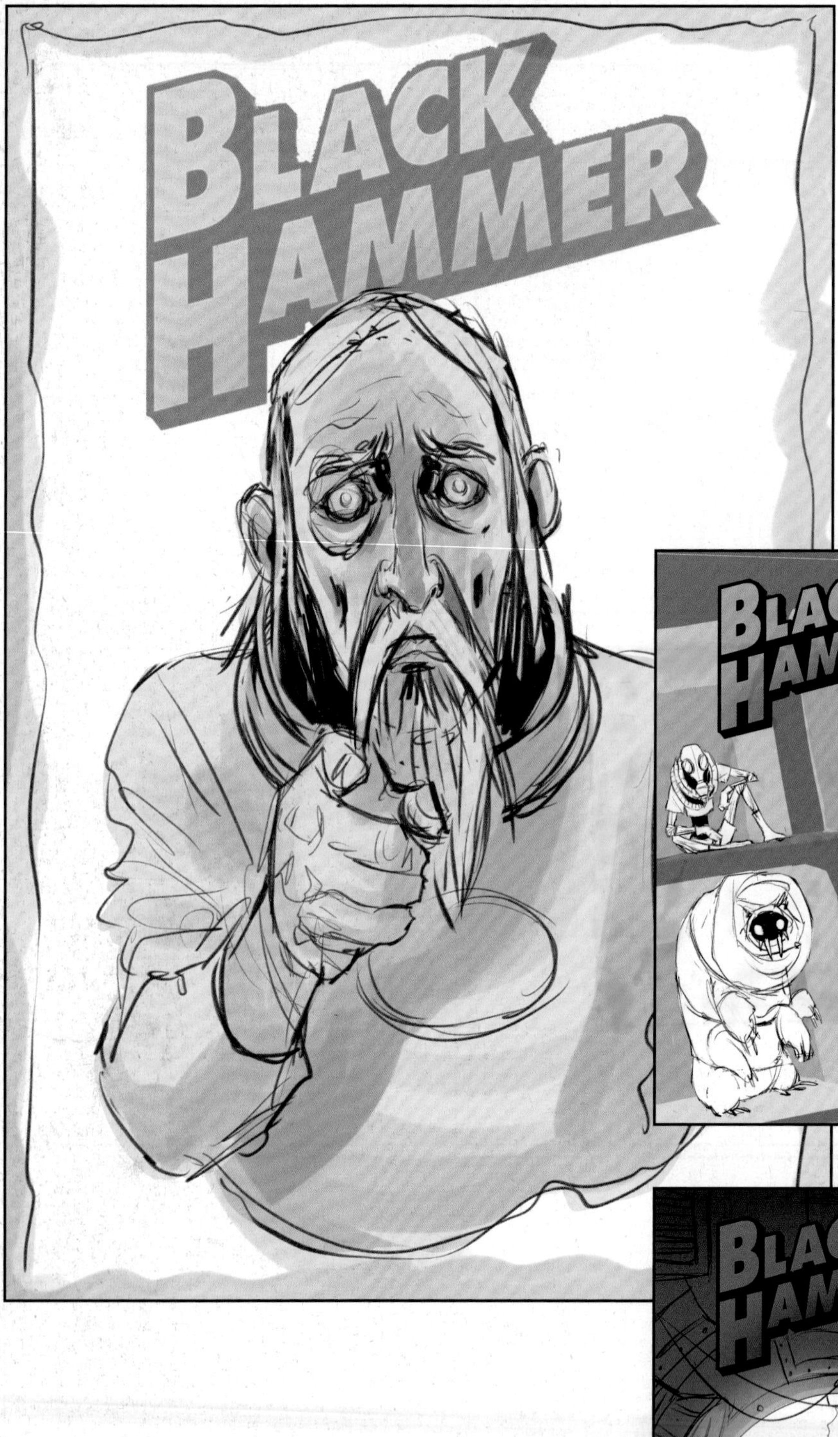
BLACK
HAMMER

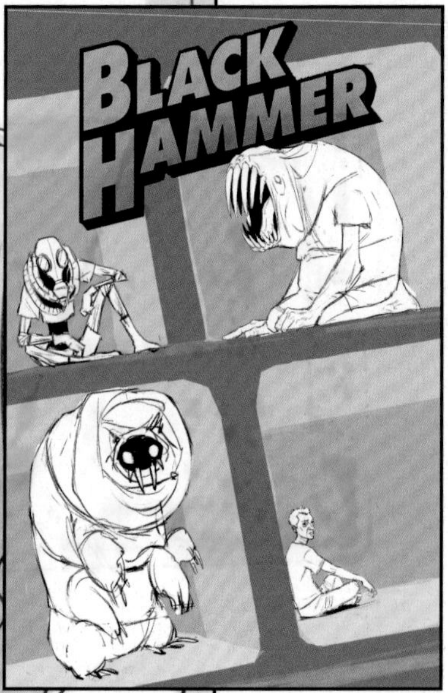
BLACK
HAMMER

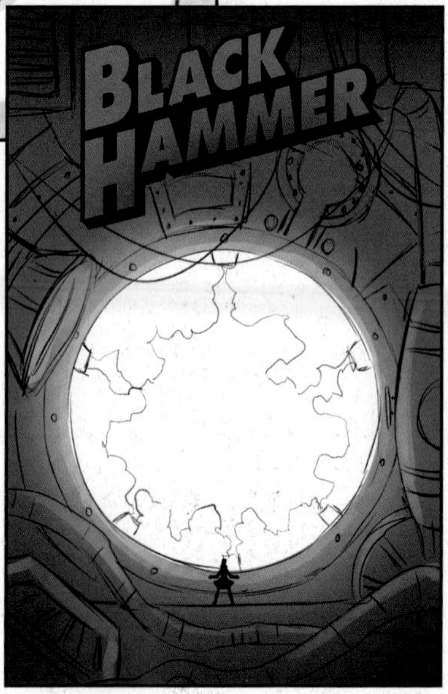
BLACK
HAMMER

For the Colonel Weird cover, I borrowed from the old wartime recruiting poster of Uncle Sam. The other covers had me looking up reference of everything from factory machinery to microscopic "water bears." Google doesn't know what to make of me.